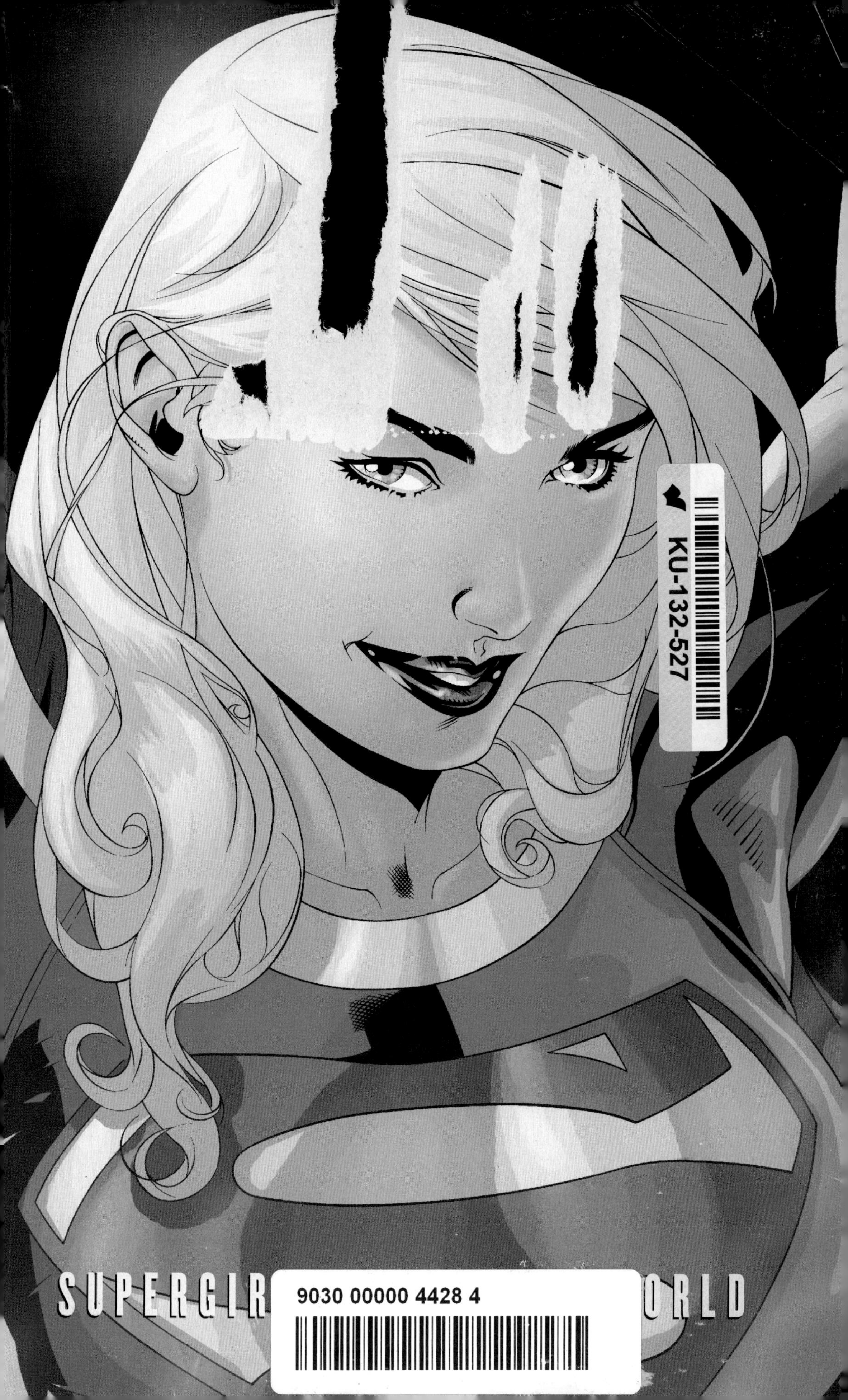
SUPERGIR
ORLD

Kelley Puckett   Will Pfeifer   James Peaty **Writers**

Ron Randall   Drew Johnson   Brad Walker **Pencillers**

Ron Randall   Ray Snyder   Jon Sibal   Jesse Delperdang   Rodney Ramos **Inkers**

Brad Anderson   Kanila Tripp   Shannon Blanchard   Edgar Delgado   Wes Dzioba **Colorists**

Travis Lanham   Sal Cipriano   Jared K. Fletcher   Pat Brosseau   Rob Clark, Jr. **Letterers**

SUPERG

WAY OF T

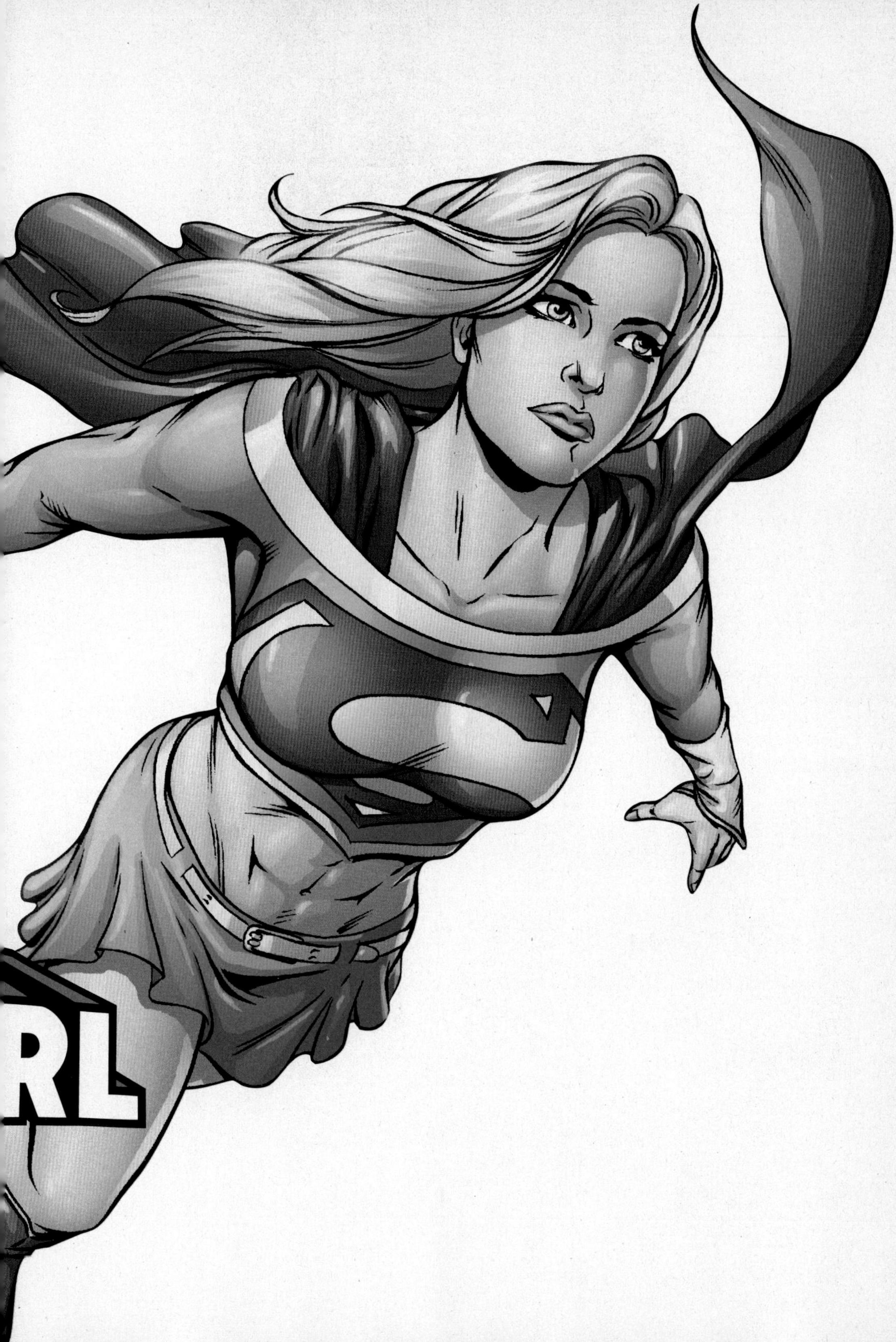
RL

IE WORLD

Dan DiDio Senior VP-Executive Editor

Matt Idelson Editor-original oeries

Nachie Castro Tom Palmer, Jr. Associate Editors-original oeries

Bob Joy Editor-collected cdition

Robbin Brosterman Senior Art Director

Paul Levitz President & Publisher

Georg Brewer VP-Design & DC Direct Creative

Richard Bruning Senior VP-Creative Director

Patrick Caldon Executive VP-Finance & Operations

Chris Caramalis VP-Finance

John Cunningham VP-Marketing

Terri Cunningham VP-Managing Editor

Amy Genkins Senior VP-Business & Legal Affairs

Alison Gill VP-Manufacturing

David Hyde VP-Publicity

Hank Kanalz VP-General Manager, WildStorm

Jim Lee Editorial Director-WildStorm

Gregory Noveck Senior VP-Creative Affairs

Sue Pohja VP-Book Trade Sales

Steve Rotterdam Senior VP-Sales & Marketing

Cheryl Rubin Senior VP-Brand Management

Alysse Soll VP-Advertising & Custom Publishing

Jeff Trojan VP-Business Development, DC Direct

Bob Wayne VP-Sales

Cover by Drew Johnson & Ray Snyder with Shannon Blanchard

SUPERGIRL: WAY OF THE WORLD
Published by DC Comics.
Cover and compilation Copyright © 2009 DC Comics.
All Rights Reserved.

Originally published in single magazine form as SUPERGIRL 28-33
Copyright © 2008 DC Comics. All Rights Reserved.
All characters, their distinctive likenesses and related elements featured in this publication are trademarks of DC Comics.
The stories, characters and incidents featured in this
publication are entirely fictional. DC Comics does not read
or accept unsolicited submissions of ideas, stories or artwork.

DC Comics, 1700 Broadway, New York, NY 10019
A Warner Bros. Entertainment Company
Printed in Canada. First Printing.

ISBN: 978-1-4012-2129-4

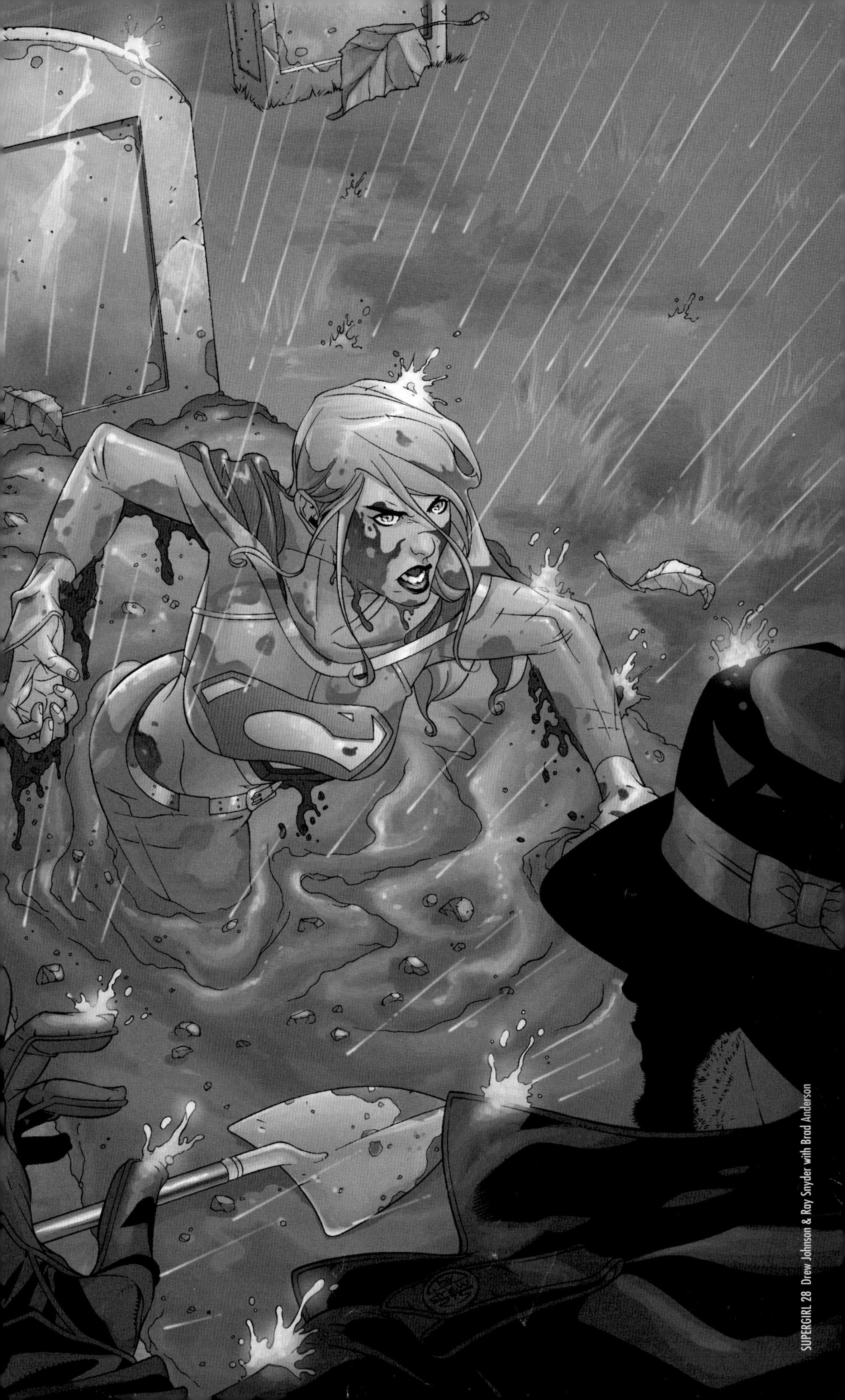

SUPERGIRL 28 Drew Johnson & Ray Snyder with Brad Anderson

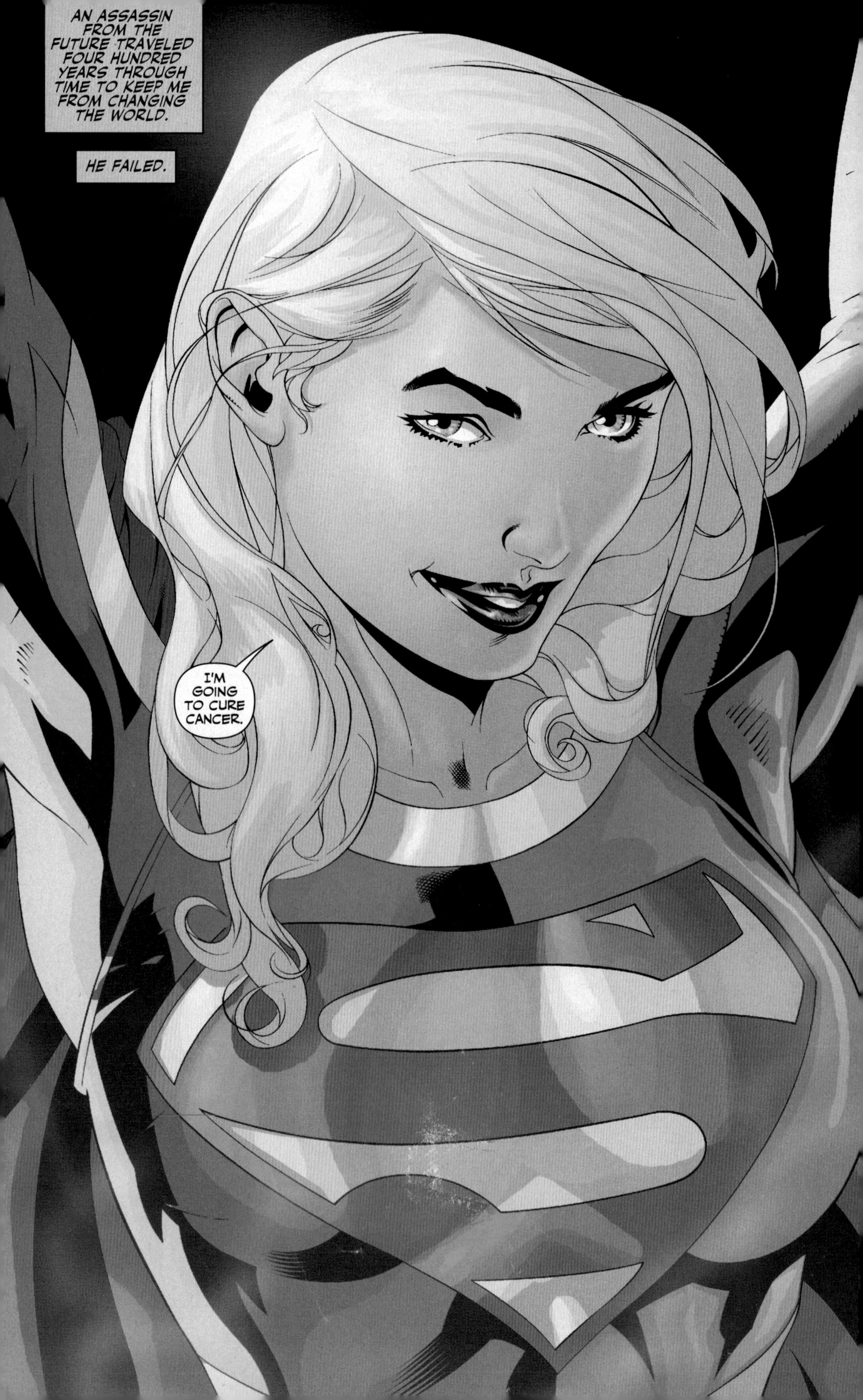
AN ASSASSIN FROM THE FUTURE TRAVELED FOUR HUNDRED YEARS THROUGH TIME TO KEEP ME FROM CHANGING THE WORLD.
HE FAILED.
I'M GOING TO CURE CANCER.

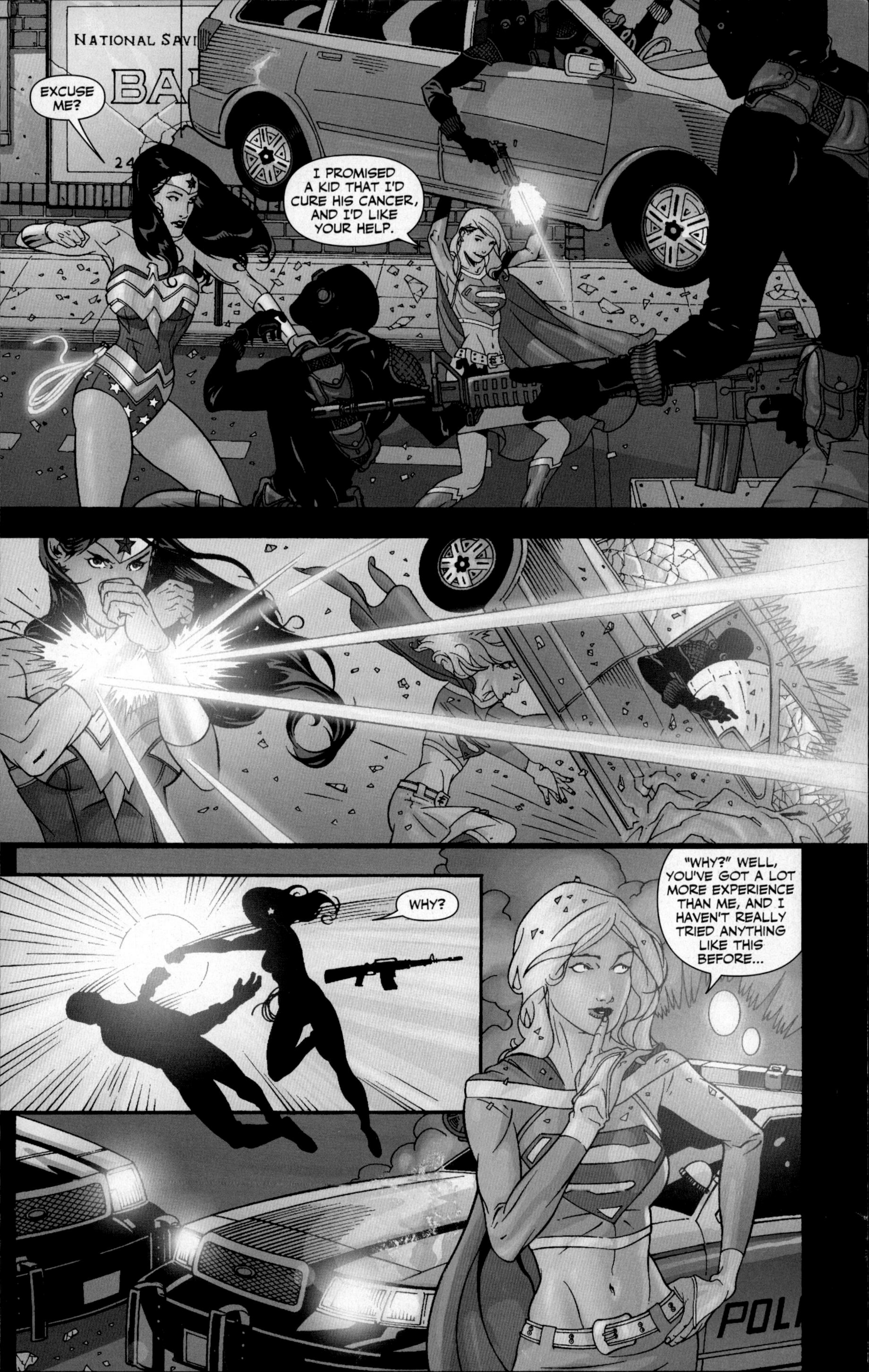
NATIONAL SAVI
BA
EXCUSE ME?
I PROMISED A KID THAT I'D CURE HIS CANCER, AND I'D LIKE YOUR HELP.
WHY?
"WHY?" WELL, YOU'VE GOT A LOT MORE EXPERIENCE THAN ME, AND I HAVEN'T REALLY TRIED ANYTHING LIKE THIS BEFORE...
POL

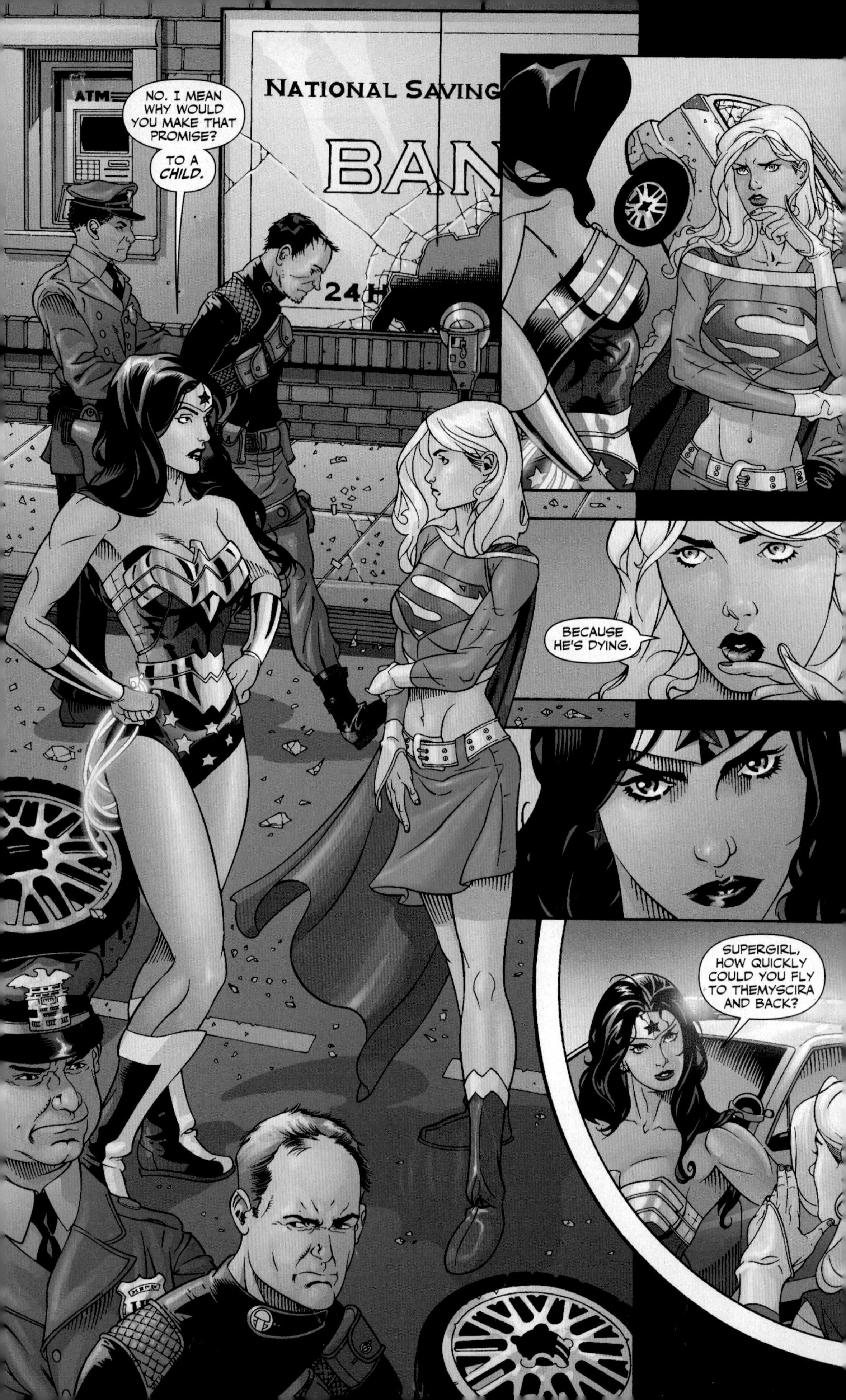
NATIONAL SAVING
BAN
24 H
ATM
NO. I MEAN WHY WOULD YOU MAKE THAT PROMISE?
TO A *CHILD.*
BECAUSE HE'S DYING.
SUPERGIRL, HOW QUICKLY COULD YOU FLY TO THEMYSCIRA AND BACK?

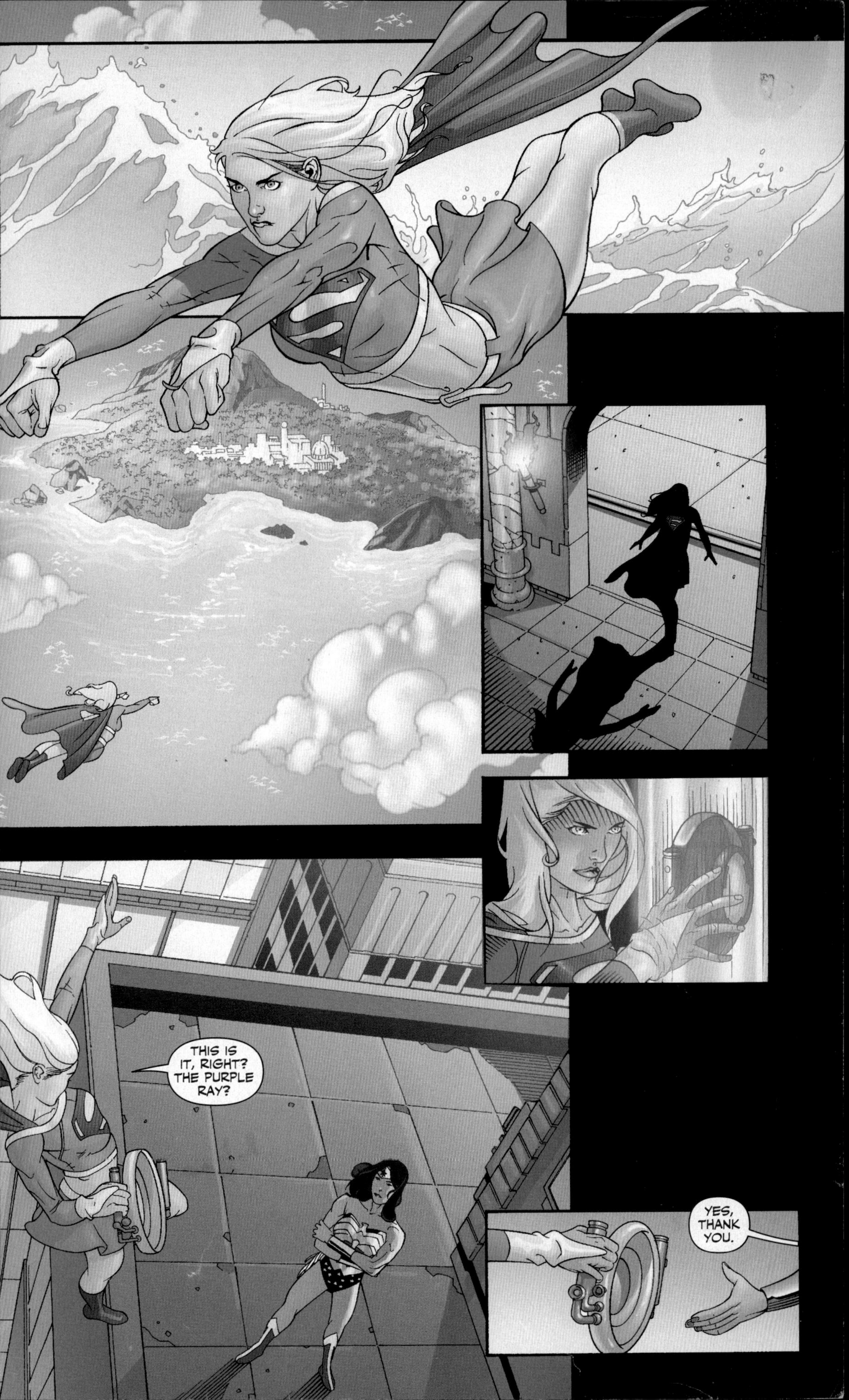
THIS IS IT, RIGHT? THE PURPLE RAY?
YES, THANK YOU.

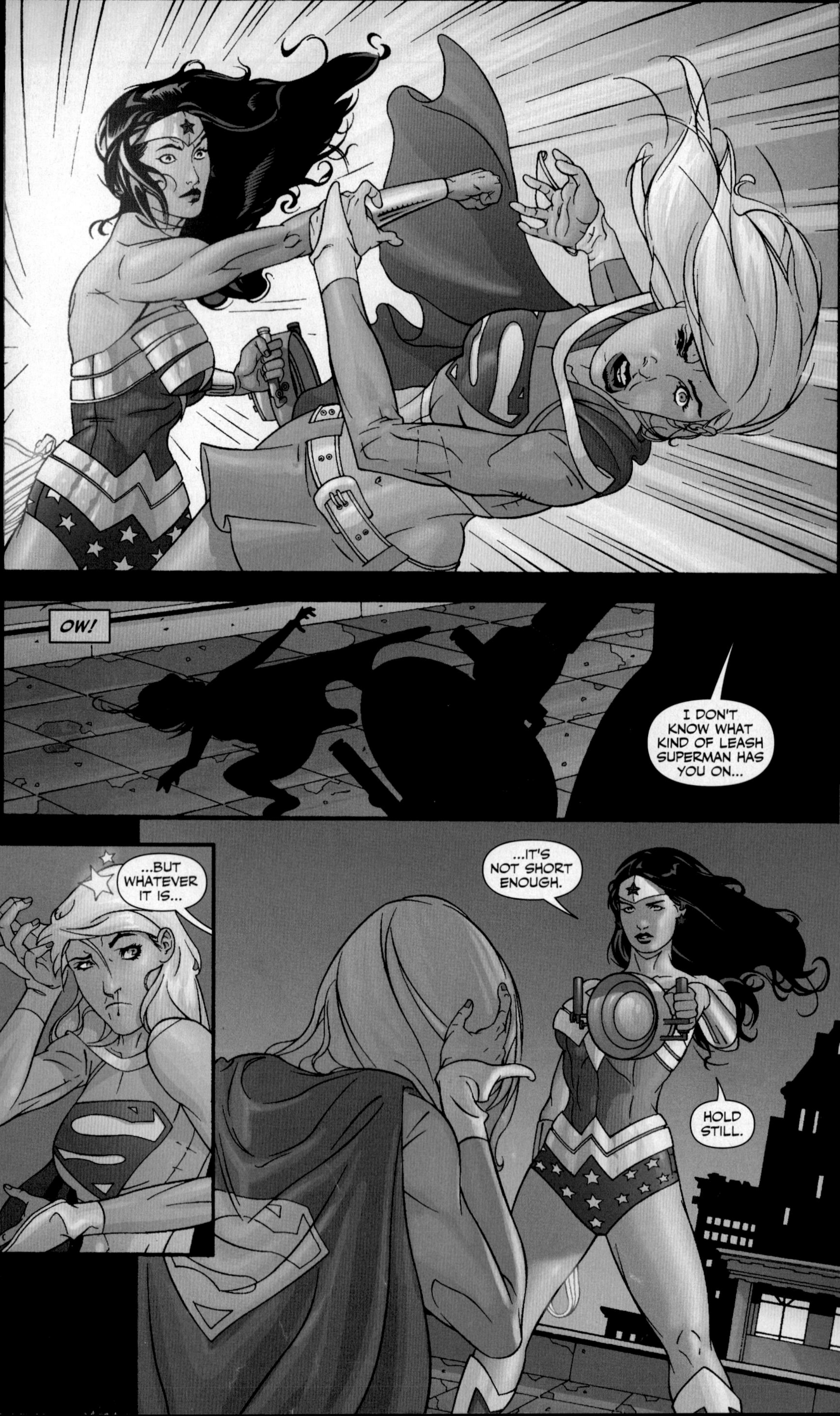
OW!
I DON'T KNOW WHAT KIND OF LEASH SUPERMAN HAS YOU ON...
...BUT WHATEVER IT IS...
...IT'S NOT SHORT ENOUGH.
HOLD STILL.

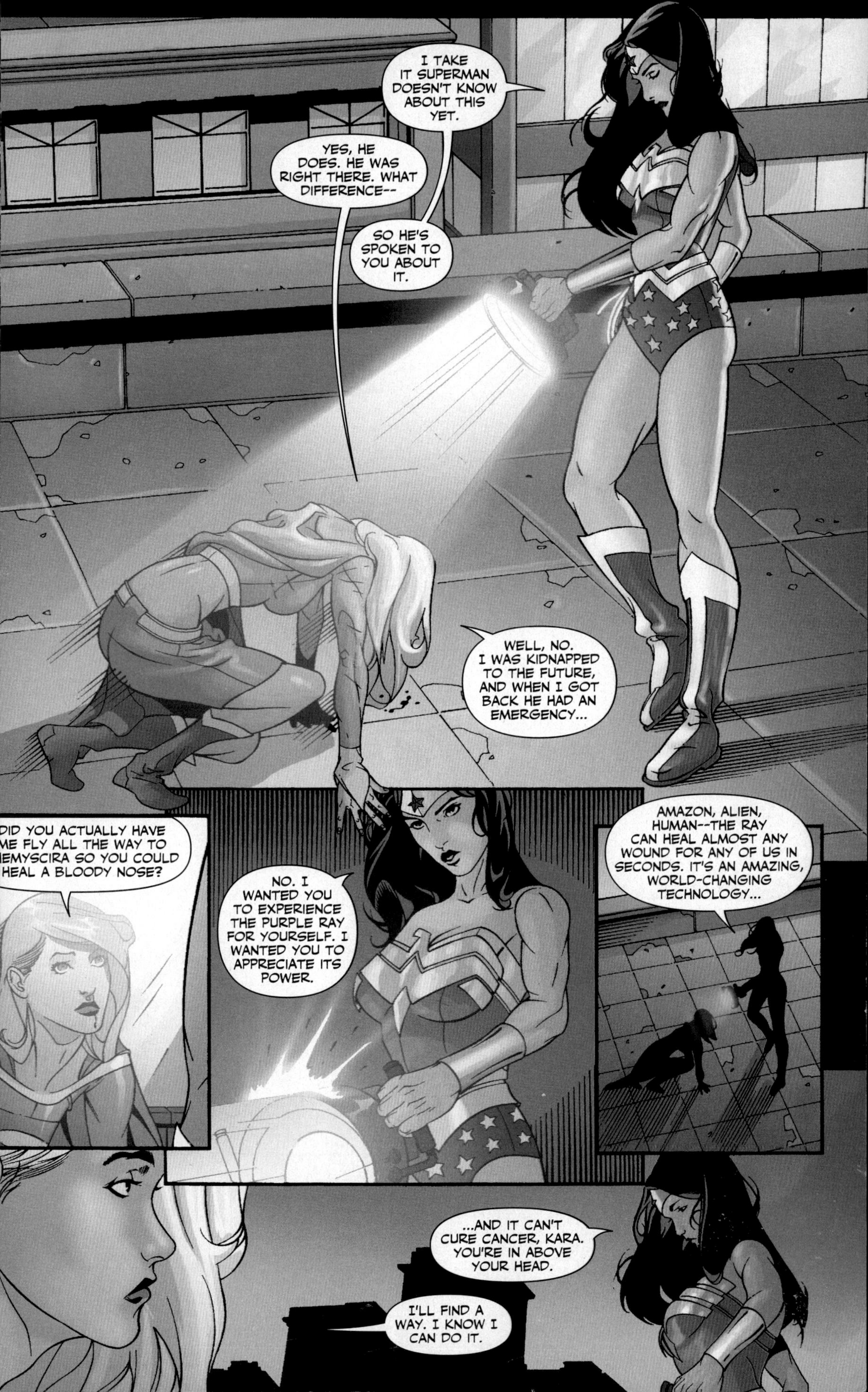
I TAKE IT SUPERMAN DOESN'T KNOW ABOUT THIS YET.
YES, HE DOES. HE WAS RIGHT THERE. WHAT DIFFERENCE--
SO HE'S SPOKEN TO YOU ABOUT IT.
WELL, NO. I WAS KIDNAPPED TO THE FUTURE, AND WHEN I GOT BACK HE HAD AN EMERGENCY...
DID YOU ACTUALLY HAVE ME FLY ALL THE WAY TO EMYSCIRA SO YOU COULD HEAL A BLOODY NOSE?
NO. I WANTED YOU TO EXPERIENCE THE PURPLE RAY FOR YOURSELF. I WANTED YOU TO APPRECIATE ITS POWER.
AMAZON, ALIEN, HUMAN--THE RAY CAN HEAL ALMOST ANY WOUND FOR ANY OF US IN SECONDS. IT'S AN AMAZING, WORLD-CHANGING TECHNOLOGY...
...AND IT CAN'T CURE CANCER, KARA. YOU'RE IN ABOVE YOUR HEAD.
I'LL FIND A WAY. I KNOW I CAN DO IT.

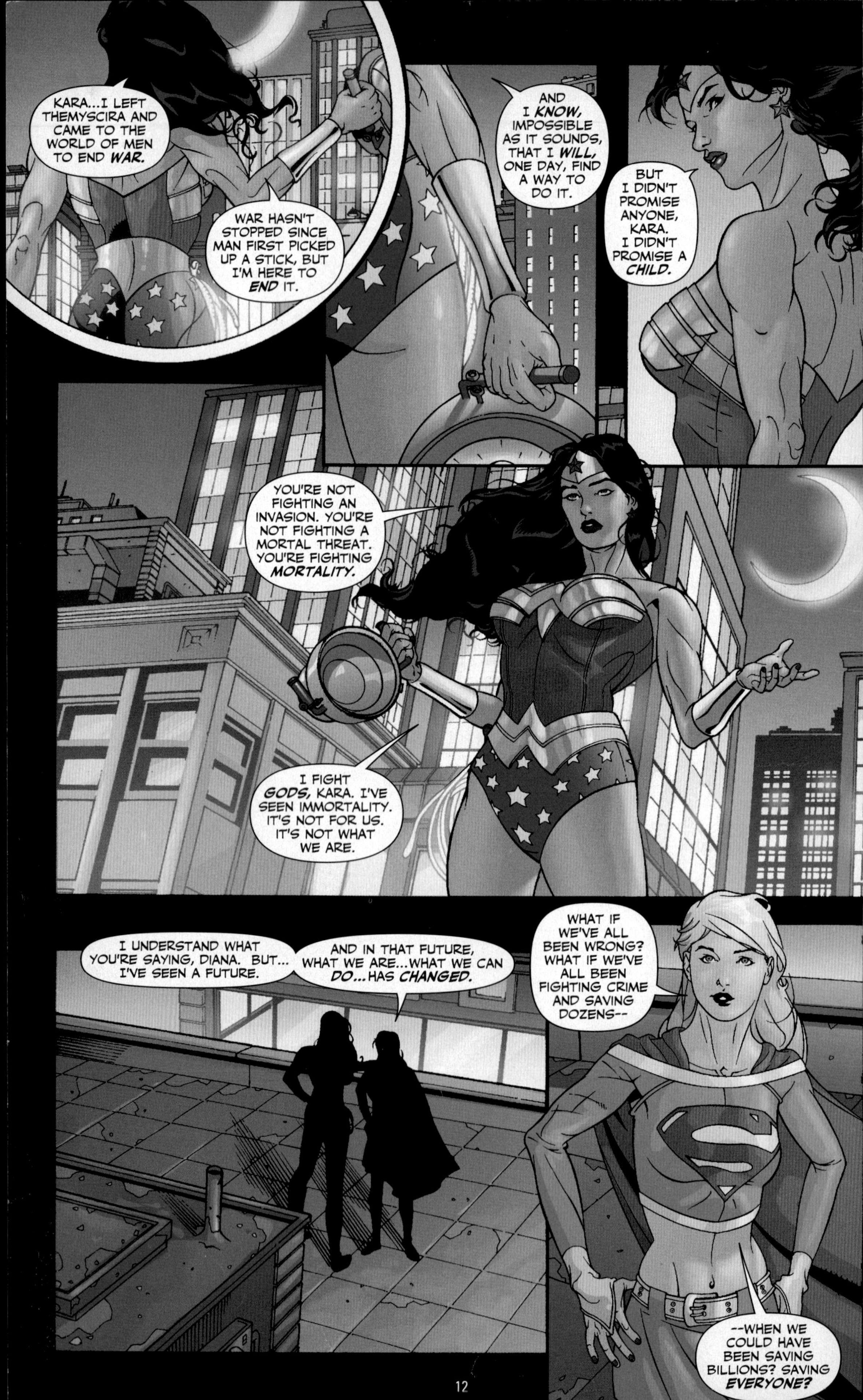
KARA...I LEFT THEMYSCIRA AND CAME TO THE WORLD OF MEN TO END WAR.
WAR HASN'T STOPPED SINCE MAN FIRST PICKED UP A STICK, BUT I'M HERE TO END IT.
AND I KNOW, IMPOSSIBLE AS IT SOUNDS, THAT I WILL, ONE DAY, FIND A WAY TO DO IT.
BUT I DIDN'T PROMISE ANYONE, KARA. I DIDN'T PROMISE A CHILD.
YOU'RE NOT FIGHTING AN INVASION. YOU'RE NOT FIGHTING A MORTAL THREAT. YOU'RE FIGHTING MORTALITY.
I FIGHT GODS, KARA. I'VE SEEN IMMORTALITY. IT'S NOT FOR US. IT'S NOT WHAT WE ARE.
I UNDERSTAND WHAT YOU'RE SAYING, DIANA. BUT... I'VE SEEN A FUTURE.
AND IN THAT FUTURE, WHAT WE ARE...WHAT WE CAN DO...HAS CHANGED.
WHAT IF WE'VE ALL BEEN WRONG? WHAT IF WE'VE ALL BEEN FIGHTING CRIME AND SAVING DOZENS--
--WHEN WE COULD HAVE BEEN SAVING BILLIONS? SAVING EVERYONE?

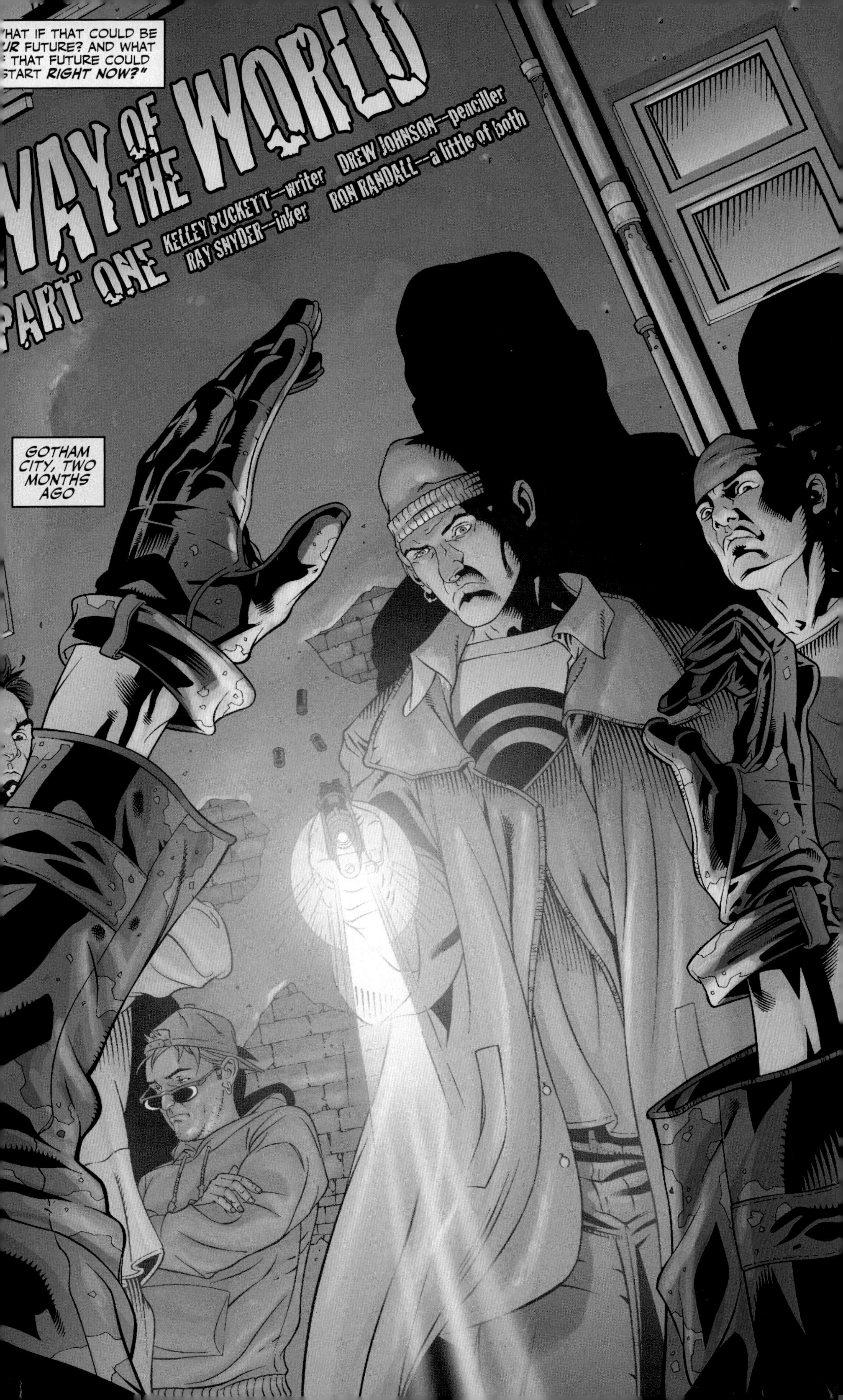
"WHAT IF THAT COULD BE YOUR FUTURE? AND WHAT IF THAT FUTURE COULD START RIGHT NOW?"
WAY OF THE WORLD
PART ONE
KELLEY PUCKETT--writer
DREW JOHNSON--penciller
RAY SNYDER--inker
RON RANDALL--a little of both
GOTHAM CITY, TWO MONTHS AGO

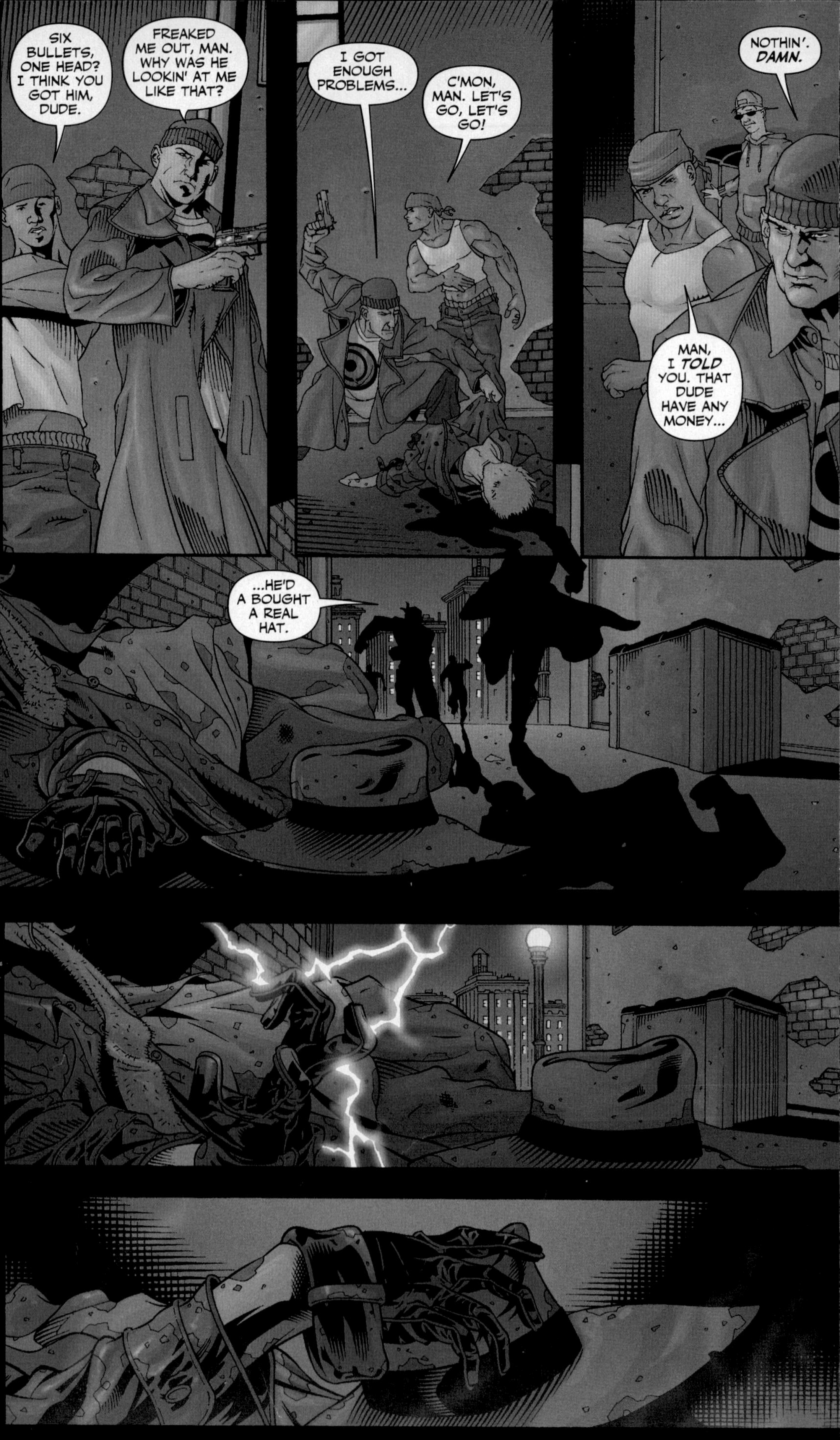
SIX BULLETS, ONE HEAD? I THINK YOU GOT HIM, DUDE.
FREAKED ME OUT, MAN. WHY WAS HE LOOKIN' AT ME LIKE THAT?
I GOT ENOUGH PROBLEMS...
C'MON, MAN. LET'S GO, LET'S GO!
NOTHIN'. *DAMN.*
MAN, I *TOLD* YOU. THAT DUDE HAVE ANY MONEY...
...HE'D A BOUGHT A REAL HAT.

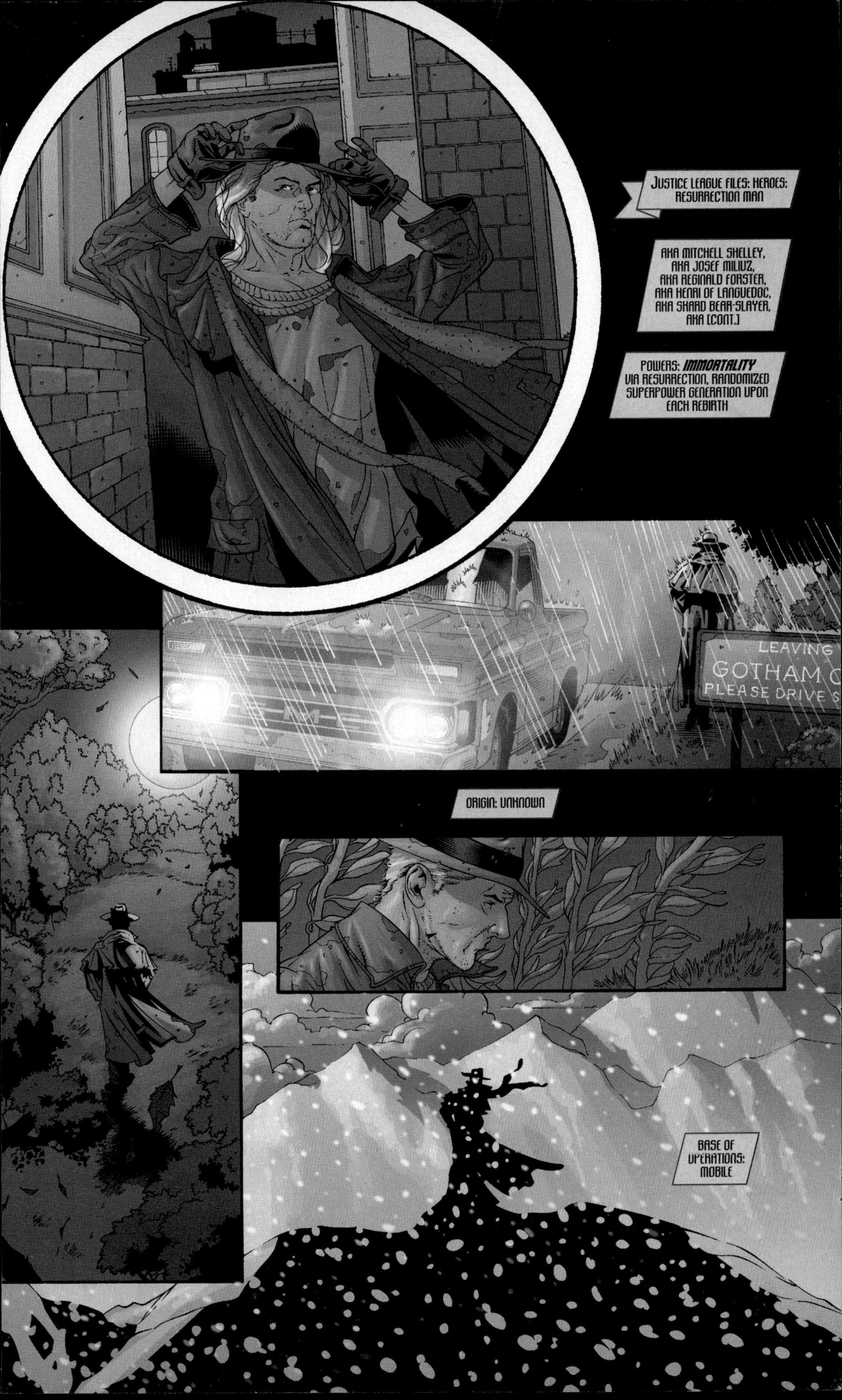
JUSTICE LEAGUE FILES: HEROES:
RESURRECTION MAN
AKA MITCHELL SHELLEY,
AKA JOSEF MILIUZ,
AKA REGINALD FORSTER,
AKA HENRI OF LANGUEDOC,
AKA SHARD BEAR-SLAYER,
AKA [CONT.]
POWERS: IMMORTALITY
VIA RESURRECTION, RANDOMIZED
SUPERPOWER GENERATION UPON
EACH REBIRTH
LEAVING
GOTHAM C
PLEASE DRIVE S
ORIGIN: UNKNOWN
BASE OF
OPERATIONS:
MOBILE

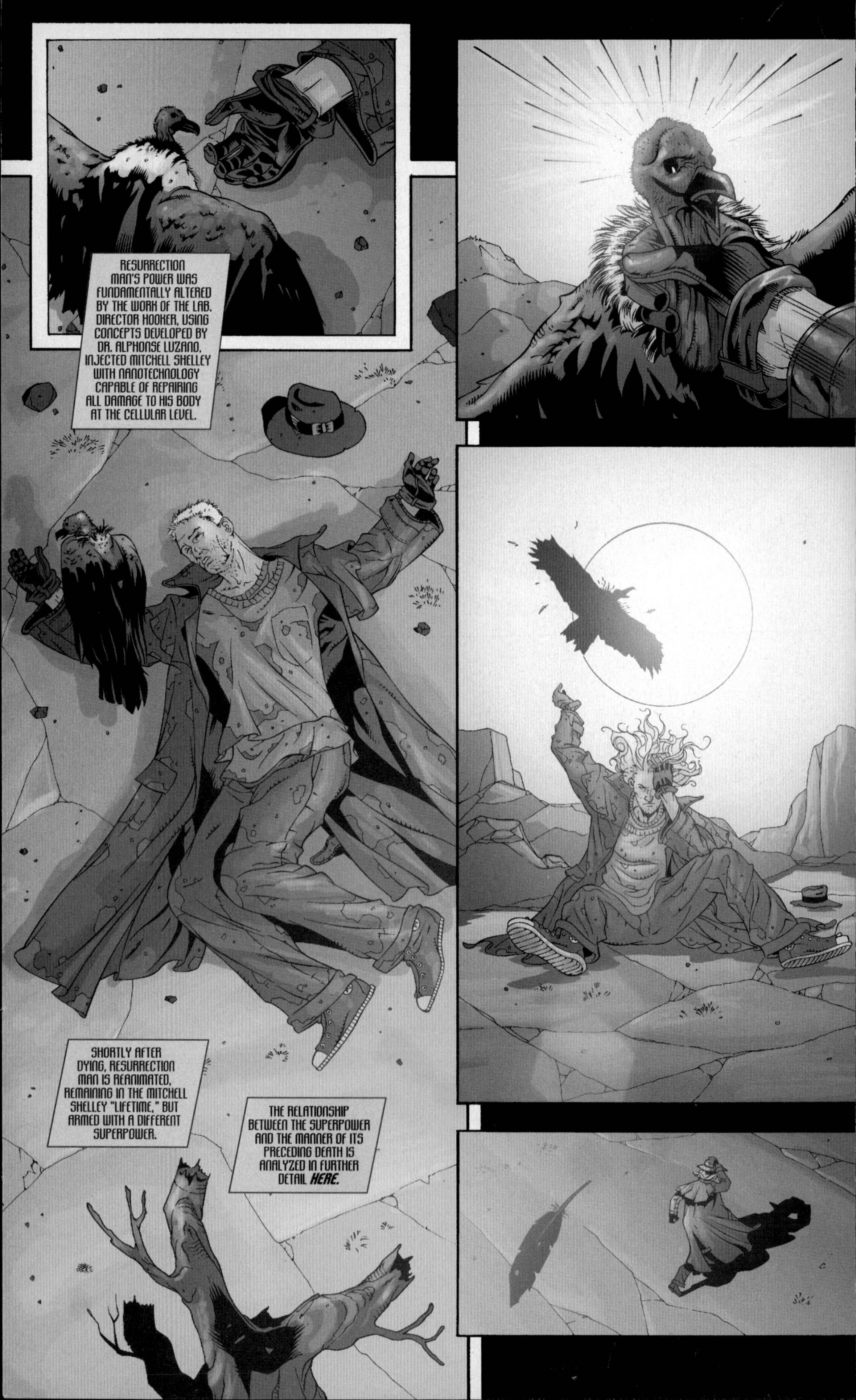
RESURRECTION MAN'S POWER WAS FUNDAMENTALLY ALTERED BY THE WORK OF THE LAB. DIRECTOR HOOKER, USING CONCEPTS DEVELOPED BY DR. ALPHONSE LUZANO, INJECTED MITCHELL SHELLEY WITH NANOTECHNOLOGY CAPABLE OF REPAIRING ALL DAMAGE TO HIS BODY AT THE CELLULAR LEVEL.
SHORTLY AFTER DYING, RESURRECTION MAN IS REANIMATED, REMAINING IN THE MITCHELL SHELLEY "LIFETIME," BUT ARMED WITH A DIFFERENT SUPERPOWER.
THE RELATIONSHIP BETWEEN THE SUPERPOWER AND THE MANNER OF ITS PRECEDING DEATH IS ANALYZED IN FURTHER DETAIL ***HERE.***

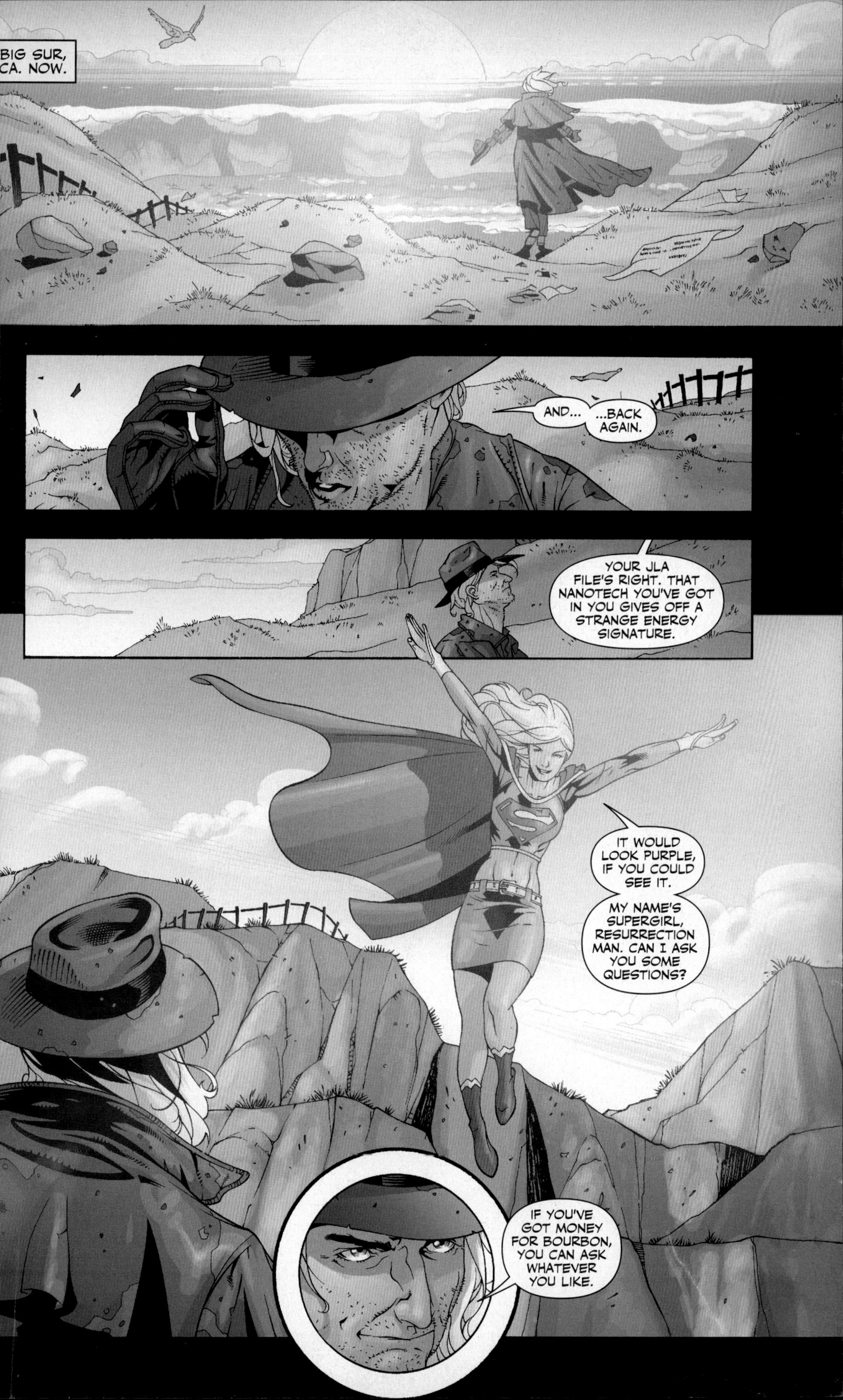
BIG SUR, CA. NOW.
AND...
...BACK AGAIN.
YOUR JLA FILE'S RIGHT. THAT NANOTECH YOU'VE GOT IN YOU GIVES OFF A STRANGE ENERGY SIGNATURE.
IT WOULD LOOK PURPLE, IF YOU COULD SEE IT.
MY NAME'S SUPERGIRL, RESURRECTION MAN. CAN I ASK YOU SOME QUESTIONS?
IF YOU'VE GOT MONEY FOR BOURBON, YOU CAN ASK WHATEVER YOU LIKE.

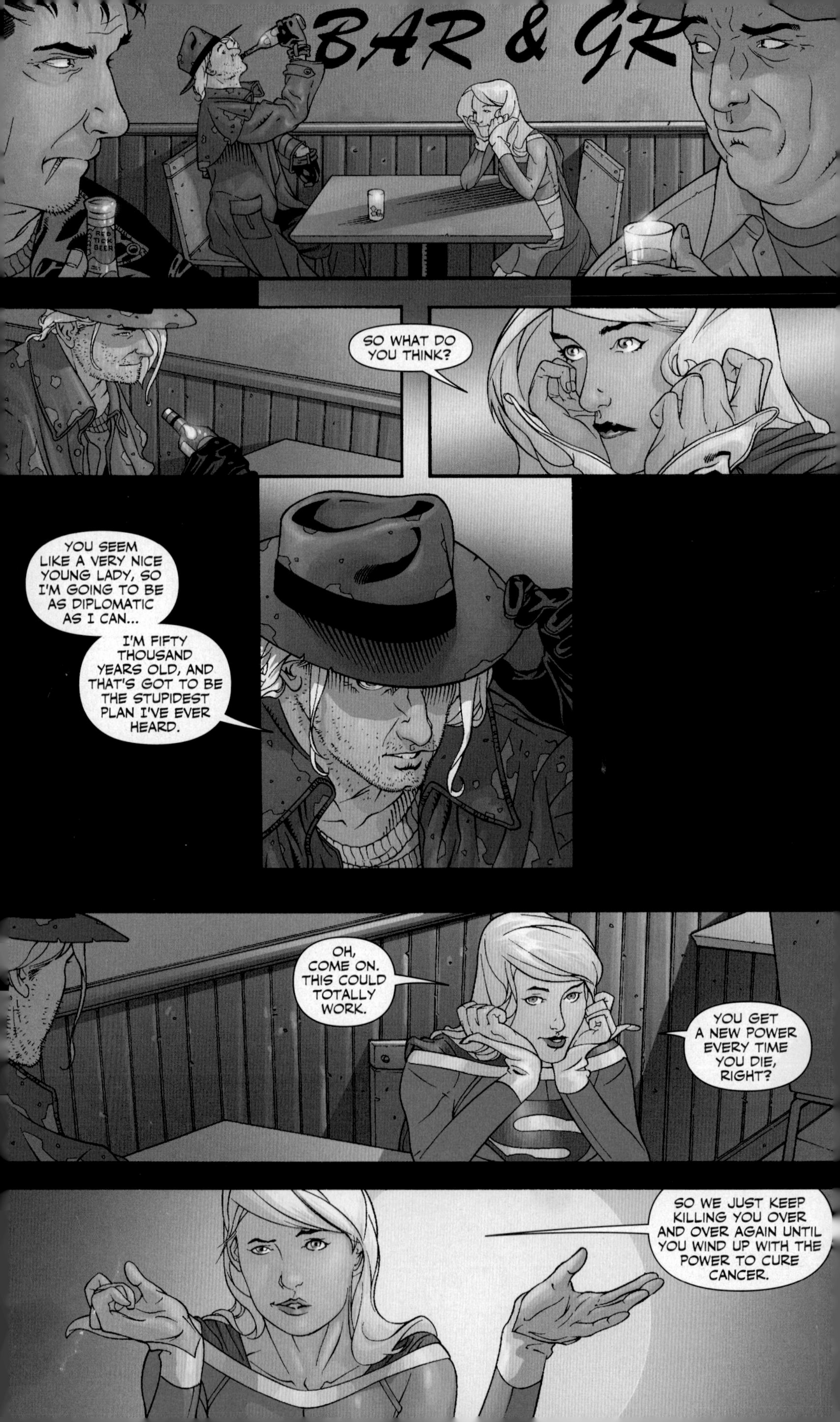
BAR & GR
RED TICK BEER
SO WHAT DO YOU THINK?
YOU SEEM LIKE A VERY NICE YOUNG LADY, SO I'M GOING TO BE AS DIPLOMATIC AS I CAN...
I'M FIFTY THOUSAND YEARS OLD, AND THAT'S GOT TO BE THE STUPIDEST PLAN I'VE EVER HEARD.
OH, COME ON. THIS COULD TOTALLY WORK.
YOU GET A NEW POWER EVERY TIME YOU DIE, RIGHT?
SO WE JUST KEEP KILLING YOU OVER AND OVER AGAIN UNTIL YOU WIND UP WITH THE POWER TO CURE CANCER.

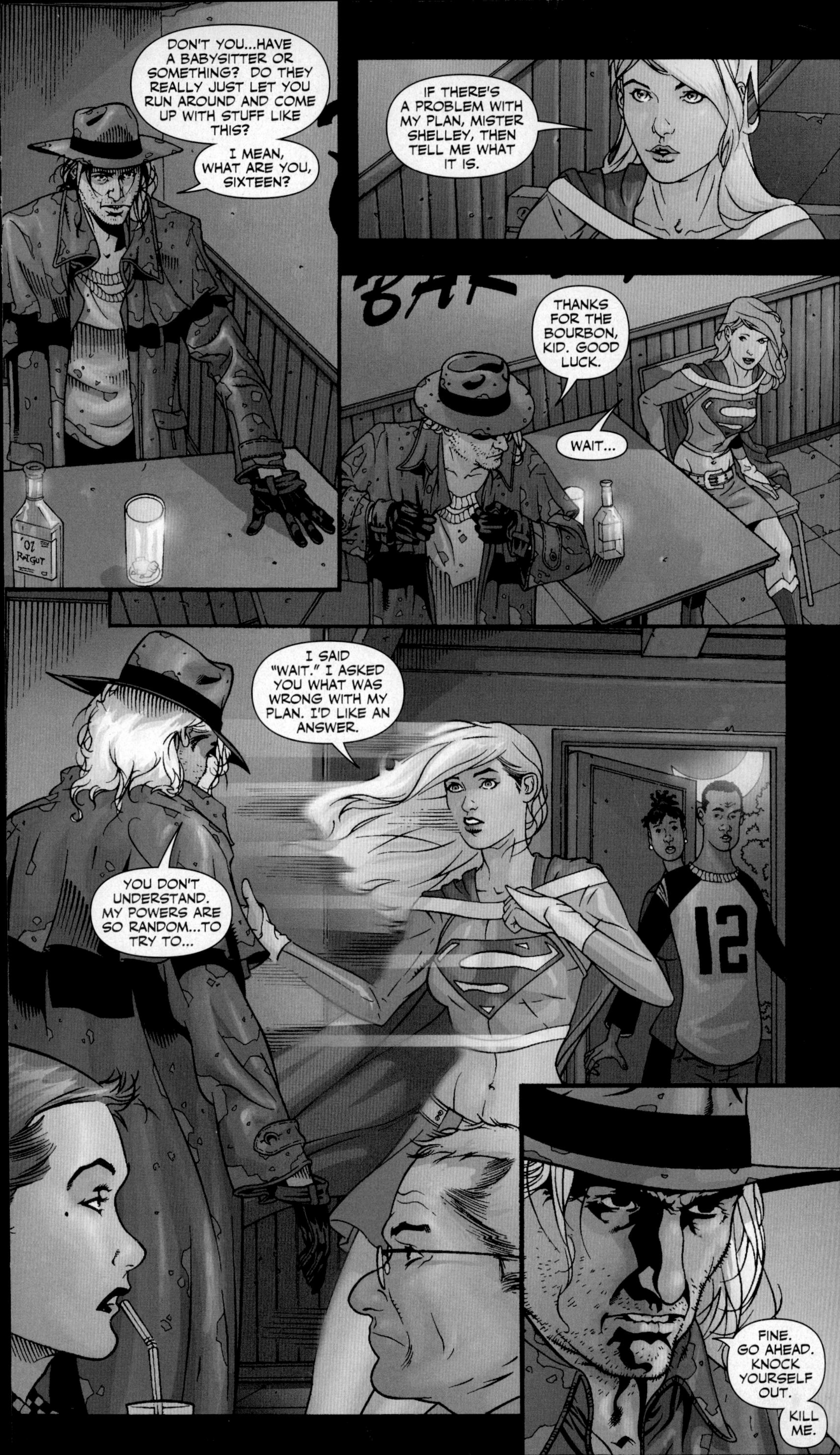
DON'T YOU...HAVE A BABYSITTER OR SOMETHING? DO THEY REALLY JUST LET YOU RUN AROUND AND COME UP WITH STUFF LIKE THIS?
I MEAN, WHAT ARE YOU, SIXTEEN?
'02 RATGUT
IF THERE'S A PROBLEM WITH MY PLAN, MISTER SHELLEY, THEN TELL ME WHAT IT IS.
THANKS FOR THE BOURBON, KID. GOOD LUCK.
WAIT...
I SAID "WAIT." I ASKED YOU WHAT WAS WRONG WITH MY PLAN. I'D LIKE AN ANSWER.
YOU DON'T UNDERSTAND. MY POWERS ARE SO RANDOM...TO TRY TO...
12
FINE. GO AHEAD. KNOCK YOURSELF OUT.
KILL ME.

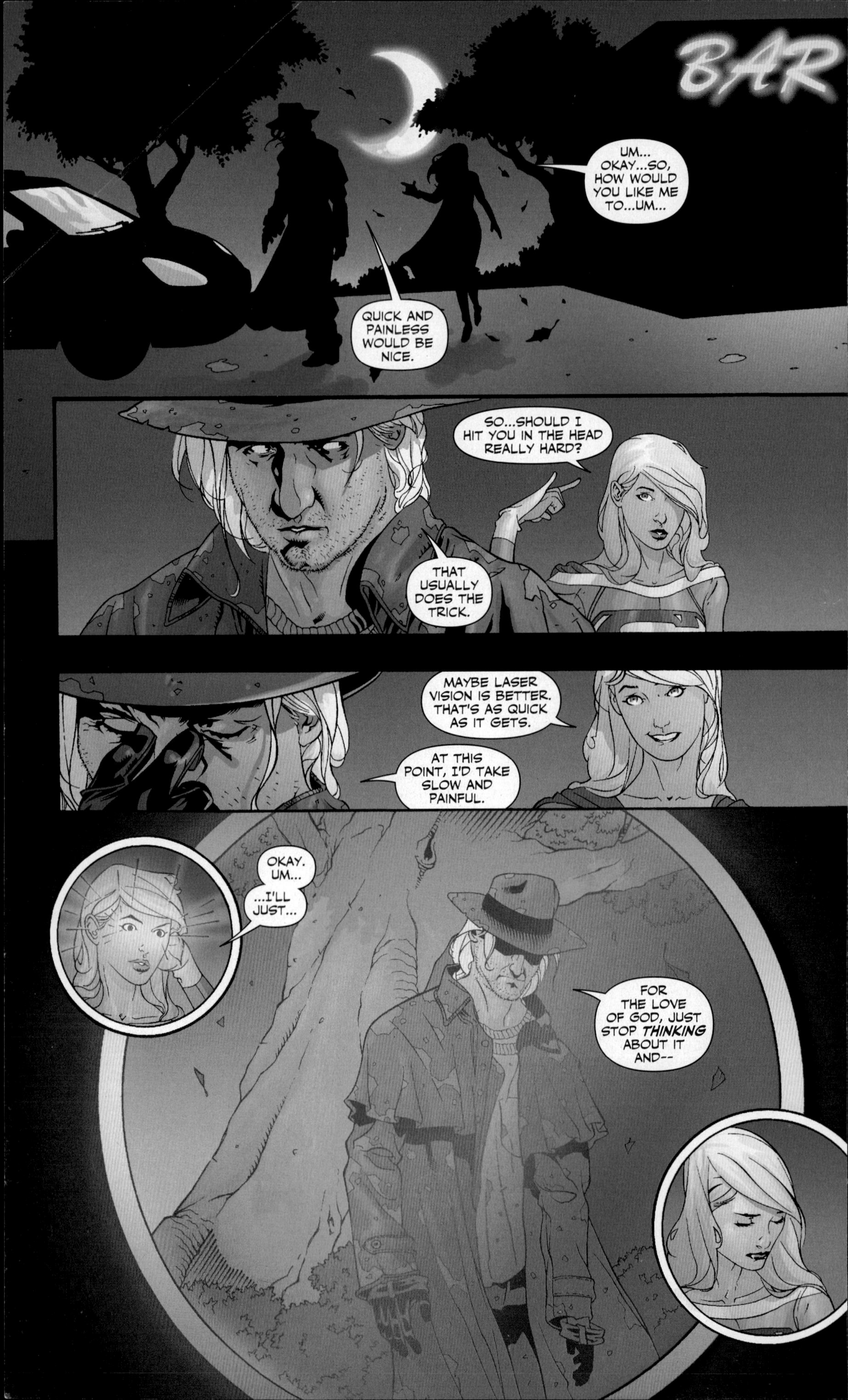
BAR
UM... OKAY...SO, HOW WOULD YOU LIKE ME TO...UM...
QUICK AND PAINLESS WOULD BE NICE.
SO...SHOULD I HIT YOU IN THE HEAD REALLY HARD?
THAT USUALLY DOES THE TRICK.
MAYBE LASER VISION IS BETTER. THAT'S AS QUICK AS IT GETS.
AT THIS POINT, I'D TAKE SLOW AND PAINFUL.
OKAY. UM... ...I'LL JUST...
FOR THE LOVE OF GOD, JUST STOP *THINKING* ABOUT IT AND--

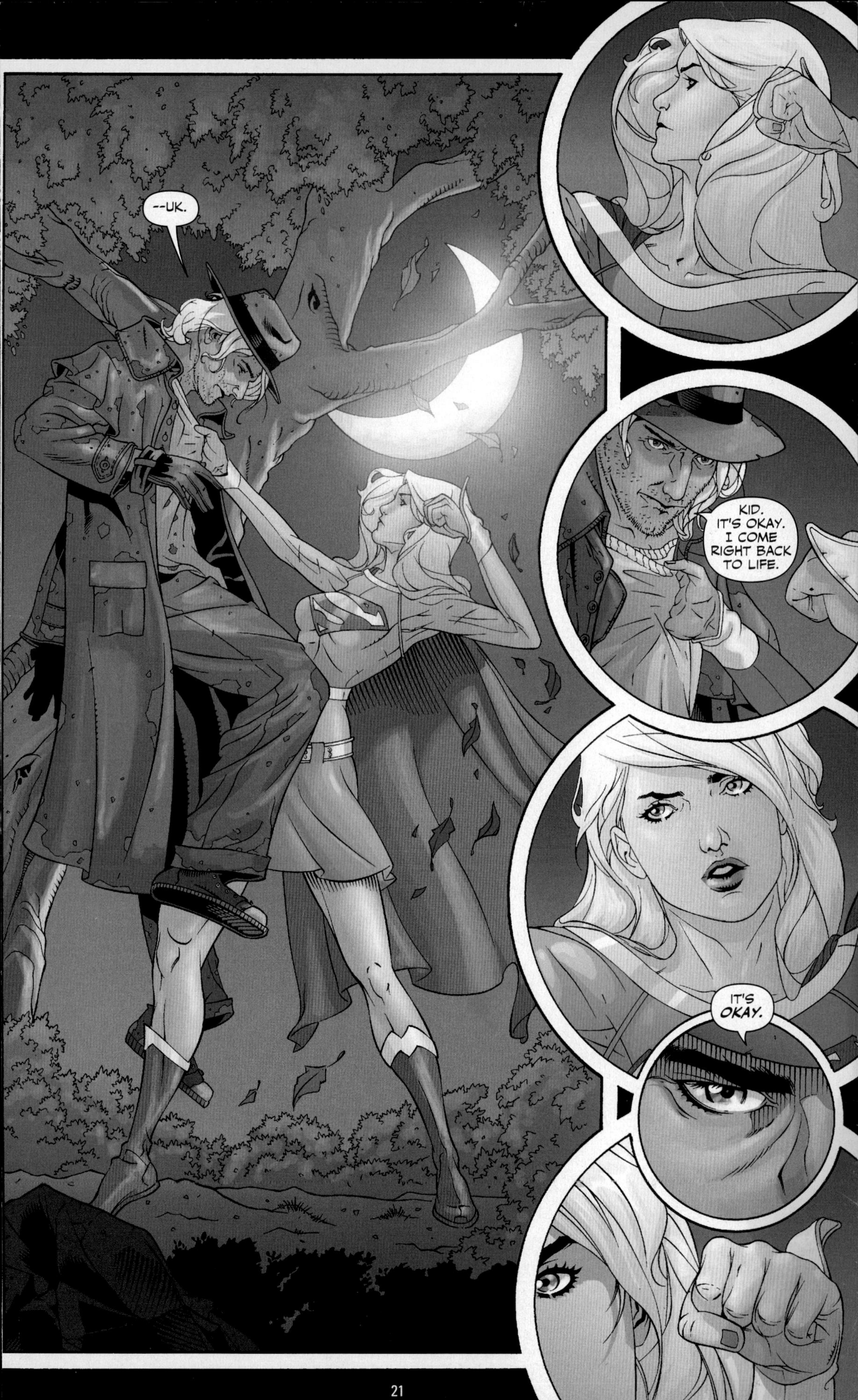
--UK.
KID. IT'S OKAY. I COME RIGHT BACK TO LIFE.
IT'S *OKAY.*

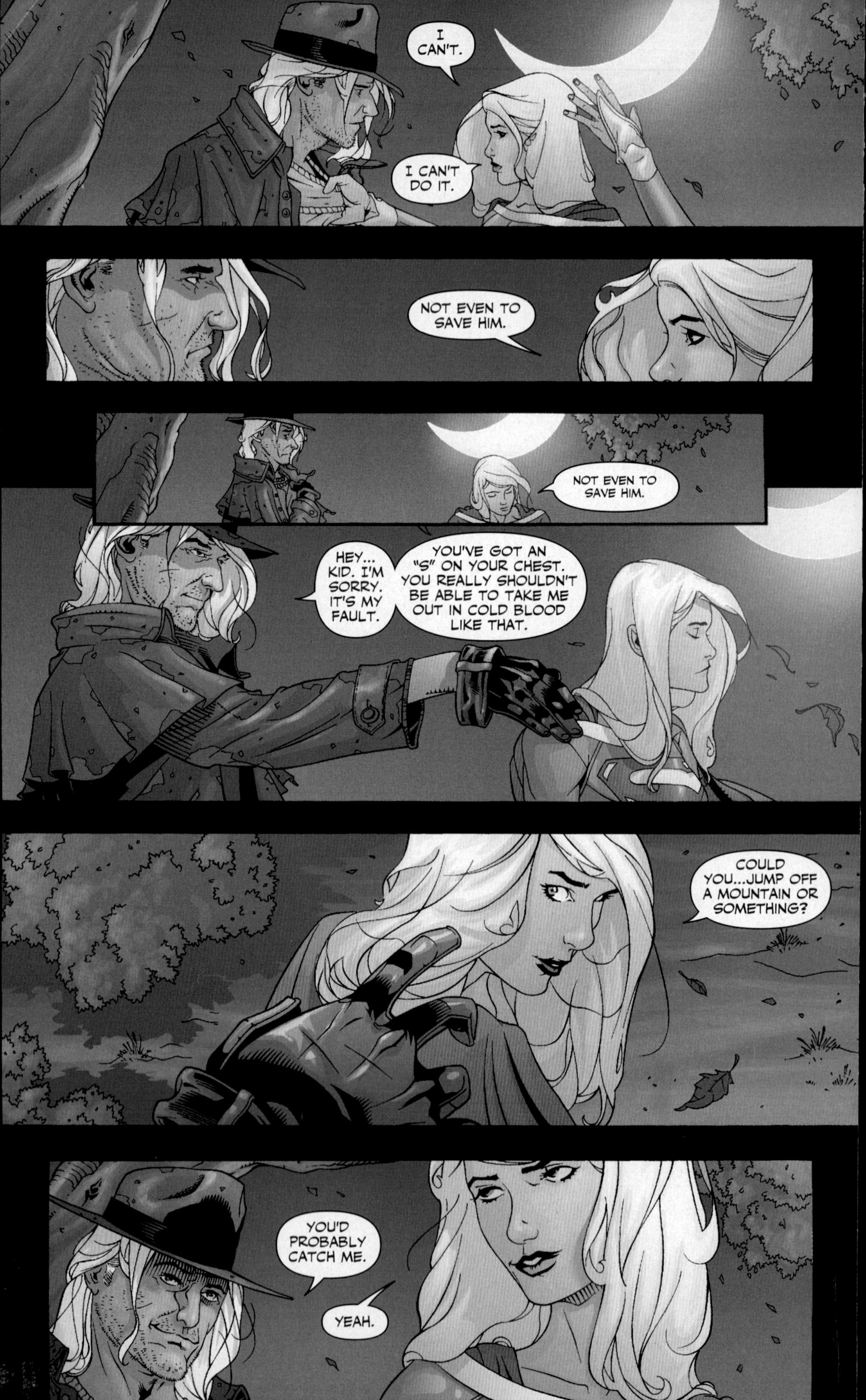
I CAN'T.
I CAN'T DO IT.
NOT EVEN TO SAVE HIM.
NOT EVEN TO SAVE HIM.
HEY... KID. I'M SORRY. IT'S MY FAULT.
YOU'VE GOT AN "S" ON YOUR CHEST. YOU REALLY SHOULDN'T BE ABLE TO TAKE ME OUT IN COLD BLOOD LIKE THAT.
COULD YOU...JUMP OFF A MOUNTAIN OR SOMETHING?
YOU'D PROBABLY CATCH ME.
YEAH.

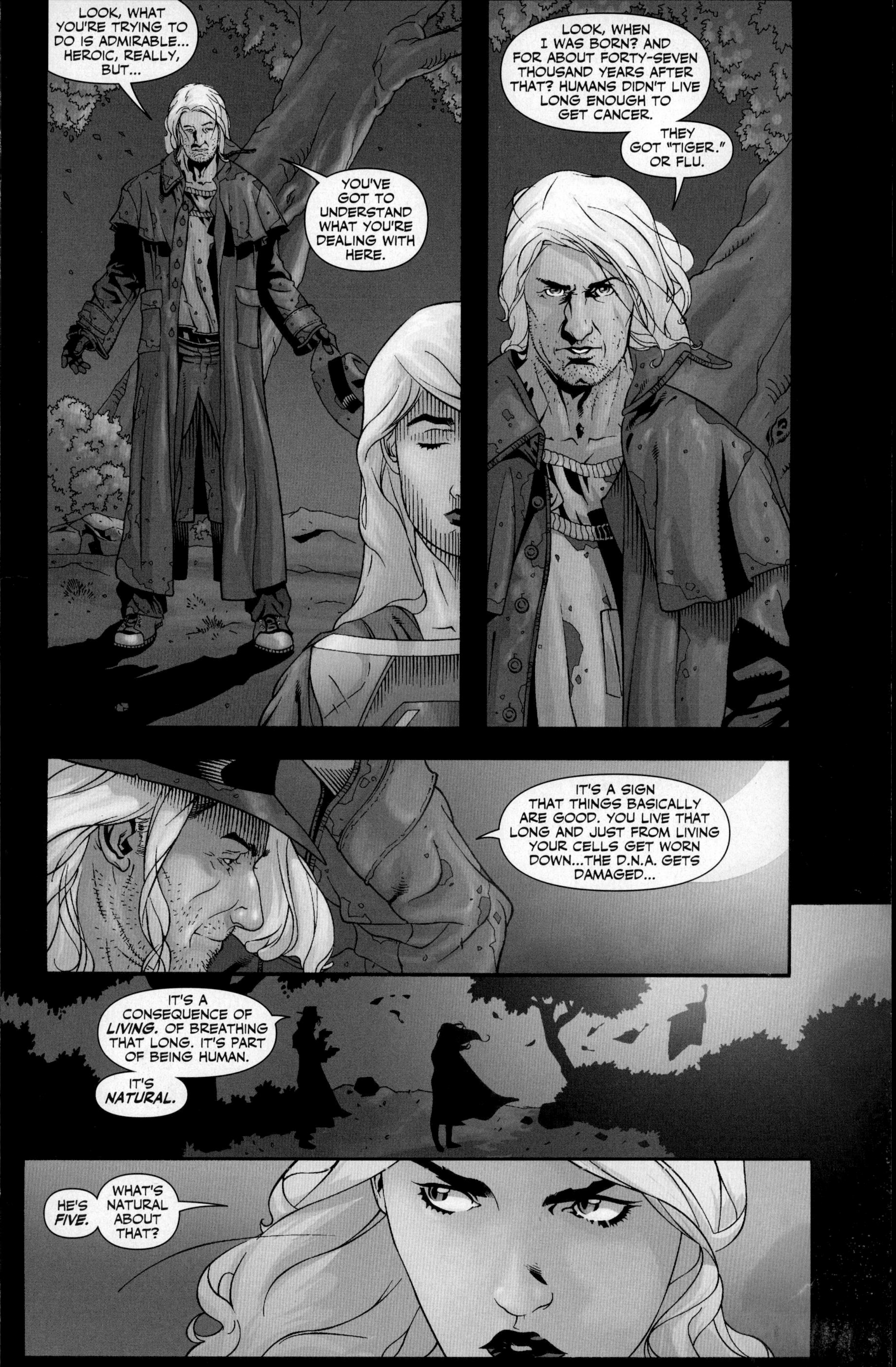
LOOK, WHAT YOU'RE TRYING TO DO IS ADMIRABLE... HEROIC, REALLY, BUT...
YOU'VE GOT TO UNDERSTAND WHAT YOU'RE DEALING WITH HERE.
LOOK, WHEN I WAS BORN? AND FOR ABOUT FORTY-SEVEN THOUSAND YEARS AFTER THAT? HUMANS DIDN'T LIVE LONG ENOUGH TO GET CANCER.
THEY GOT "TIGER." OR FLU.
IT'S A SIGN THAT THINGS BASICALLY ARE GOOD. YOU LIVE THAT LONG AND JUST FROM LIVING YOUR CELLS GET WORN DOWN...THE D.N.A. GETS DAMAGED...
IT'S A CONSEQUENCE OF *LIVING.* OF BREATHING THAT LONG. IT'S PART OF BEING HUMAN.
IT'S *NATURAL.*
HE'S *FIVE.*
WHAT'S NATURAL ABOUT THAT?

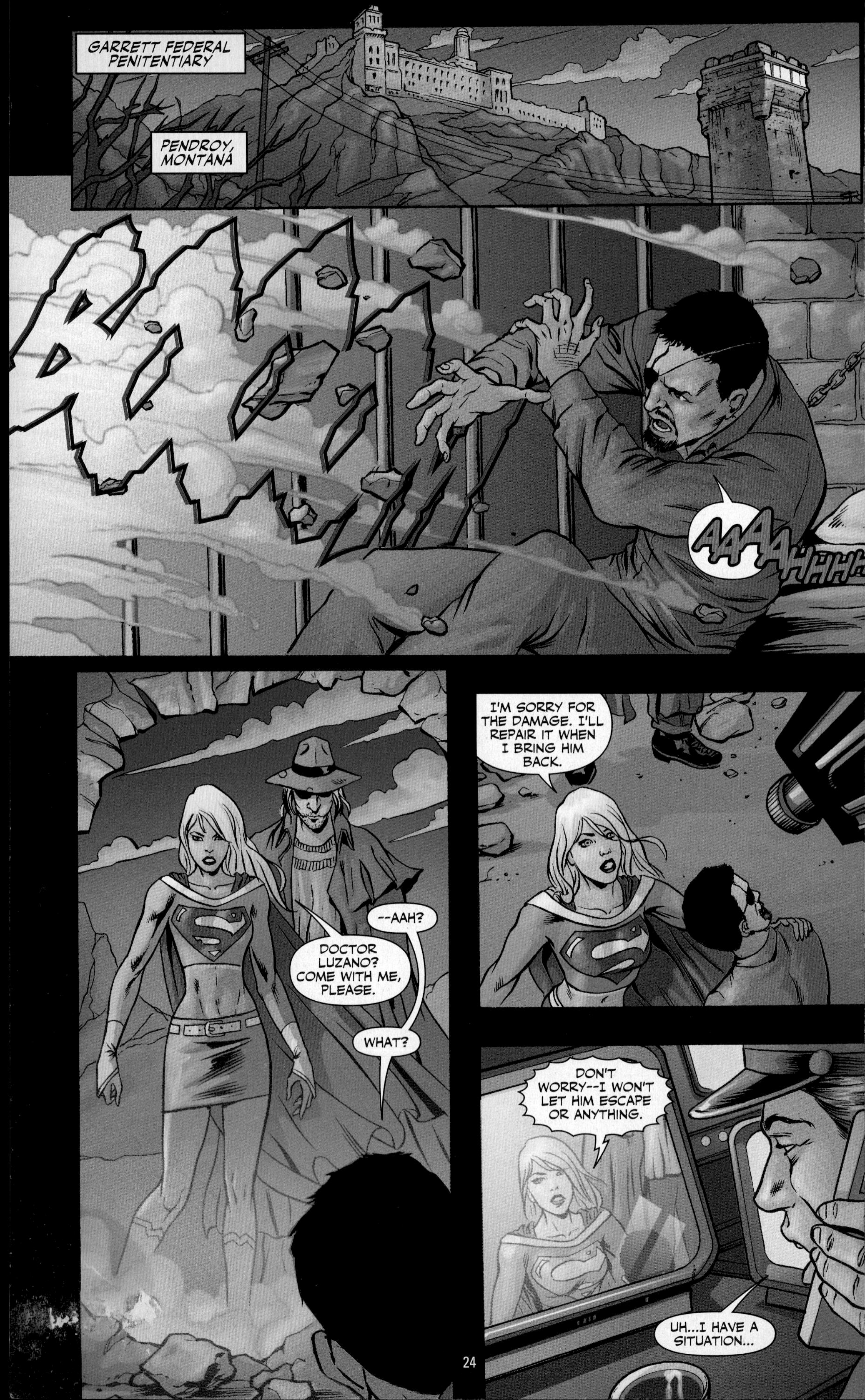
GARRETT FEDERAL PENITENTIARY
PENDROY, MONTANA
AAAAHHHH
--AAH?
DOCTOR LUZANO? COME WITH ME, PLEASE.
WHAT?
I'M SORRY FOR THE DAMAGE. I'LL REPAIR IT WHEN I BRING HIM BACK.
DON'T WORRY--I WON'T LET HIM ESCAPE OR ANYTHING.
UH...I HAVE A SITUATION...

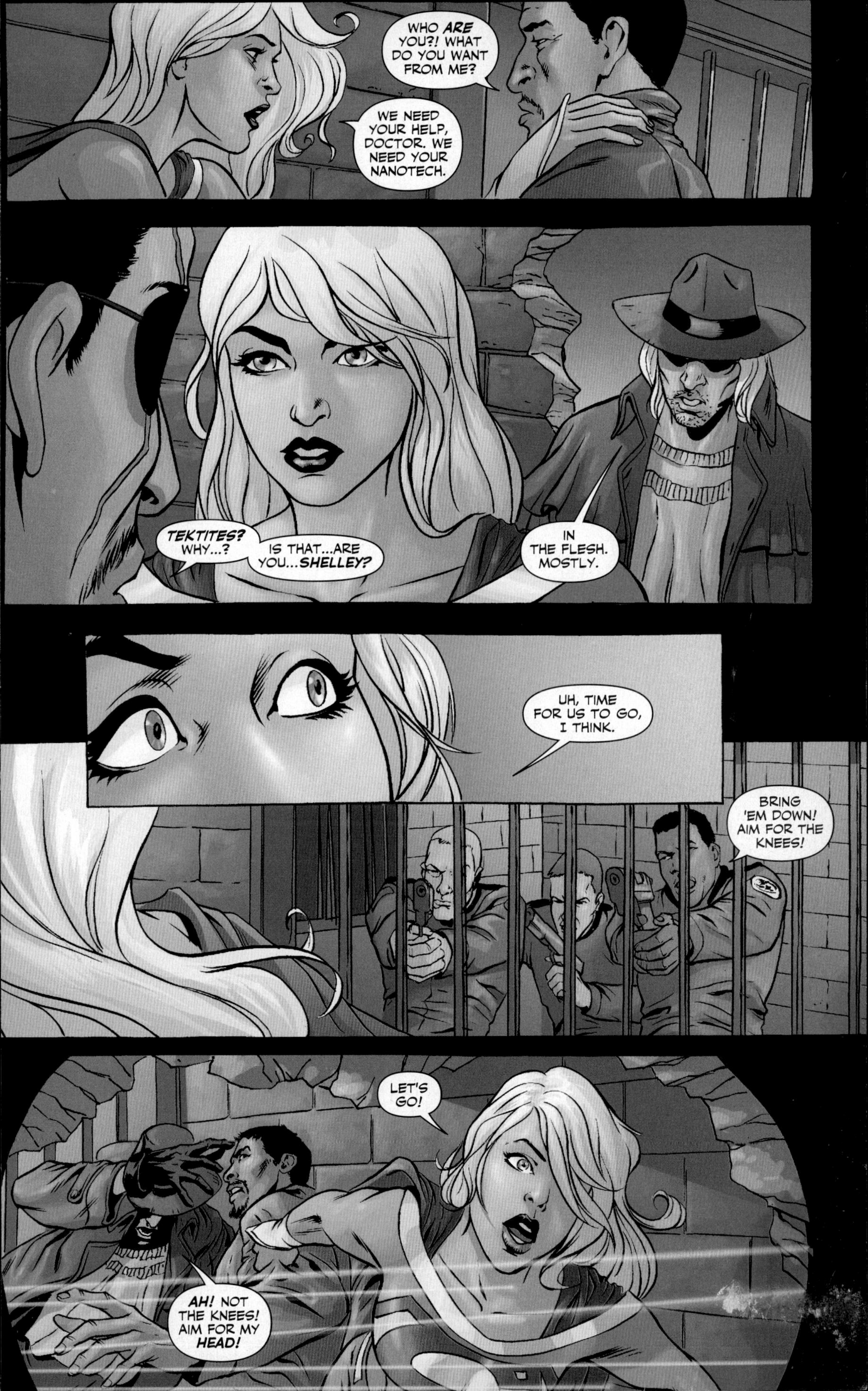
WHO ARE YOU?! WHAT DO YOU WANT FROM ME?
WE NEED YOUR HELP, DOCTOR. WE NEED YOUR NANOTECH.
TEKTITES? WHY...?
IS THAT...ARE YOU...SHELLEY?
IN THE FLESH. MOSTLY.
UH, TIME FOR US TO GO, I THINK.
BRING 'EM DOWN! AIM FOR THE KNEES!
LET'S GO!
AH! NOT THE KNEES! AIM FOR MY HEAD!

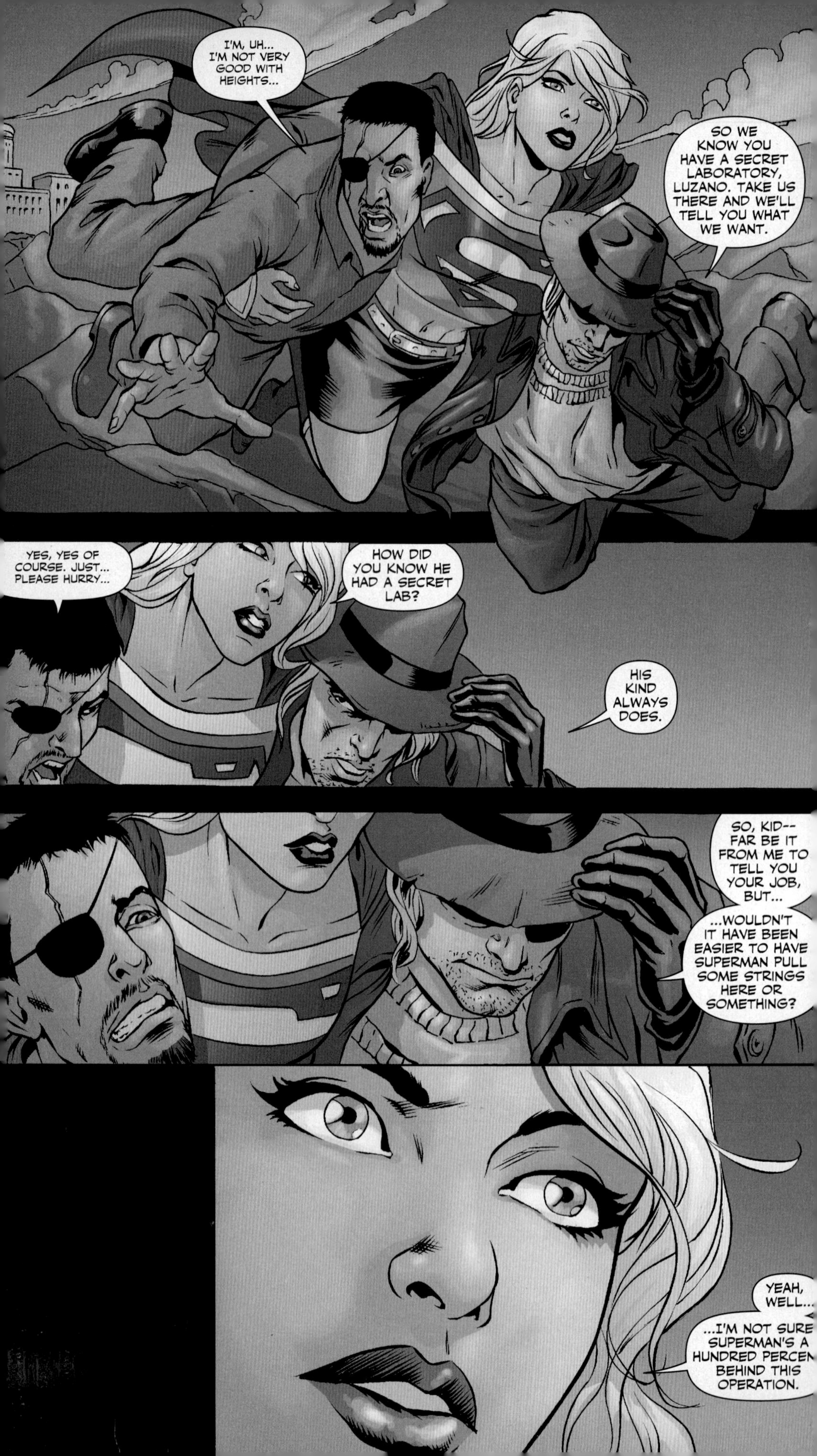
I'M, UH... I'M NOT VERY GOOD WITH HEIGHTS...
SO WE KNOW YOU HAVE A SECRET LABORATORY, LUZANO. TAKE US THERE AND WE'LL TELL YOU WHAT WE WANT.
YES, YES OF COURSE. JUST... PLEASE HURRY...
HOW DID YOU KNOW HE HAD A SECRET LAB?
HIS KIND ALWAYS DOES.
SO, KID-- FAR BE IT FROM ME TO TELL YOU YOUR JOB, BUT...
...WOULDN'T IT HAVE BEEN EASIER TO HAVE SUPERMAN PULL SOME STRINGS HERE OR SOMETHING?
YEAH, WELL...
...I'M NOT SURE SUPERMAN'S A HUNDRED PERCEN BEHIND THIS OPERATION.

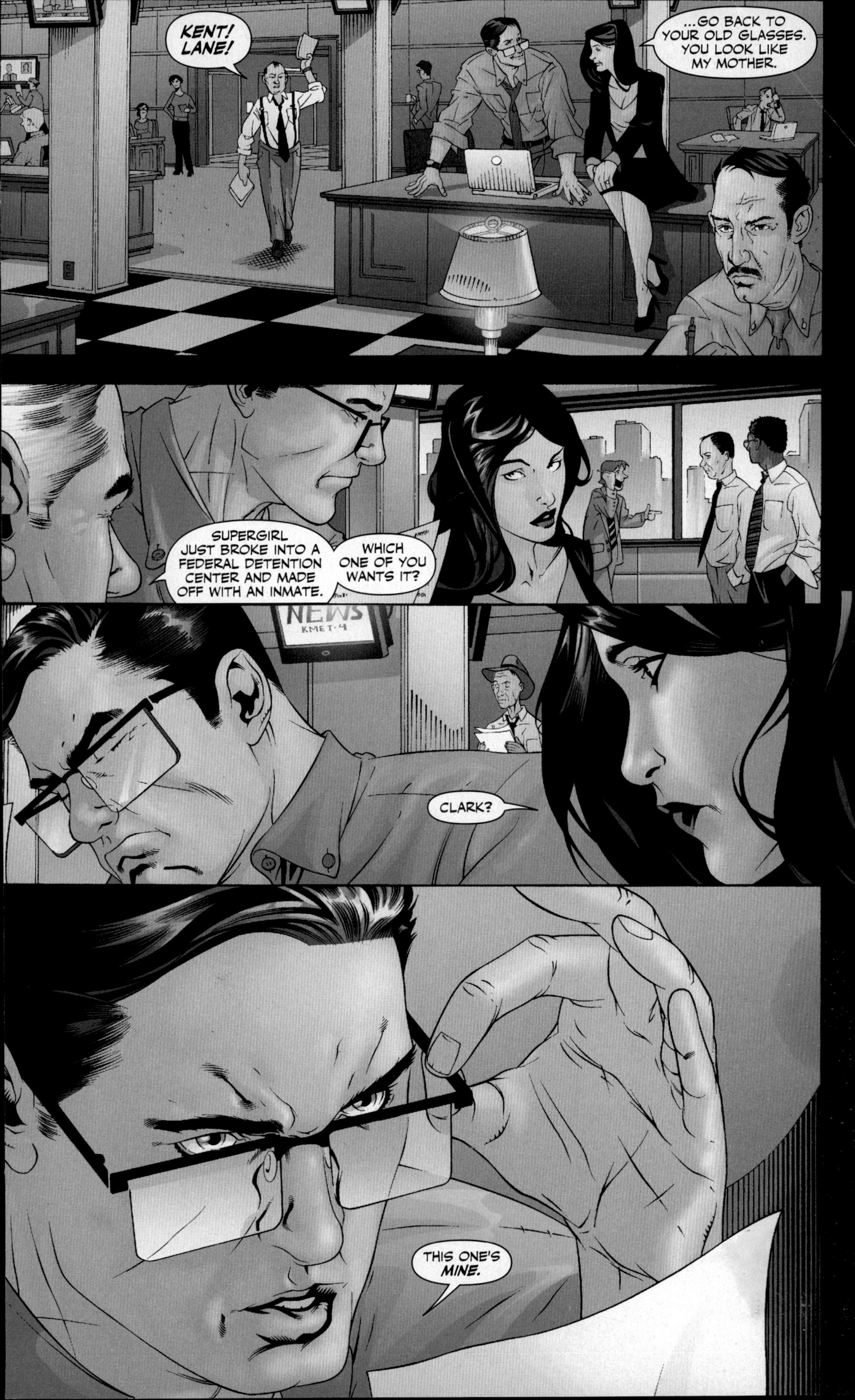
KENT! LANE!
...GO BACK TO YOUR OLD GLASSES. YOU LOOK LIKE MY MOTHER.
SUPERGIRL JUST BROKE INTO A FEDERAL DETENTION CENTER AND MADE OFF WITH AN INMATE.
WHICH ONE OF YOU WANTS IT?
NEWS
KMET·4
CLARK?
THIS ONE'S MINE.

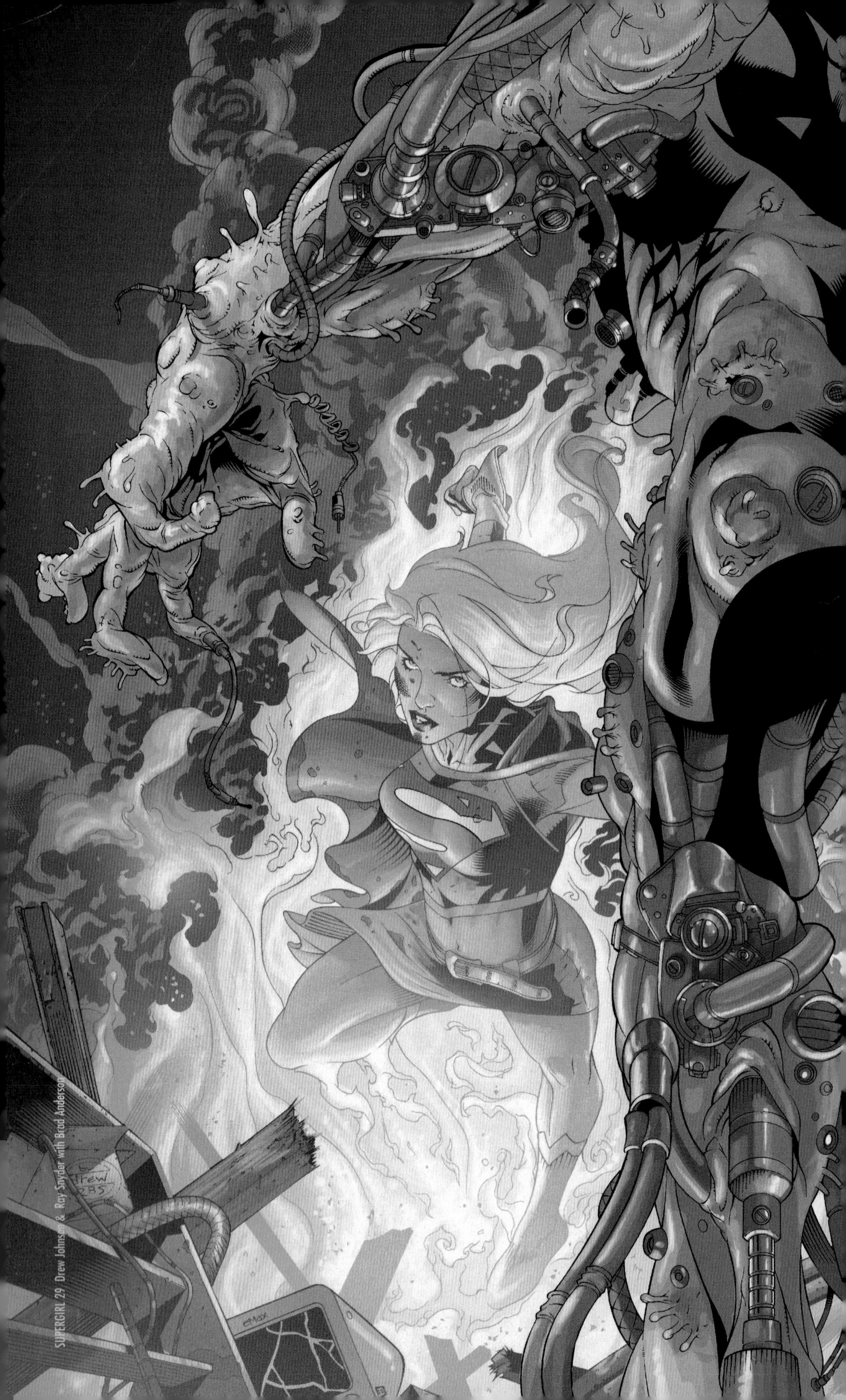

SUPERGIRL 29 Drew Johnson & Roy Snyder with Brad Anderson

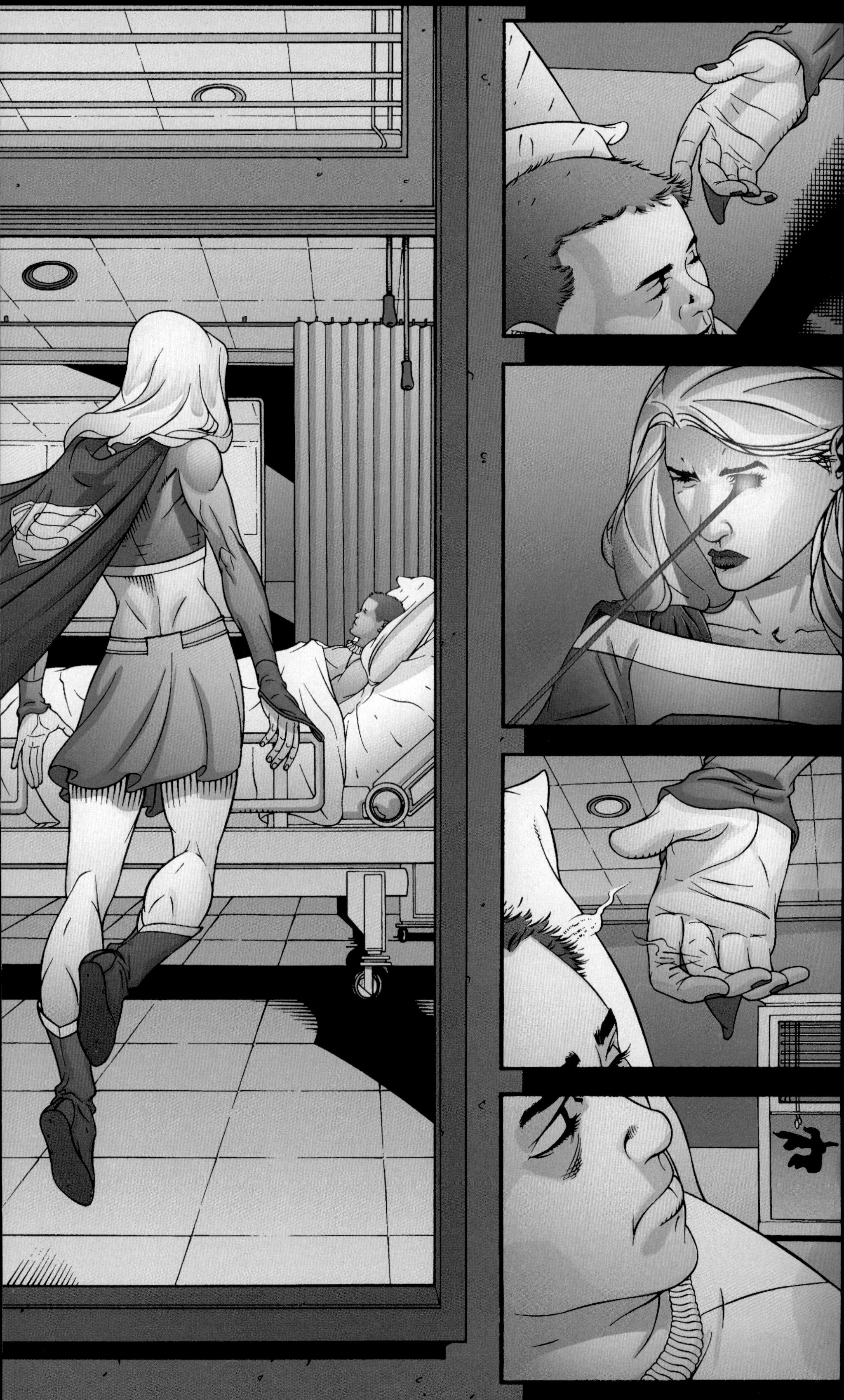

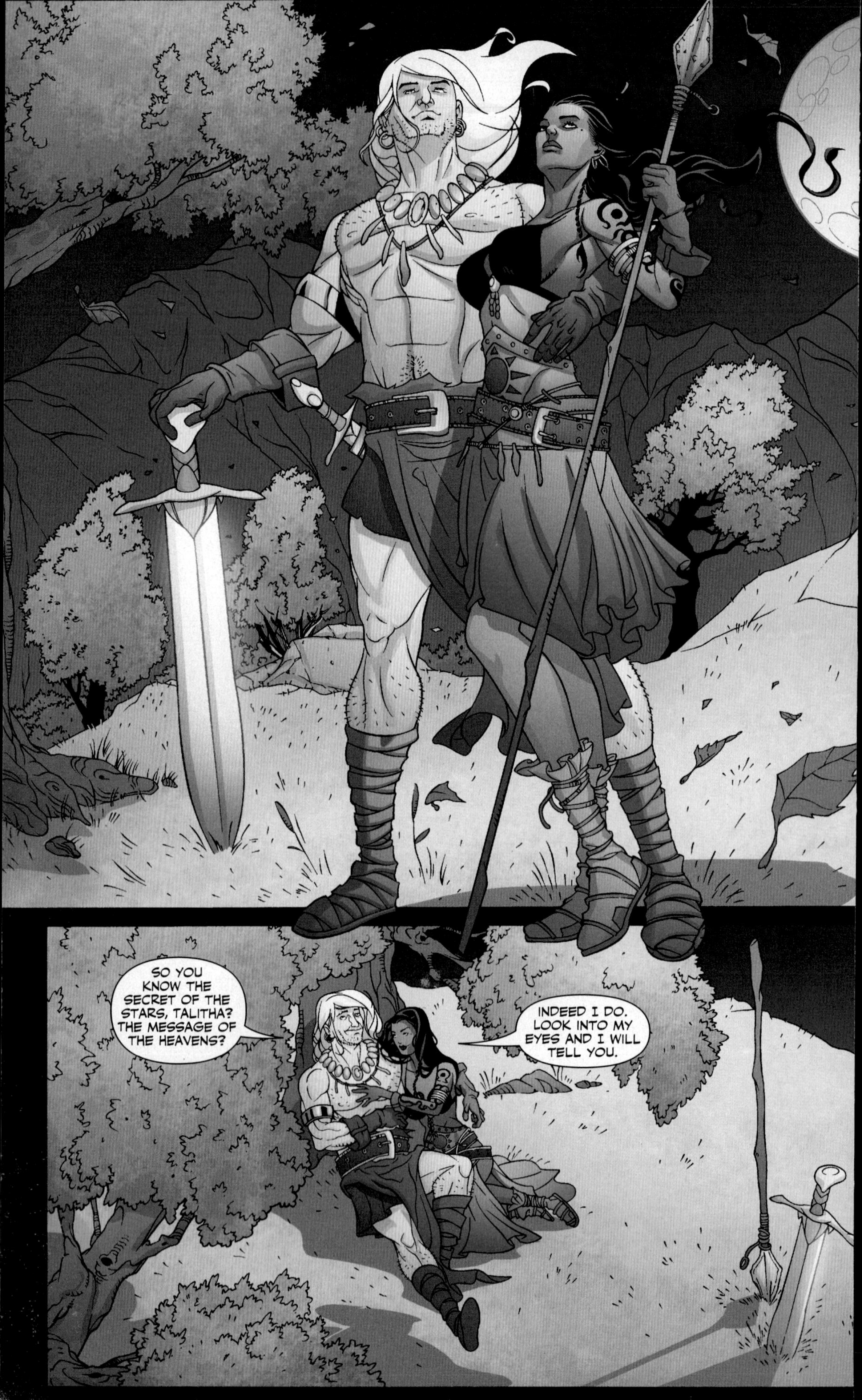
SO YOU KNOW THE SECRET OF THE STARS, TALITHA? THE MESSAGE OF THE HEAVENS?
INDEED I DO. LOOK INTO MY EYES AND I WILL TELL YOU.

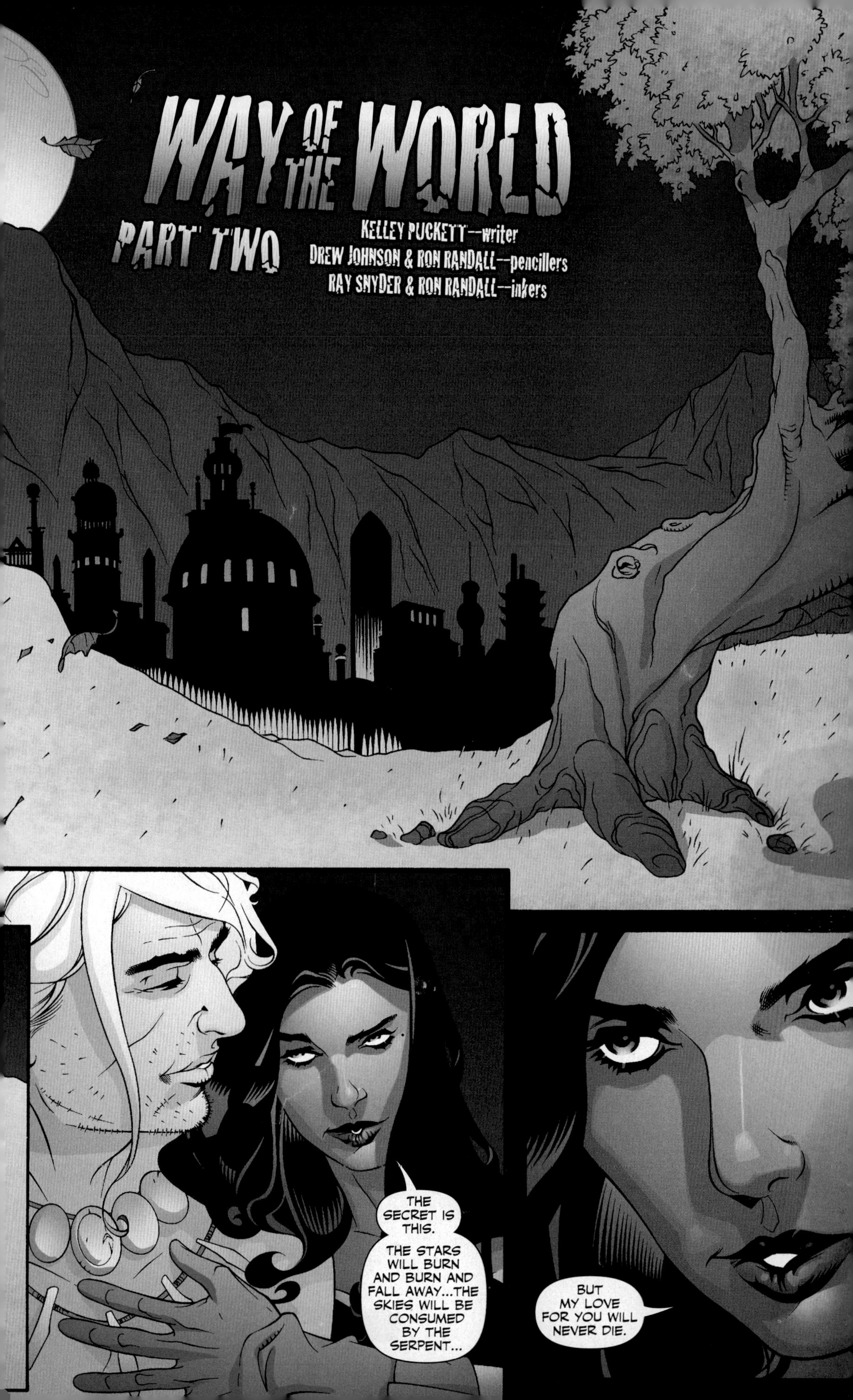
WAY OF THE WORLD
PART TWO
KELLEY PUCKETT--writer
DREW JOHNSON & RON RANDALL--pencillers
RAY SNYDER & RON RANDALL--inkers
THE SECRET IS THIS.
THE STARS WILL BURN AND BURN AND FALL AWAY...THE SKIES WILL BE CONSUMED BY THE SERPENT...
BUT MY LOVE FOR YOU WILL NEVER DIE.

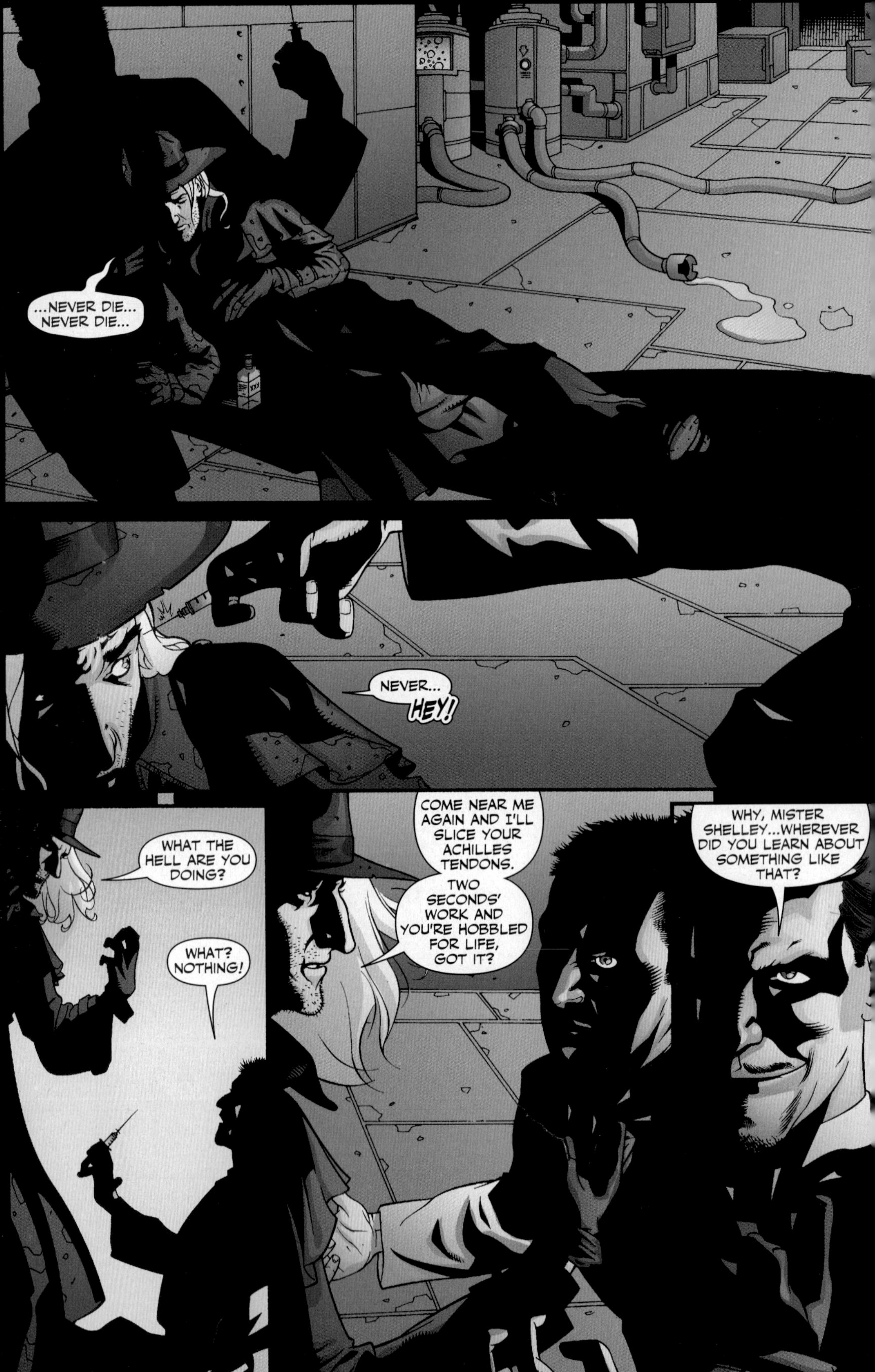
...NEVER DIE...
NEVER DIE...
NEVER...
HEY!
WHAT THE HELL ARE YOU DOING?
WHAT? NOTHING!
COME NEAR ME AGAIN AND I'LL SLICE YOUR ACHILLES TENDONS.
TWO SECONDS' WORK AND YOU'RE HOBBLED FOR LIFE, GOT IT?
WHY, MISTER SHELLEY...WHEREVER DID YOU LEARN ABOUT SOMETHING LIKE THAT?

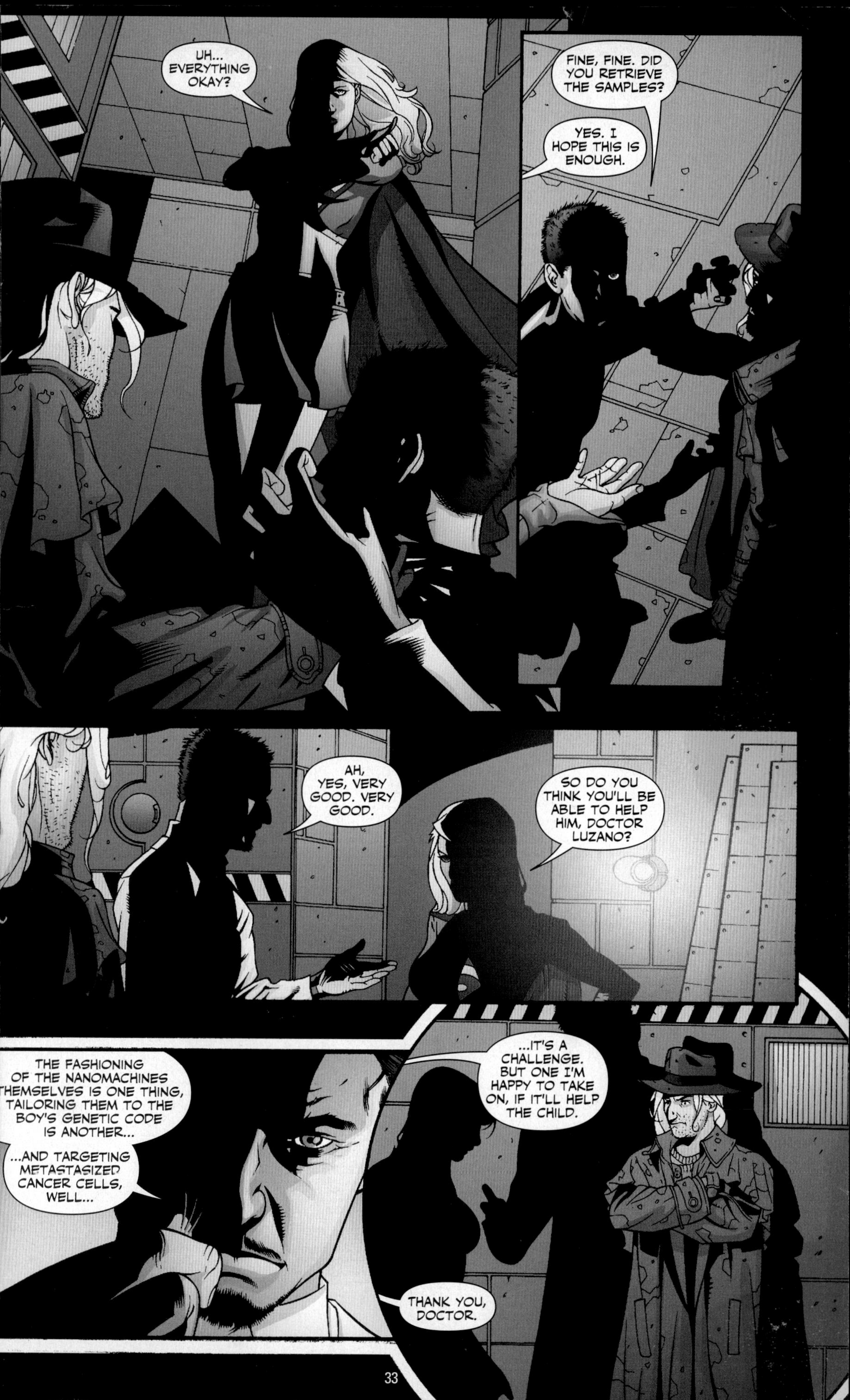

UH... EVERYTHING OKAY?
FINE, FINE. DID YOU RETRIEVE THE SAMPLES?
YES. I HOPE THIS IS ENOUGH.
AH, YES, VERY GOOD. VERY GOOD.
SO DO YOU THINK YOU'LL BE ABLE TO HELP HIM, DOCTOR LUZANO?
THE FASHIONING OF THE NANOMACHINES THEMSELVES IS ONE THING, TAILORING THEM TO THE BOY'S GENETIC CODE IS ANOTHER...
...AND TARGETING METASTASIZED CANCER CELLS, WELL...
...IT'S A CHALLENGE. BUT ONE I'M HAPPY TO TAKE ON, IF IT'LL HELP THE CHILD.
THANK YOU, DOCTOR.

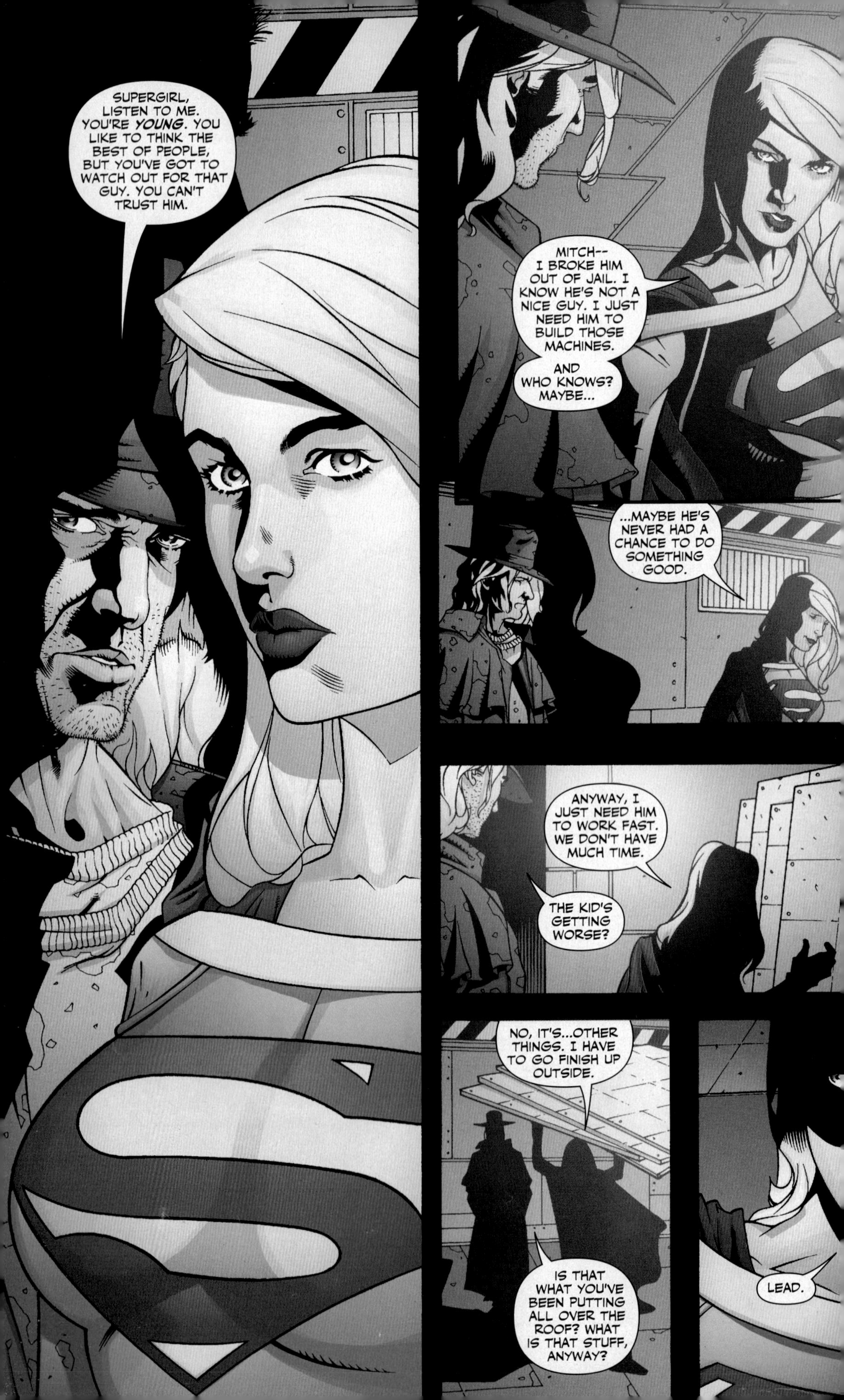
SUPERGIRL, LISTEN TO ME. YOU'RE *YOUNG*. YOU LIKE TO THINK THE BEST OF PEOPLE, BUT YOU'VE GOT TO WATCH OUT FOR THAT GUY. YOU CAN'T TRUST HIM.
MITCH-- I BROKE HIM OUT OF JAIL. I KNOW HE'S NOT A NICE GUY. I JUST NEED HIM TO BUILD THOSE MACHINES.
AND WHO KNOWS? MAYBE...
...MAYBE HE'S NEVER HAD A CHANCE TO DO SOMETHING GOOD.
ANYWAY, I JUST NEED HIM TO WORK FAST. WE DON'T HAVE MUCH TIME.
THE KID'S GETTING WORSE?
NO, IT'S...OTHER THINGS. I HAVE TO GO FINISH UP OUTSIDE.
IS THAT WHAT YOU'VE BEEN PUTTING ALL OVER THE ROOF? WHAT IS THAT STUFF, ANYWAY?
LEAD.

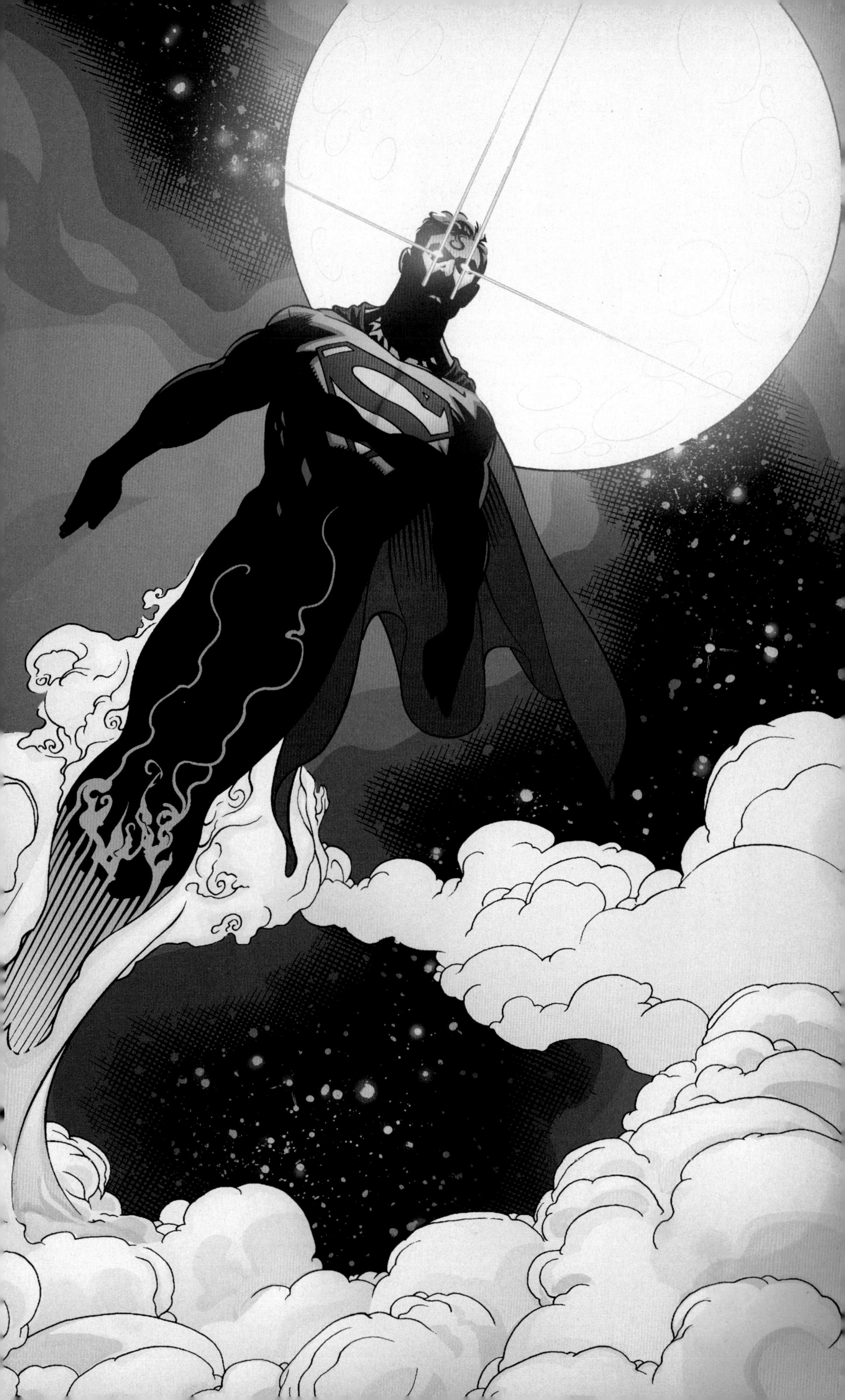

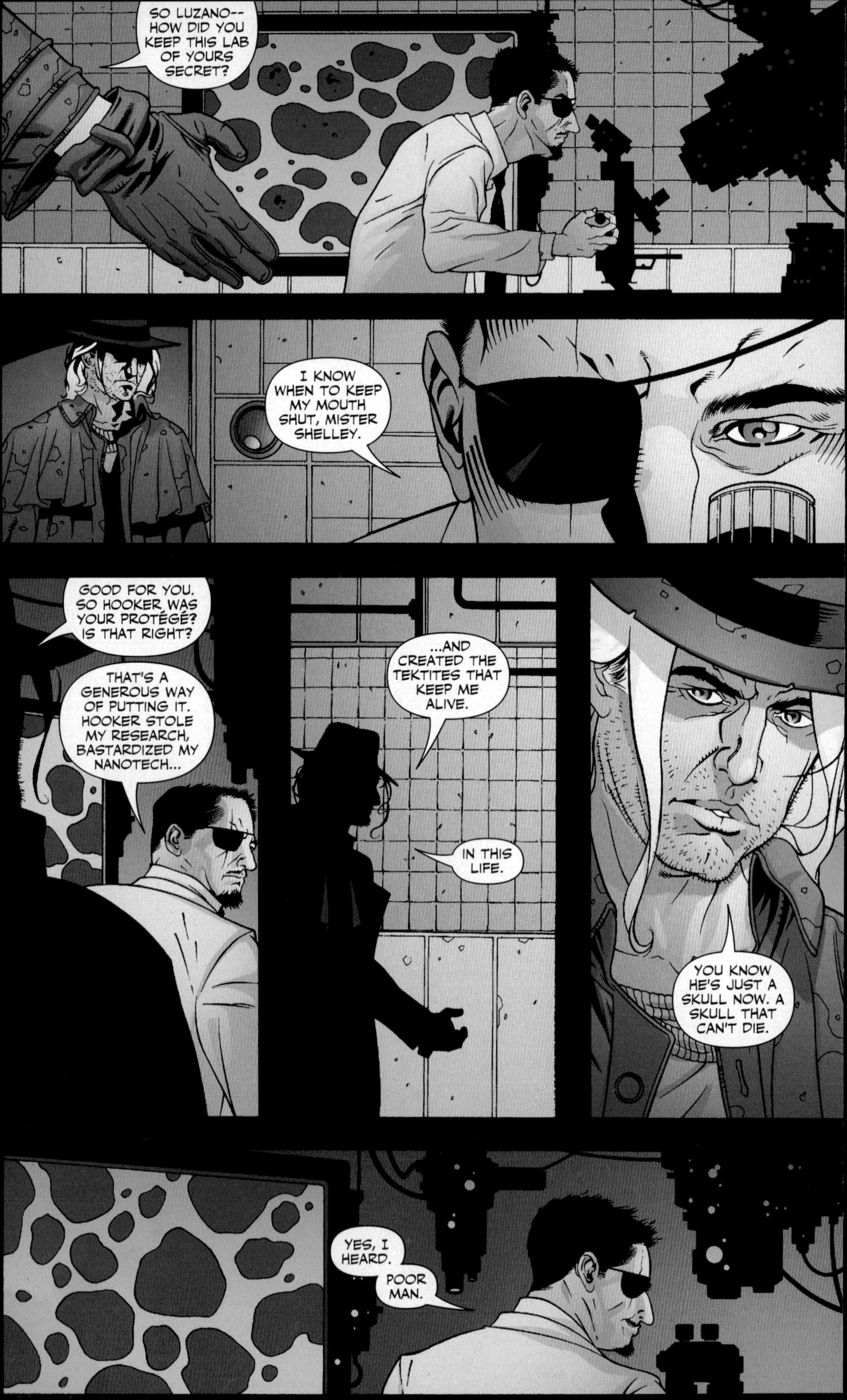
SO LUZANO-- HOW DID YOU KEEP THIS LAB OF YOURS SECRET?
I KNOW WHEN TO KEEP MY MOUTH SHUT, MISTER SHELLEY.
GOOD FOR YOU. SO HOOKER WAS YOUR PROTÉGÉ? IS THAT RIGHT?
THAT'S A GENEROUS WAY OF PUTTING IT. HOOKER STOLE MY RESEARCH, BASTARDIZED MY NANOTECH...
...AND CREATED THE TEKTITES THAT KEEP ME ALIVE.
IN THIS LIFE.
YOU KNOW HE'S JUST A SKULL NOW. A SKULL THAT CAN'T DIE.
YES, I HEARD.
POOR MAN.

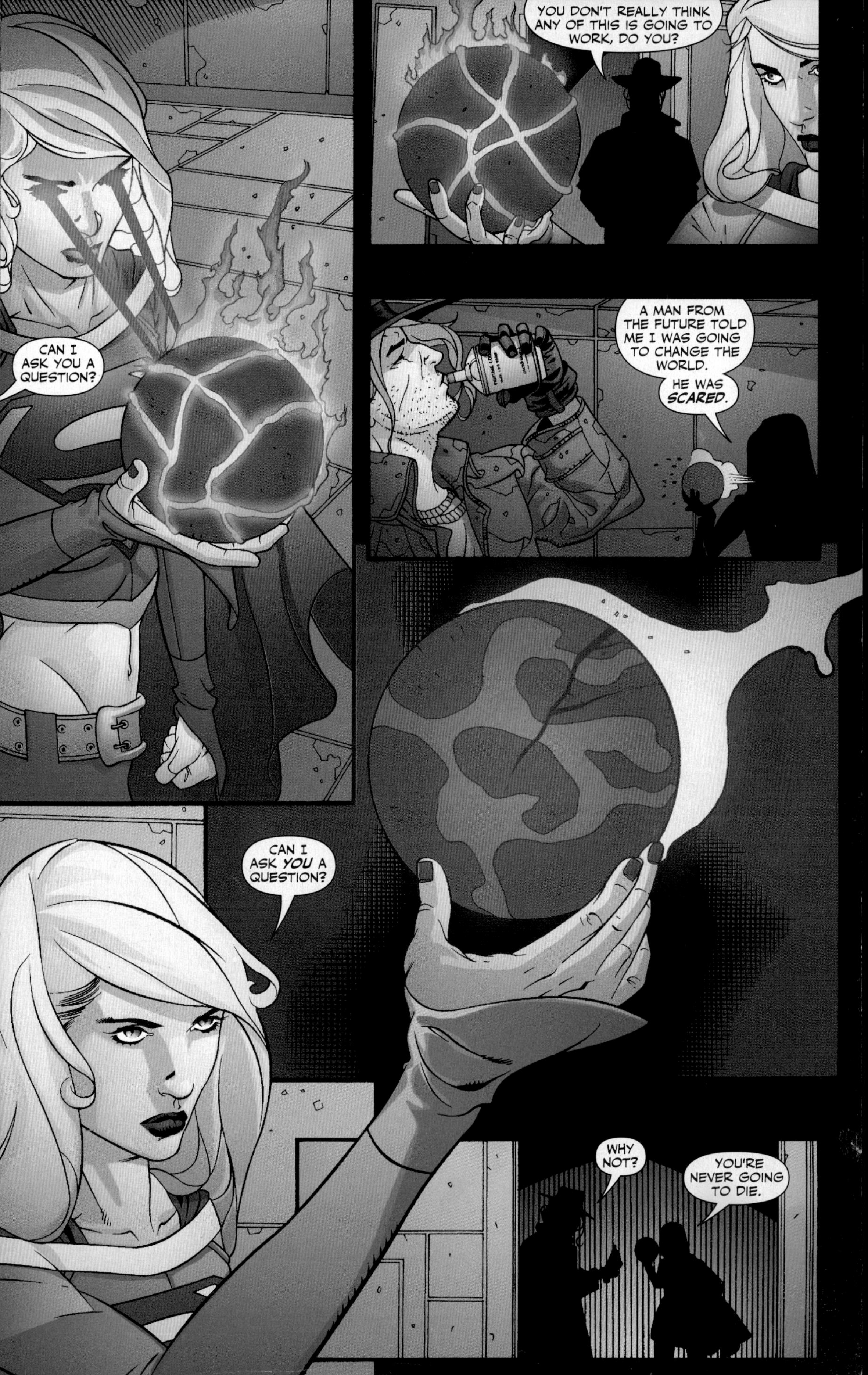
CAN I ASK YOU A QUESTION?
YOU DON'T REALLY THINK ANY OF THIS IS GOING TO WORK, DO YOU?
A MAN FROM THE FUTURE TOLD ME I WAS GOING TO CHANGE THE WORLD.
HE WAS *SCARED*.
CAN I ASK *YOU* A QUESTION?
WHY NOT?
YOU'RE NEVER GOING TO DIE.

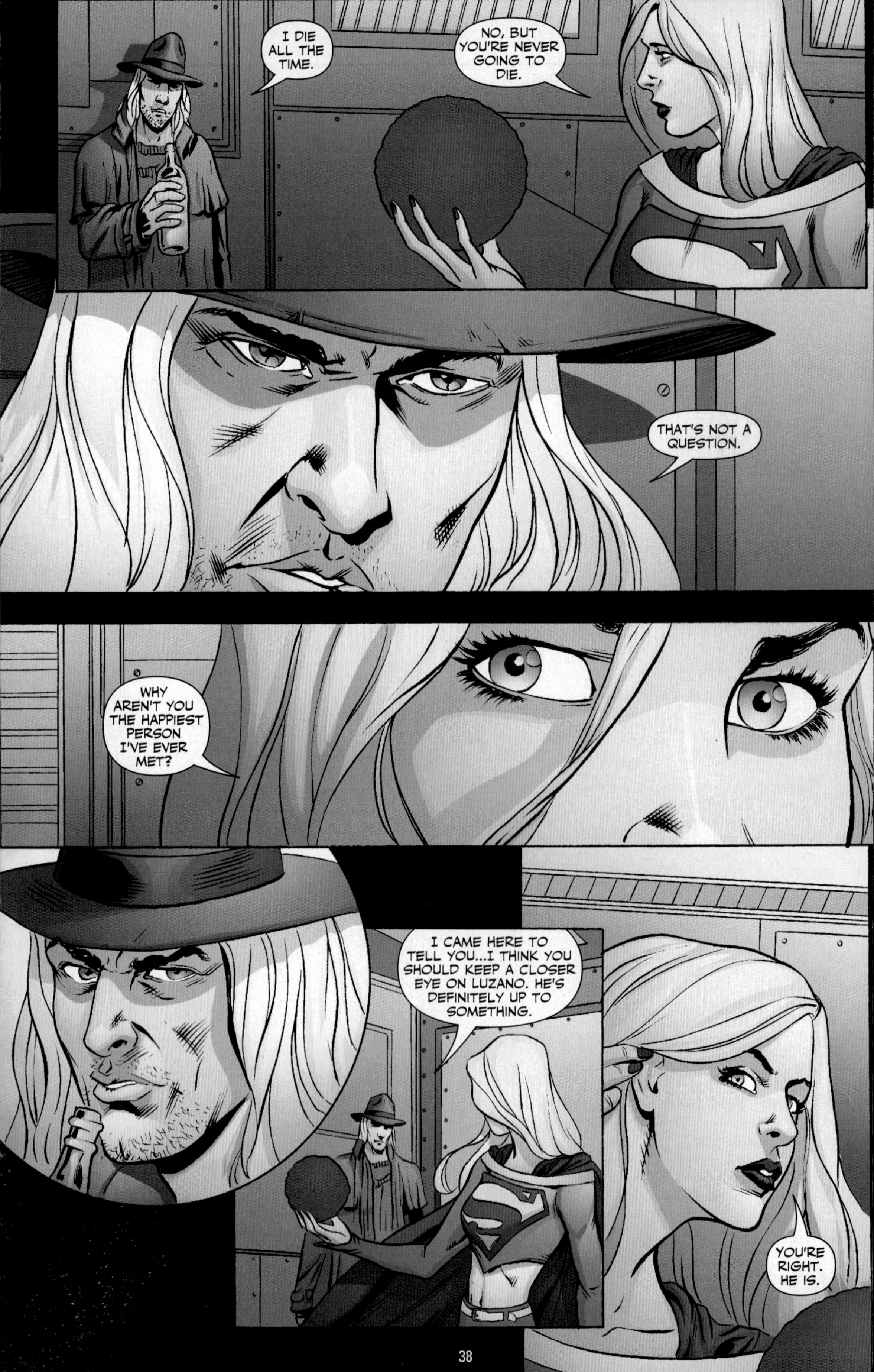

I DIE ALL THE TIME.
NO, BUT YOU'RE NEVER GOING TO DIE.
THAT'S NOT A QUESTION.
WHY AREN'T YOU THE HAPPIEST PERSON I'VE EVER MET?
I CAME HERE TO TELL YOU...I THINK YOU SHOULD KEEP A CLOSER EYE ON LUZANO. HE'S DEFINITELY UP TO SOMETHING.
YOU'RE RIGHT. HE IS.

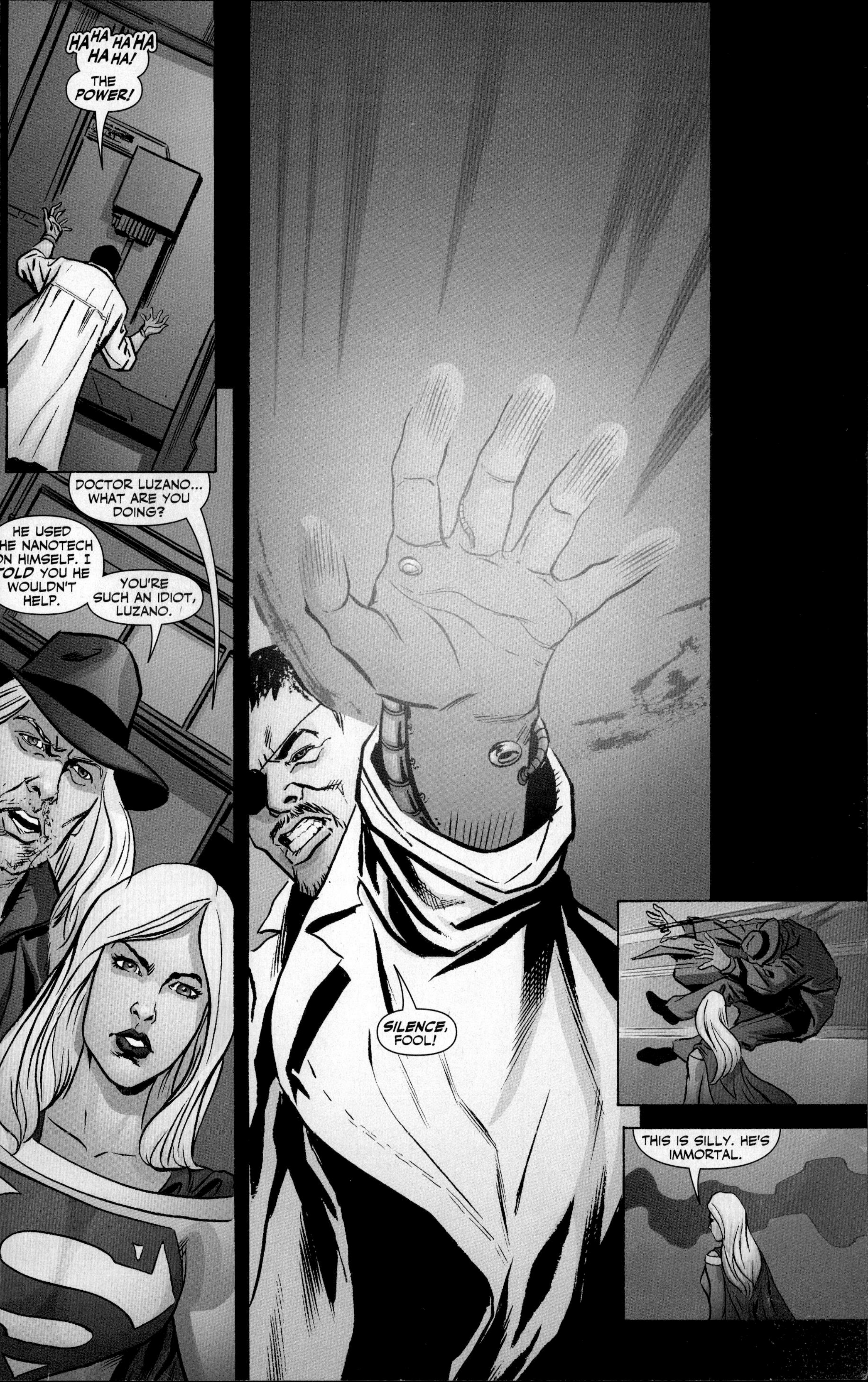
HAHA HAHA HAHA!
THE POWER!
DOCTOR LUZANO... WHAT ARE YOU DOING?
HE USED THE NANOTECH ON HIMSELF. I TOLD YOU HE WOULDN'T HELP.
YOU'RE SUCH AN IDIOT, LUZANO.
SILENCE, FOOL!
THIS IS SILLY. HE'S IMMORTAL.

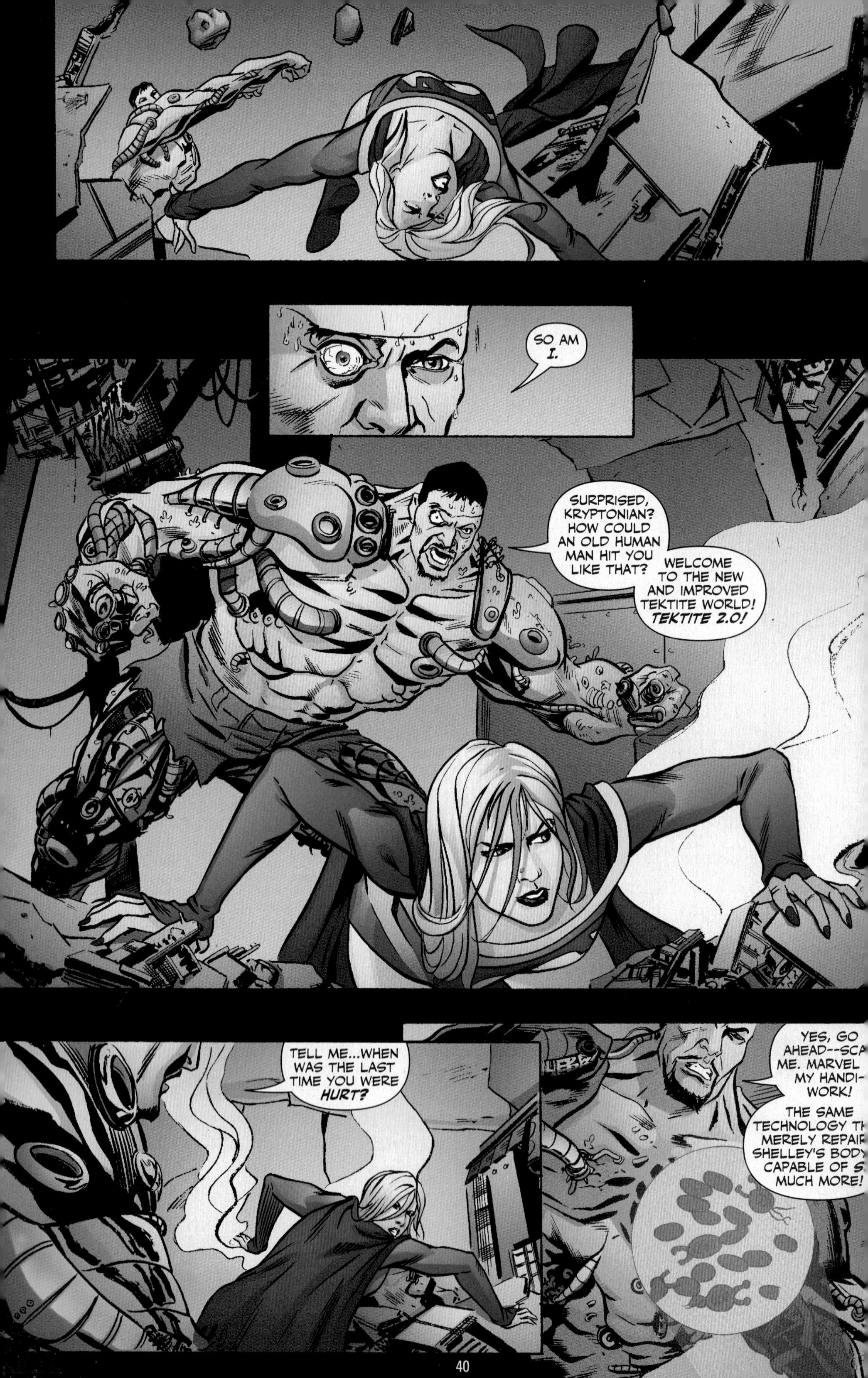
SO AM *I.*
SURPRISED, KRYPTONIAN? HOW COULD AN OLD HUMAN MAN HIT YOU LIKE THAT?
WELCOME TO THE NEW AND IMPROVED TEKTITE WORLD! ***TEKTITE 2.0!***
TELL ME...WHEN WAS THE LAST TIME YOU WERE ***HURT?***
YES, GO AHEAD--SCA ME. MARVEL MY HANDI-WORK!
THE SAME TECHNOLOGY T MERELY REPAIR SHELLEY'S BODY CAPABLE OF S MUCH MORE!

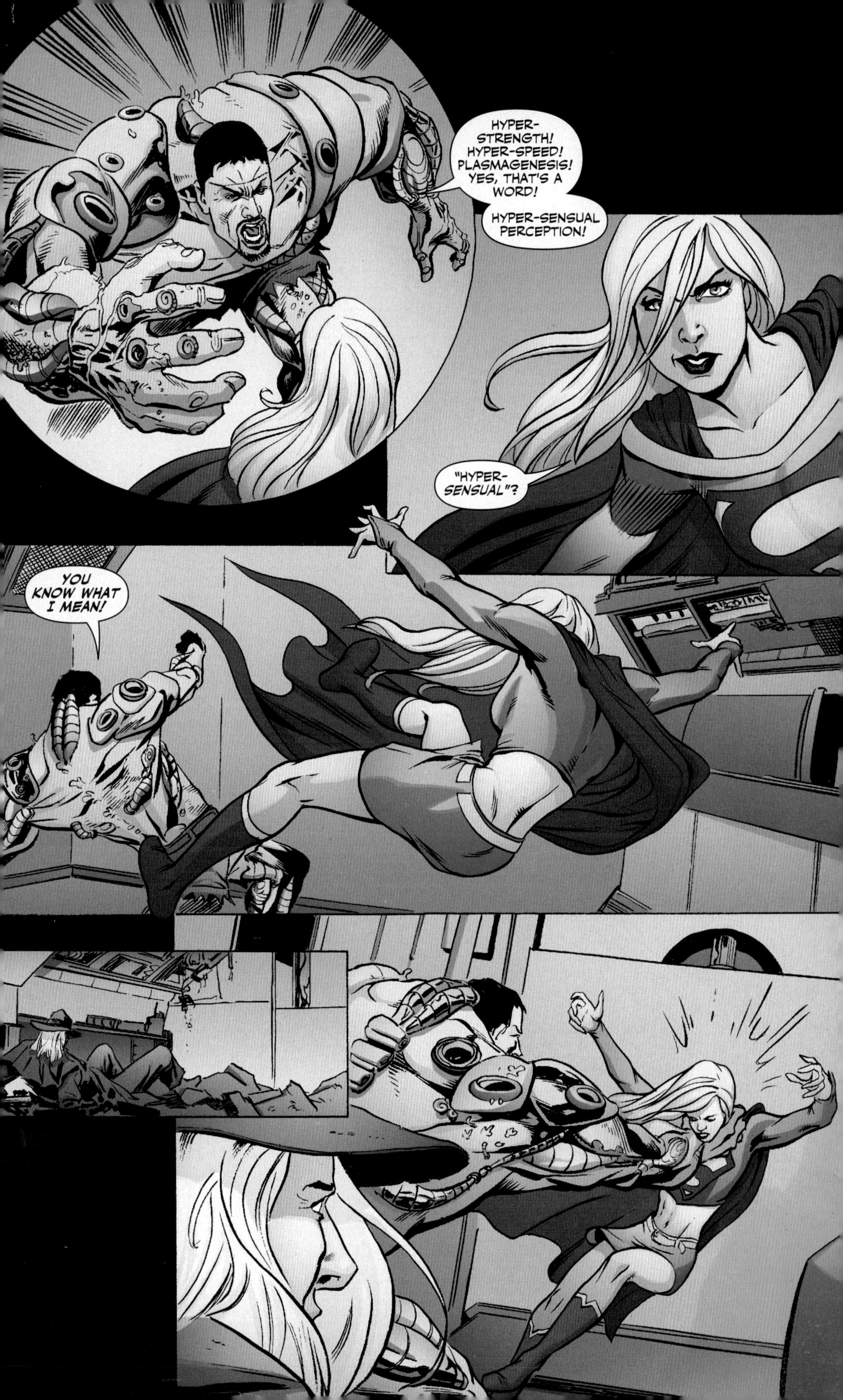
HYPER-STRENGTH! HYPER-SPEED! PLASMAGENESIS! YES, THAT'S A WORD!
HYPER-SENSUAL PERCEPTION!
"HYPER-SENSUAL"?
YOU KNOW WHAT I MEAN!

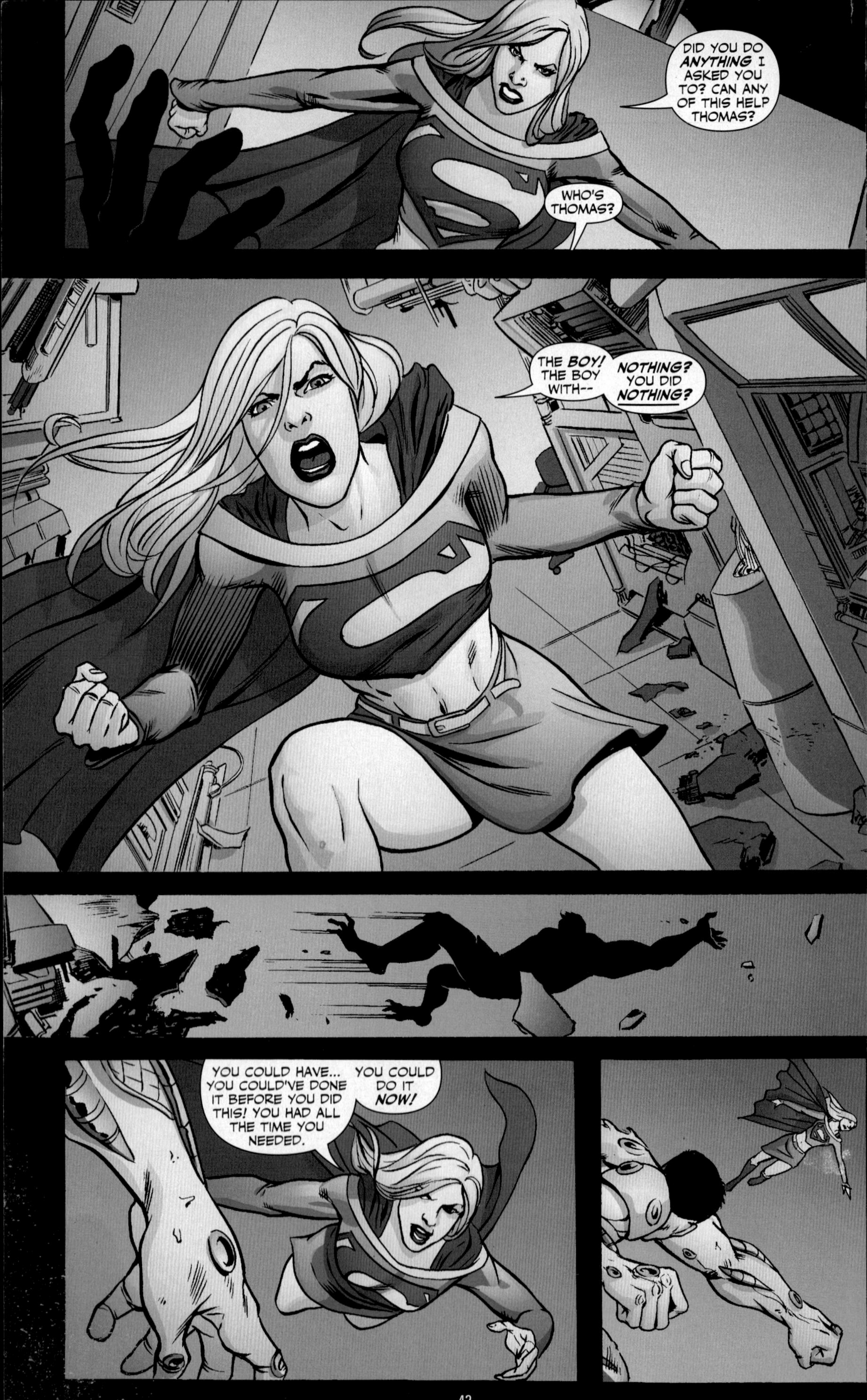
DID YOU DO ANYTHING I ASKED YOU TO? CAN ANY OF THIS HELP THOMAS?
WHO'S THOMAS?
THE BOY! THE BOY WITH--
NOTHING? YOU DID NOTHING?
YOU COULD HAVE... YOU COULD'VE DONE IT BEFORE YOU DID THIS! YOU HAD ALL THE TIME YOU NEEDED.
YOU COULD DO IT NOW!

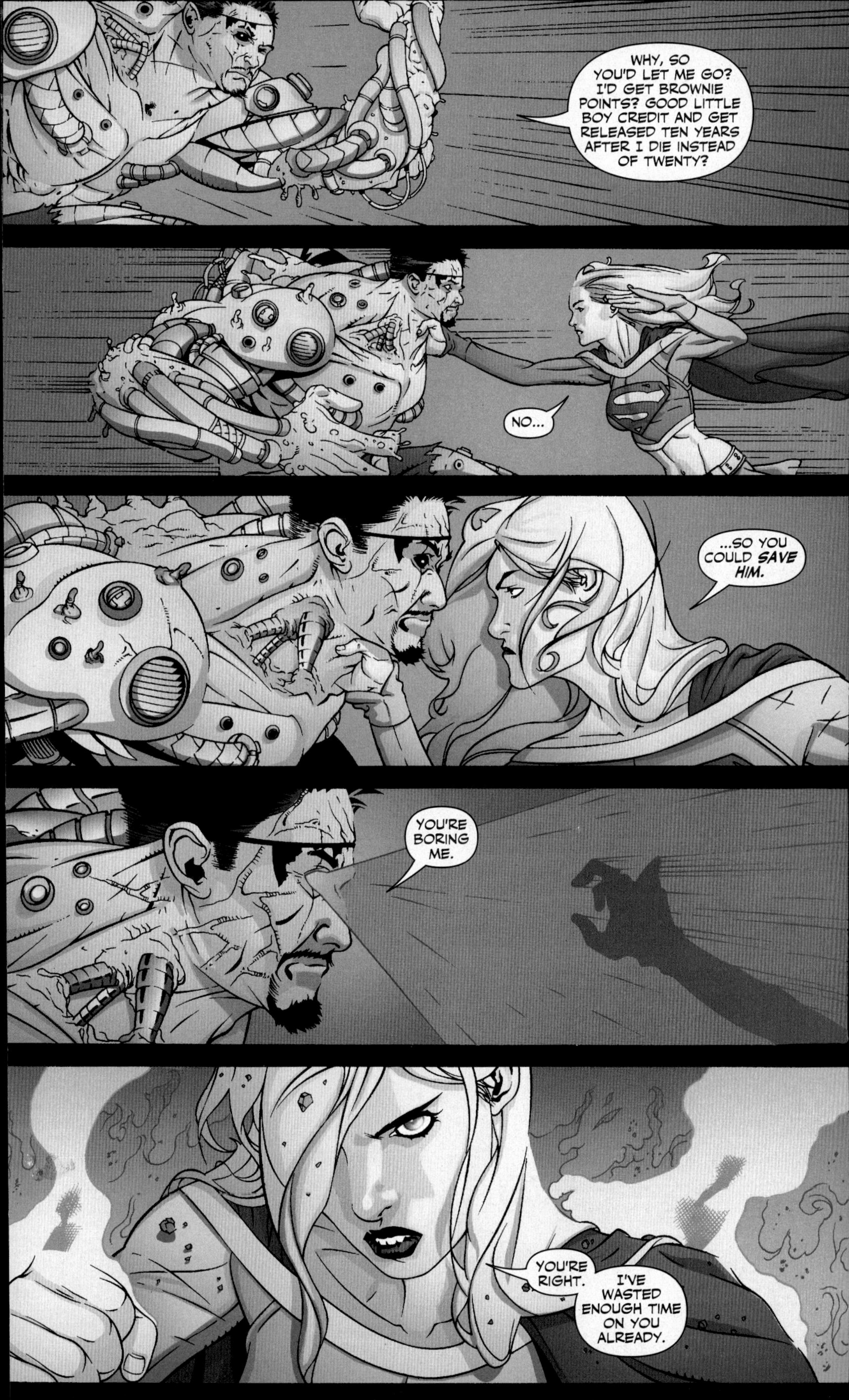
WHY, SO YOU'D LET ME GO? I'D GET BROWNIE POINTS? GOOD LITTLE BOY CREDIT AND GET RELEASED TEN YEARS AFTER I DIE INSTEAD OF TWENTY?
NO...
...SO YOU COULD SAVE HIM.
YOU'RE BORING ME.
YOU'RE RIGHT.
I'VE WASTED ENOUGH TIME ON YOU ALREADY.

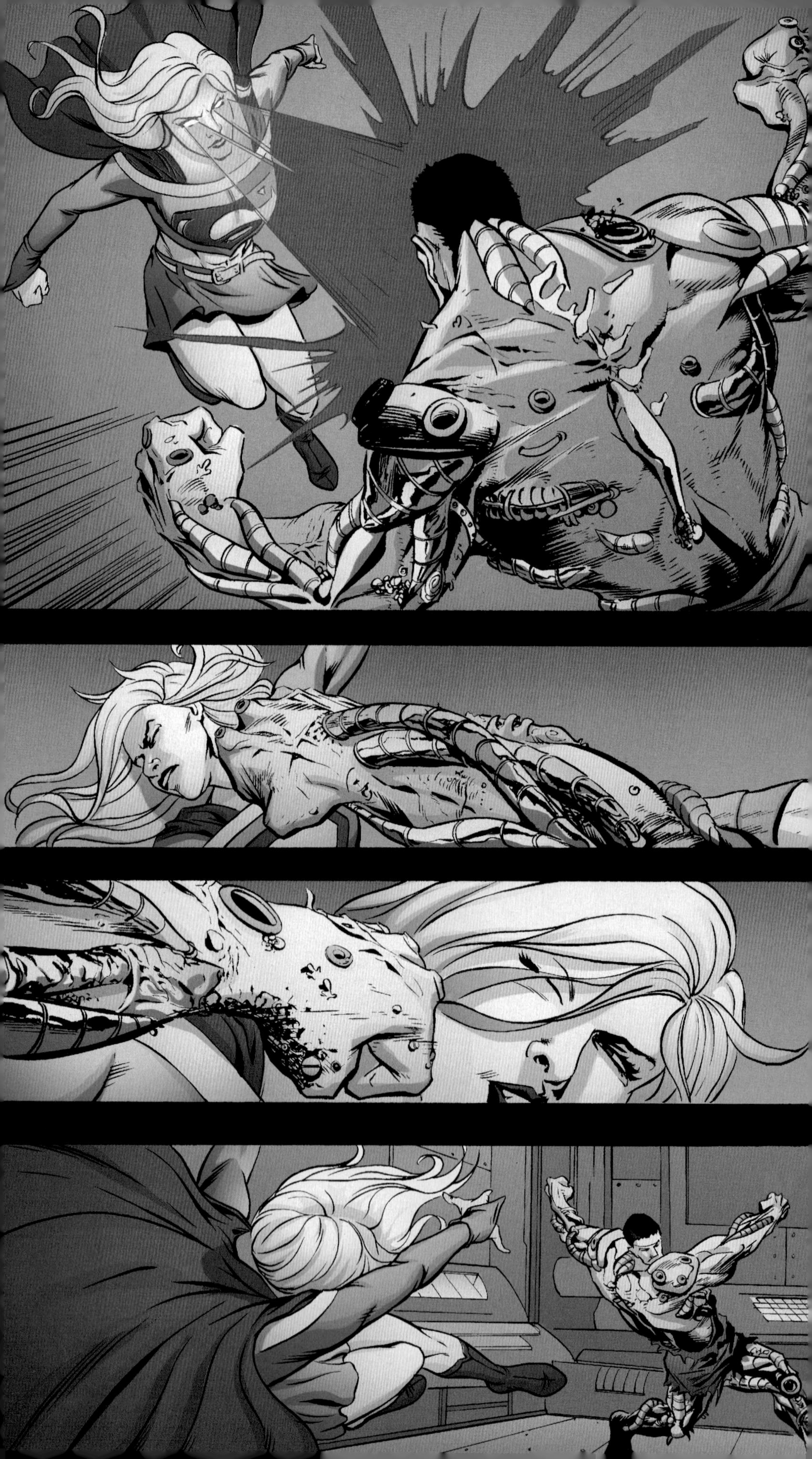

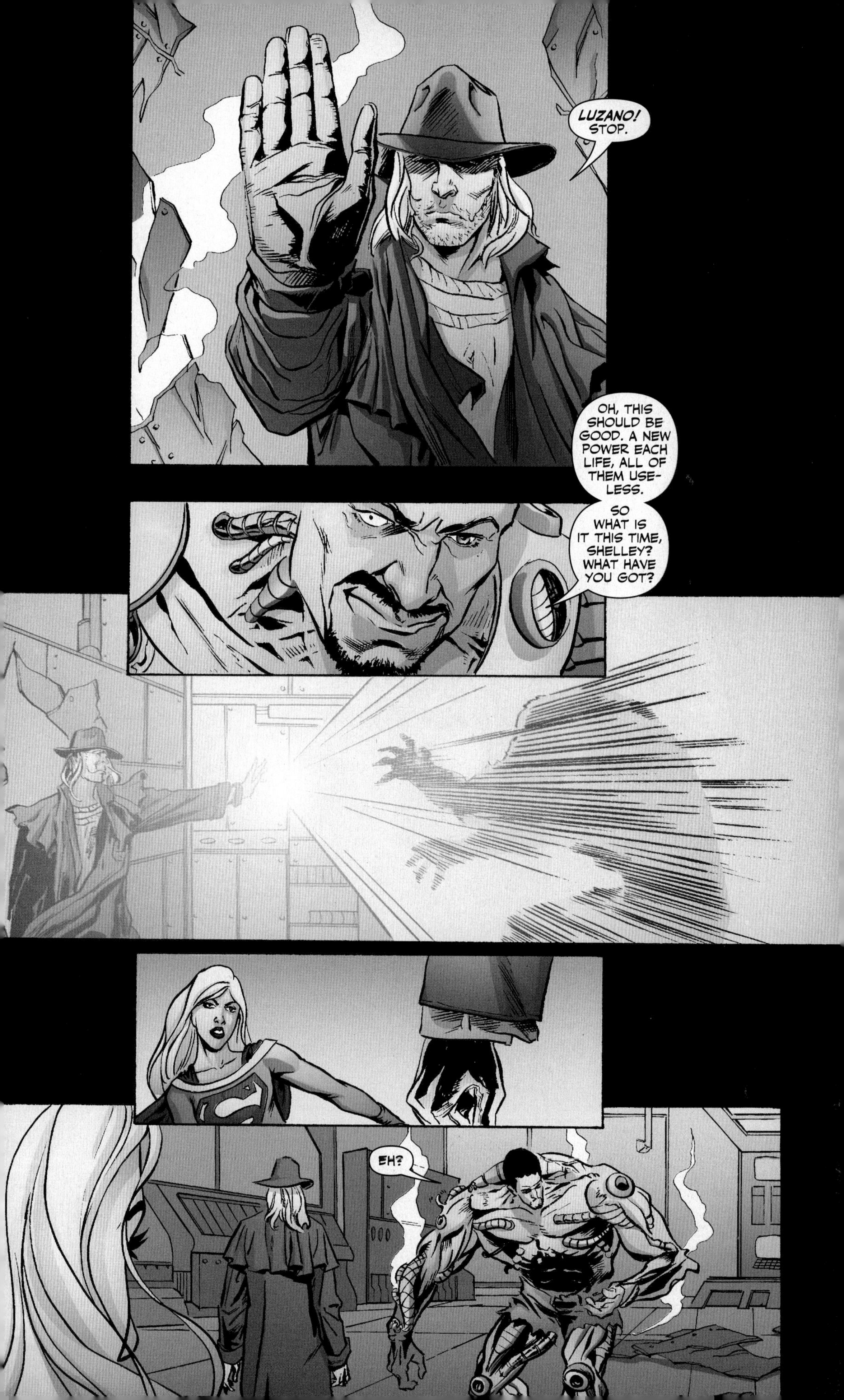
LUZANO! STOP.
OH, THIS SHOULD BE GOOD. A NEW POWER EACH LIFE, ALL OF THEM USE-LESS.
SO WHAT IS IT THIS TIME, SHELLEY? WHAT HAVE YOU GOT?
EH?

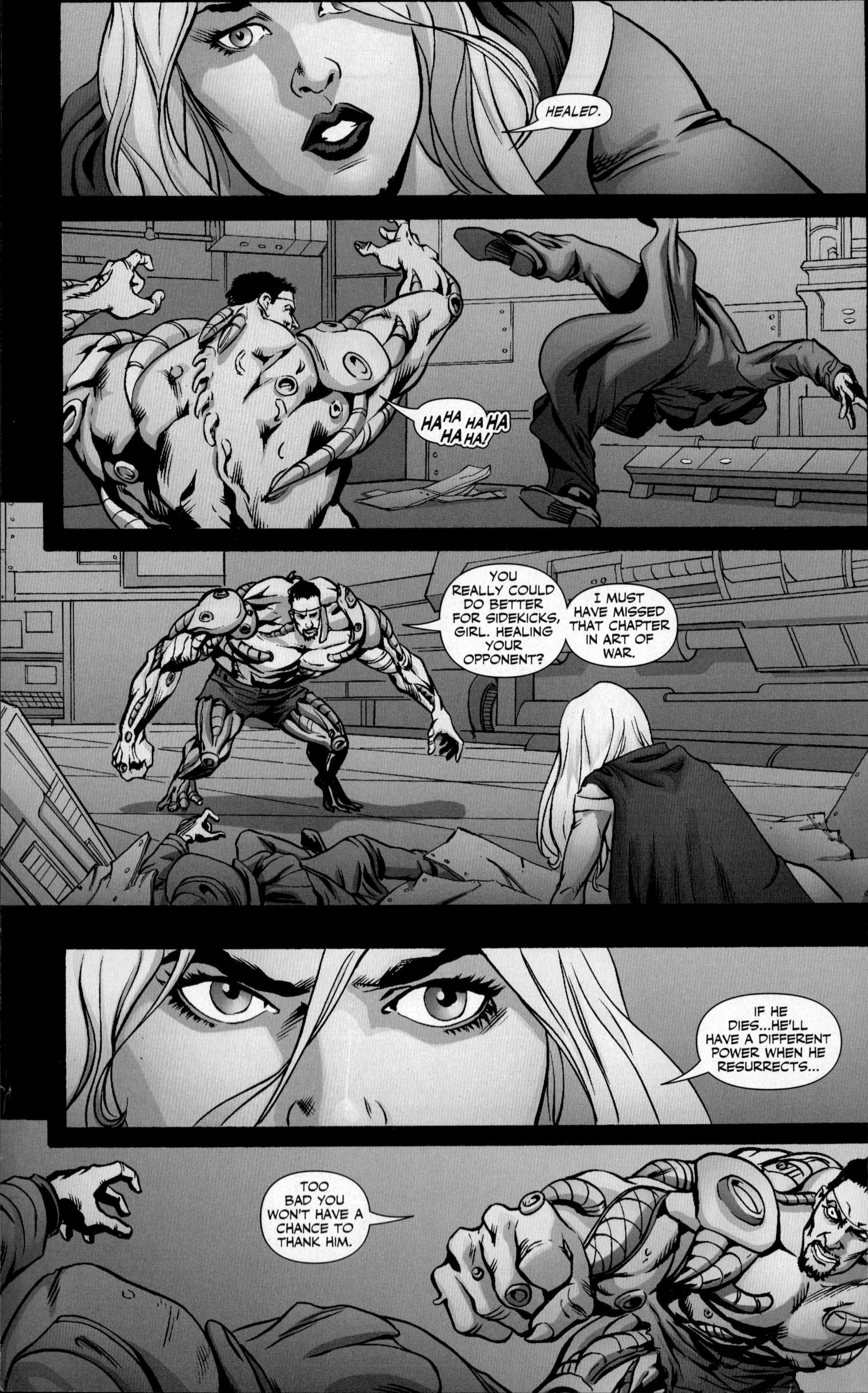
HEALED.
HAHA HAHA HAHA!
YOU REALLY COULD DO BETTER FOR SIDEKICKS, GIRL. HEALING YOUR OPPONENT?
I MUST HAVE MISSED THAT CHAPTER IN ART OF WAR.
IF HE DIES...HE'LL HAVE A DIFFERENT POWER WHEN HE RESURRECTS...
TOO BAD YOU WON'T HAVE A CHANCE TO THANK HIM.

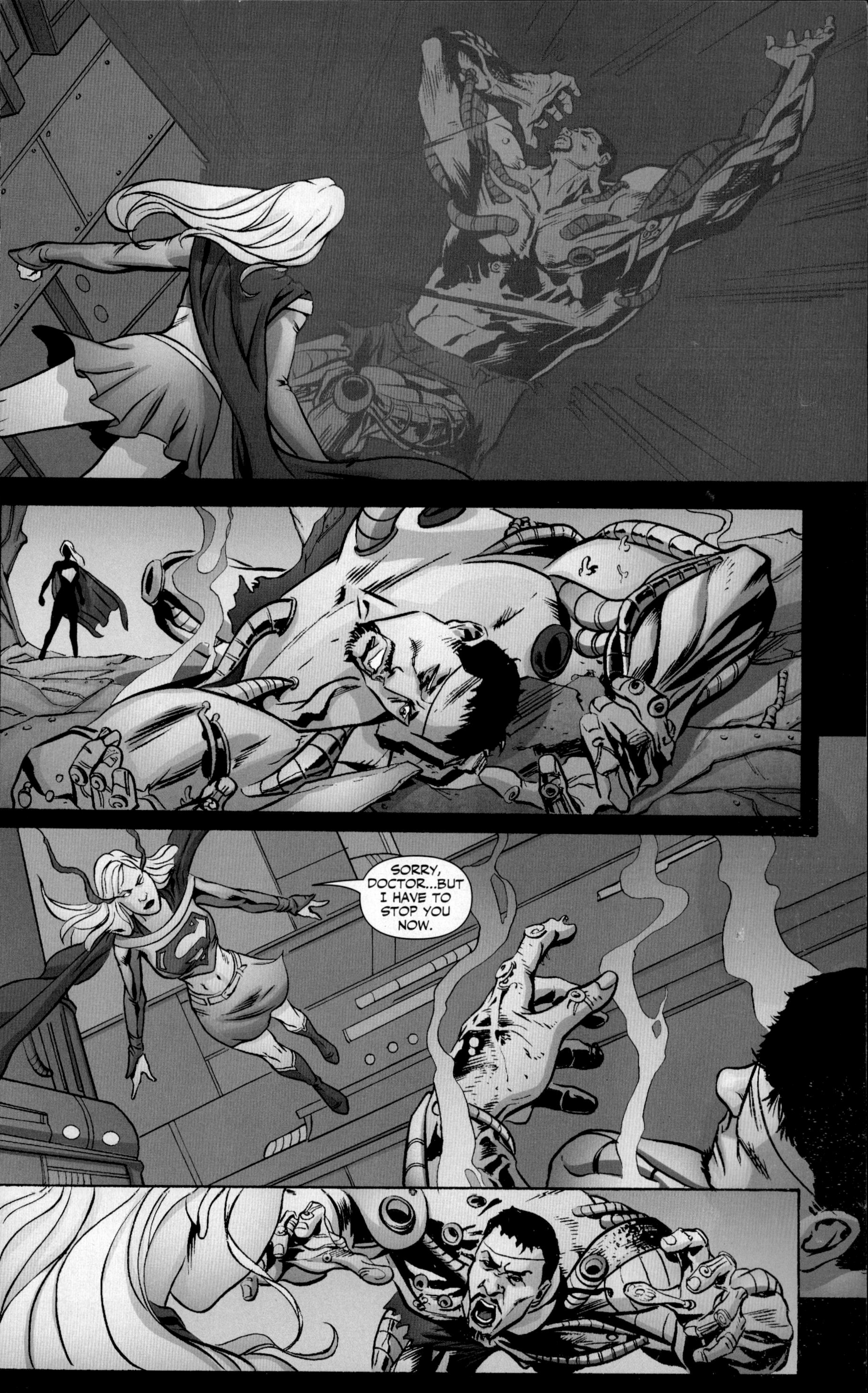
SORRY, DOCTOR...BUT I HAVE TO STOP YOU NOW.

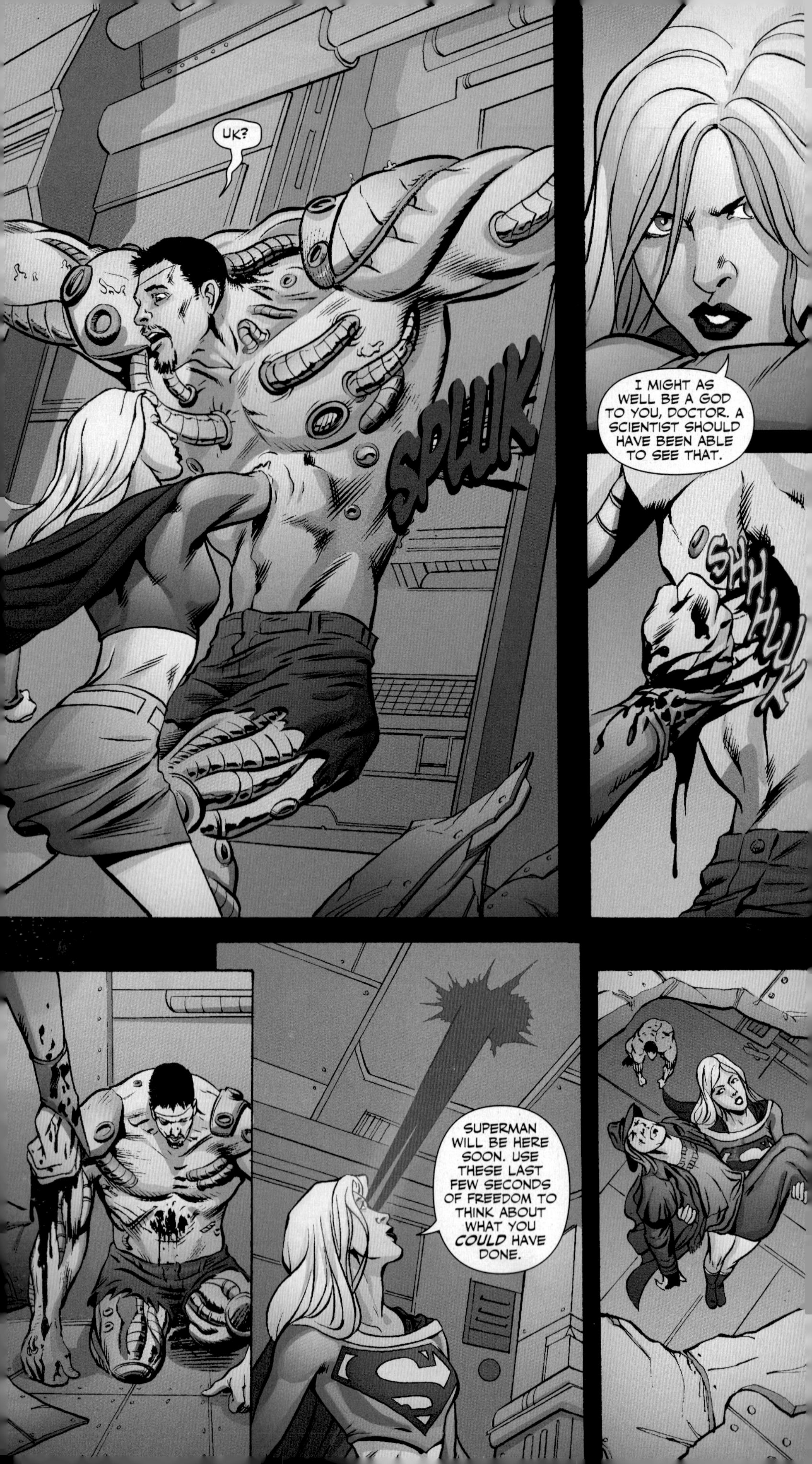
UK?
SPLUK
I MIGHT AS WELL BE A GOD TO YOU, DOCTOR. A SCIENTIST SHOULD HAVE BEEN ABLE TO SEE THAT.
SHHHLUK
SUPERMAN WILL BE HERE SOON. USE THESE LAST FEW SECONDS OF FREEDOM TO THINK ABOUT WHAT YOU *COULD* HAVE DONE.

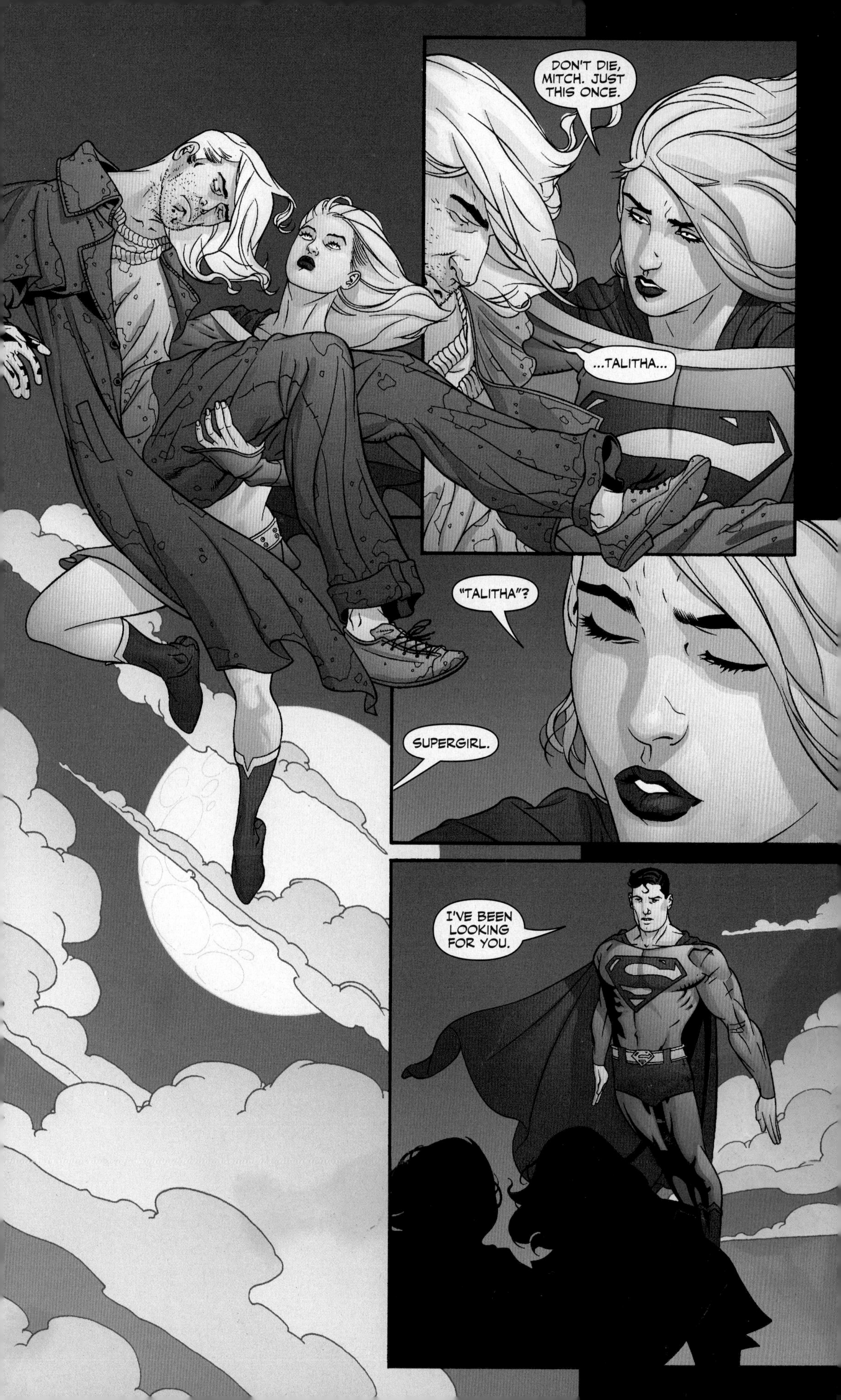
DON'T DIE, MITCH. JUST THIS ONCE.
...TALITHA...
"TALITHA"?
SUPERGIRL.
I'VE BEEN LOOKING FOR YOU.

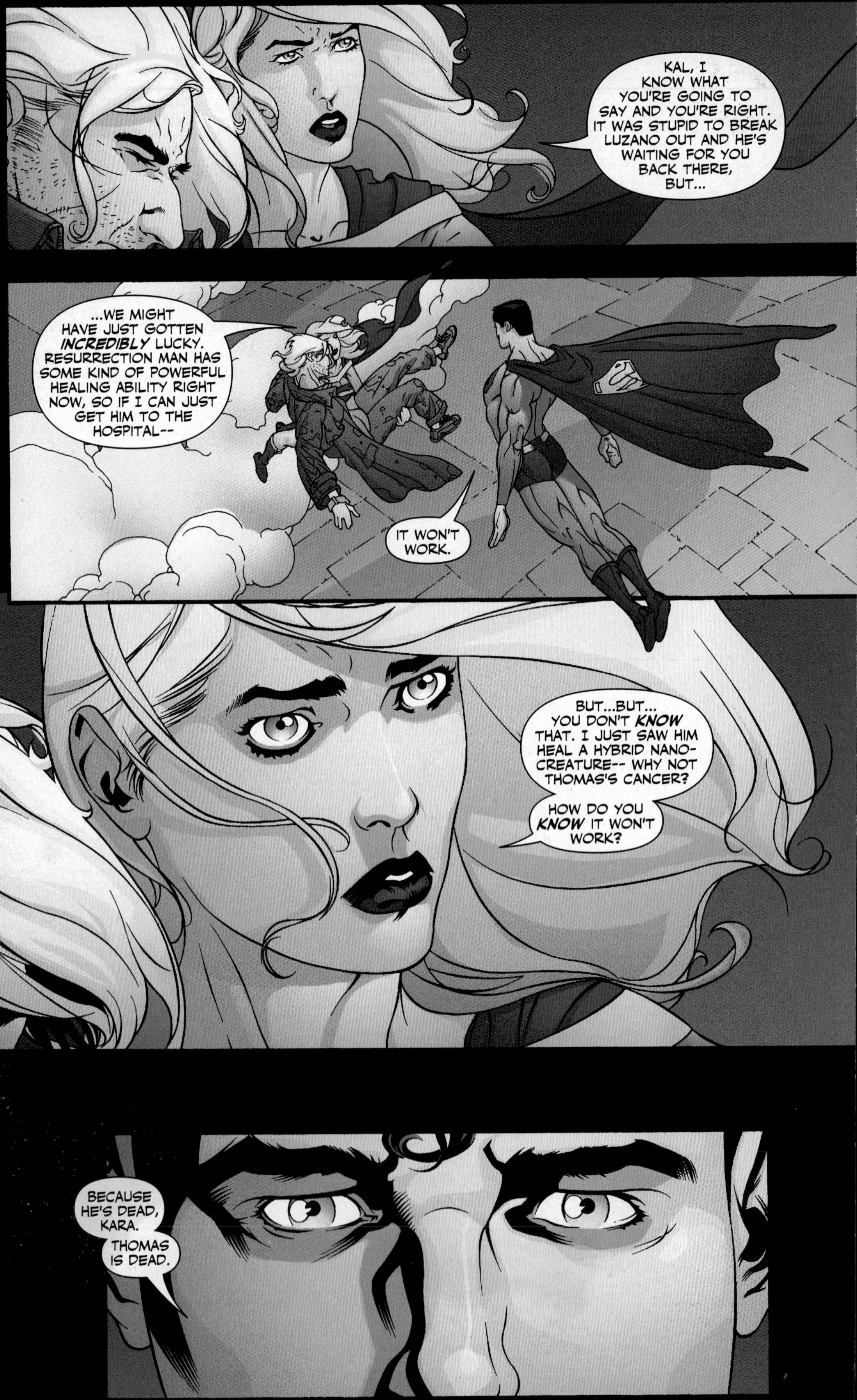
KAL, I KNOW WHAT YOU'RE GOING TO SAY AND YOU'RE RIGHT. IT WAS STUPID TO BREAK LUZANO OUT AND HE'S WAITING FOR YOU BACK THERE, BUT...
...WE MIGHT HAVE JUST GOTTEN *INCREDIBLY* LUCKY. RESURRECTION MAN HAS SOME KIND OF POWERFUL HEALING ABILITY RIGHT NOW, SO IF I CAN JUST GET HIM TO THE HOSPITAL--
IT WON'T WORK.
BUT...BUT... YOU DON'T *KNOW* THAT. I JUST SAW HIM HEAL A HYBRID NANO-CREATURE-- WHY NOT THOMAS'S CANCER?
HOW DO YOU *KNOW* IT WON'T WORK?
BECAUSE HE'S DEAD, KARA.
THOMAS IS DEAD.

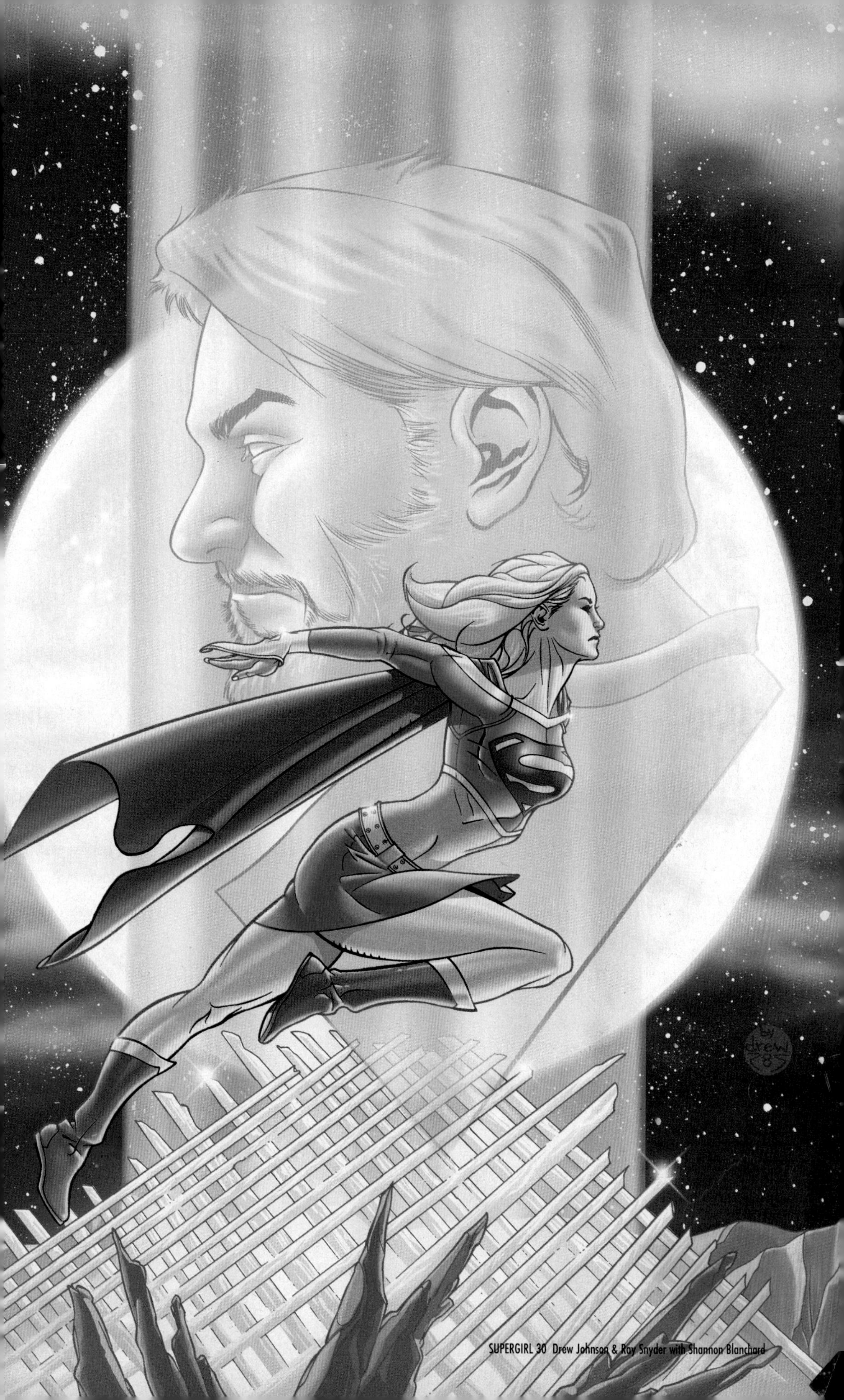

SUPERGIRL 30 Drew Johnson & Ray Snyder with Shannon Blanchard

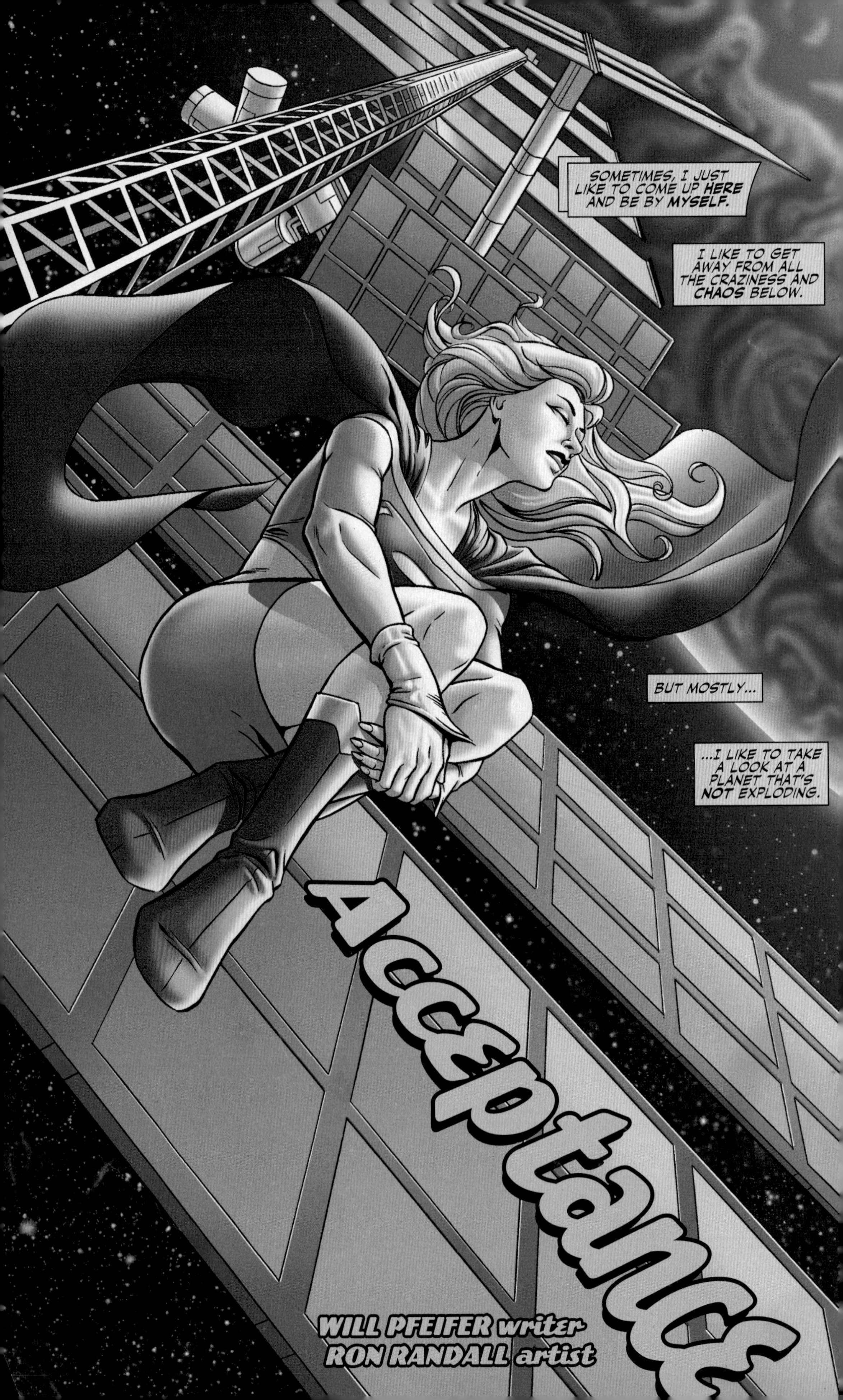
SOMETIMES, I JUST LIKE TO COME UP HERE AND BE BY MYSELF.
I LIKE TO GET AWAY FROM ALL THE CRAZINESS AND CHAOS BELOW.
BUT MOSTLY...
...I LIKE TO TAKE A LOOK AT A PLANET THAT'S NOT EXPLODING.
ACCEPTANCE
WILL PFEIFER writer
RON RANDALL artist

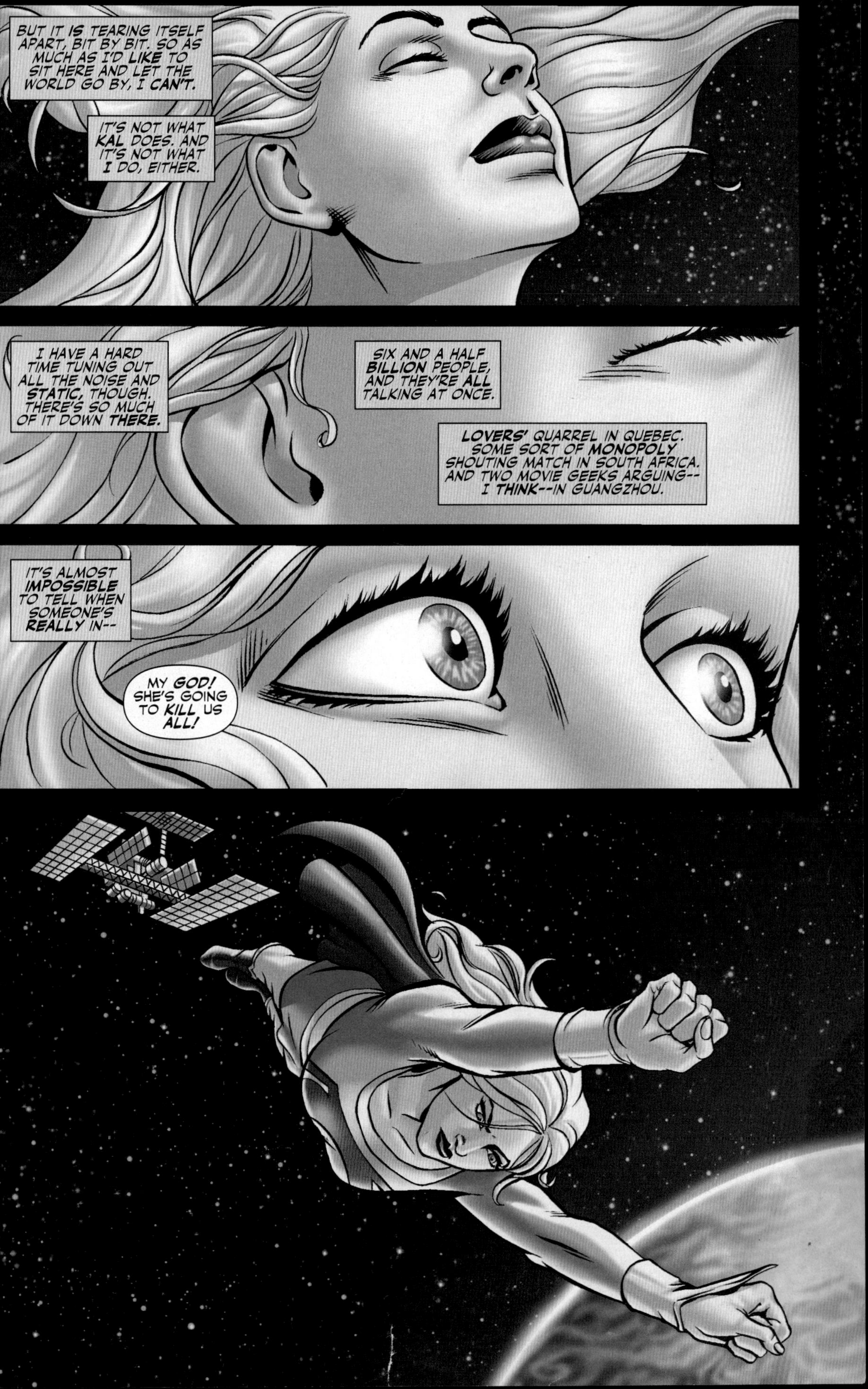

BUT IT IS TEARING ITSELF APART, BIT BY BIT. SO AS MUCH AS I'D LIKE TO SIT HERE AND LET THE WORLD GO BY, I CAN'T.
IT'S NOT WHAT KAL DOES. AND IT'S NOT WHAT I DO, EITHER.
I HAVE A HARD TIME TUNING OUT ALL THE NOISE AND STATIC, THOUGH. THERE'S SO MUCH OF IT DOWN THERE.
SIX AND A HALF BILLION PEOPLE, AND THEY'RE ALL TALKING AT ONCE.
LOVERS' QUARREL IN QUEBEC. SOME SORT OF MONOPOLY SHOUTING MATCH IN SOUTH AFRICA. AND TWO MOVIE GEEKS ARGUING-- I THINK--IN GUANGZHOU.
IT'S ALMOST IMPOSSIBLE TO TELL WHEN SOMEONE'S REALLY IN--
MY GOD! SHE'S GOING TO KILL US ALL!

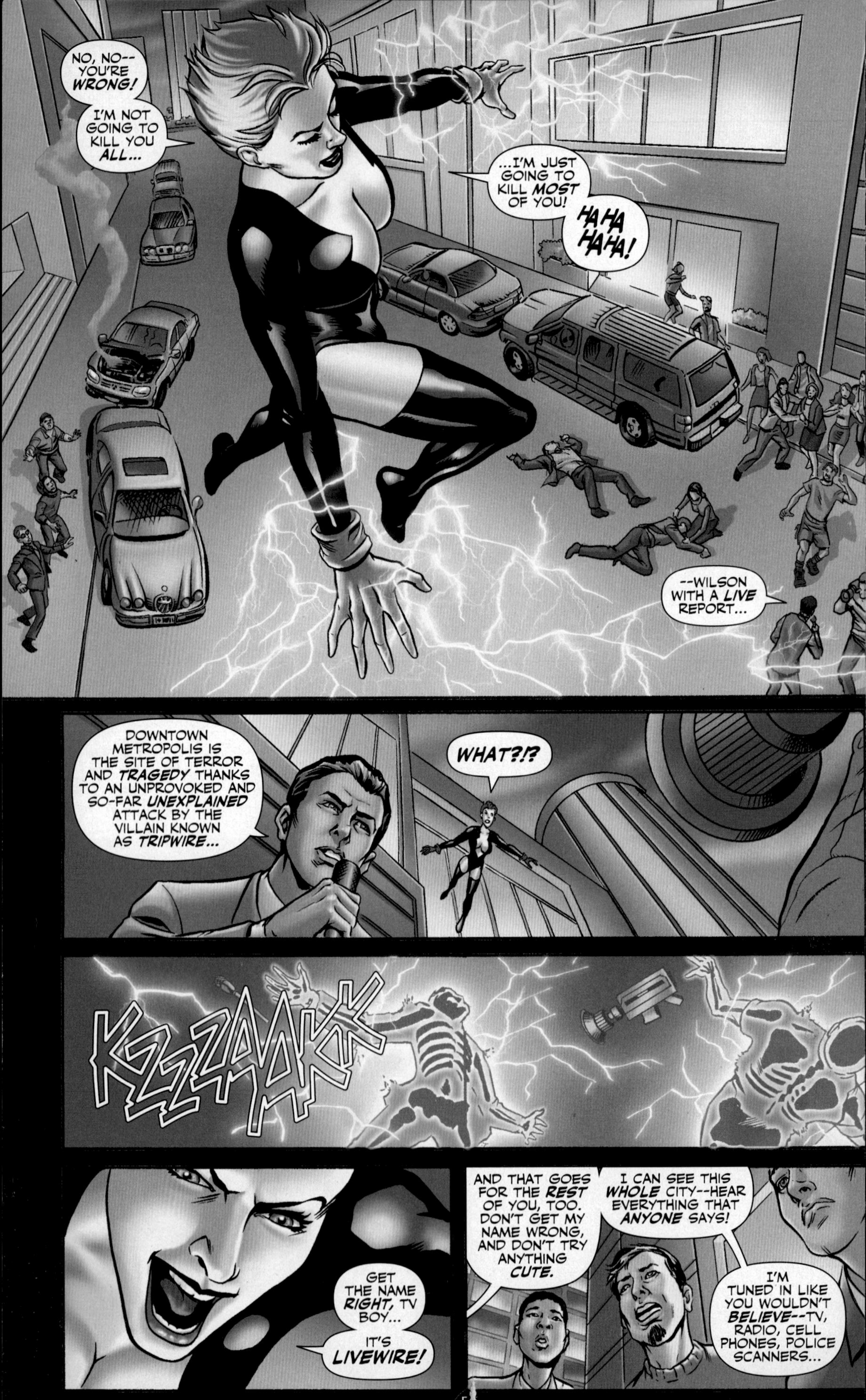
NO, NO-- YOU'RE WRONG!
I'M NOT GOING TO KILL YOU ALL...
...I'M JUST GOING TO KILL MOST OF YOU!
HA HA HA HA!
--WILSON WITH A LIVE REPORT...
DOWNTOWN METROPOLIS IS THE SITE OF TERROR AND TRAGEDY THANKS TO AN UNPROVOKED AND SO-FAR UNEXPLAINED ATTACK BY THE VILLAIN KNOWN AS TRIPWIRE...
WHAT?!?
KZZZAAKK
GET THE NAME RIGHT, TV BOY...
IT'S LIVEWIRE!
AND THAT GOES FOR THE REST OF YOU, TOO. DON'T GET MY NAME WRONG, AND DON'T TRY ANYTHING CUTE.
I CAN SEE THIS WHOLE CITY--HEAR EVERYTHING THAT ANYONE SAYS!
I'M TUNED IN LIKE YOU WOULDN'T BELIEVE--TV, RADIO, CELL PHONES, POLICE SCANNERS...

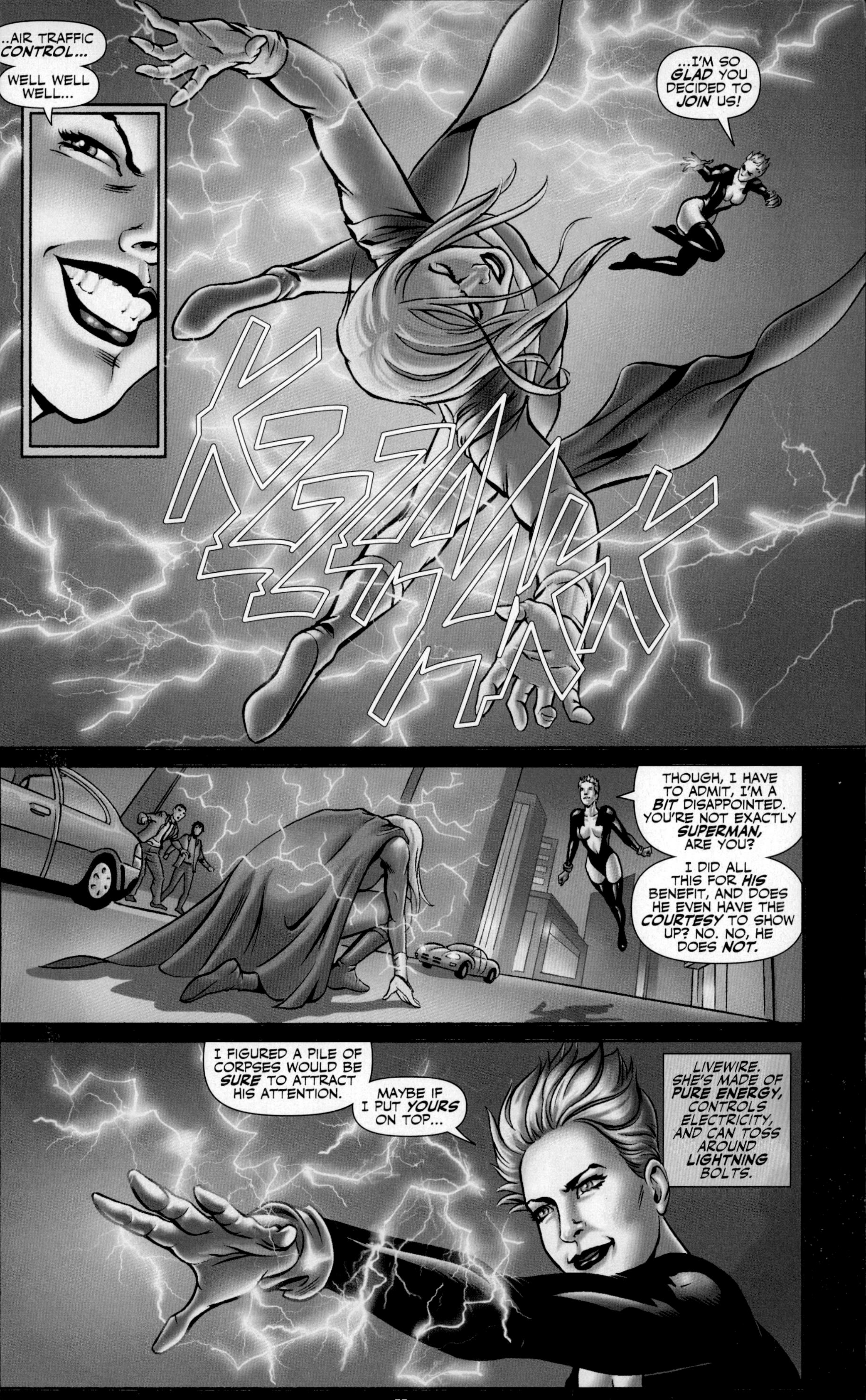
..AIR TRAFFIC CONTROL...
WELL WELL WELL...
...I'M SO GLAD YOU DECIDED TO JOIN US!
THOUGH, I HAVE TO ADMIT, I'M A BIT DISAPPOINTED. YOU'RE NOT EXACTLY SUPERMAN, ARE YOU?
I DID ALL THIS FOR HIS BENEFIT, AND DOES HE EVEN HAVE THE COURTESY TO SHOW UP? NO. NO, HE DOES NOT.
I FIGURED A PILE OF CORPSES WOULD BE SURE TO ATTRACT HIS ATTENTION.
MAYBE IF I PUT YOURS ON TOP...
LIVEWIRE. SHE'S MADE OF PURE ENERGY, CONTROLS ELECTRICITY, AND CAN TOSS AROUND LIGHTNING BOLTS.

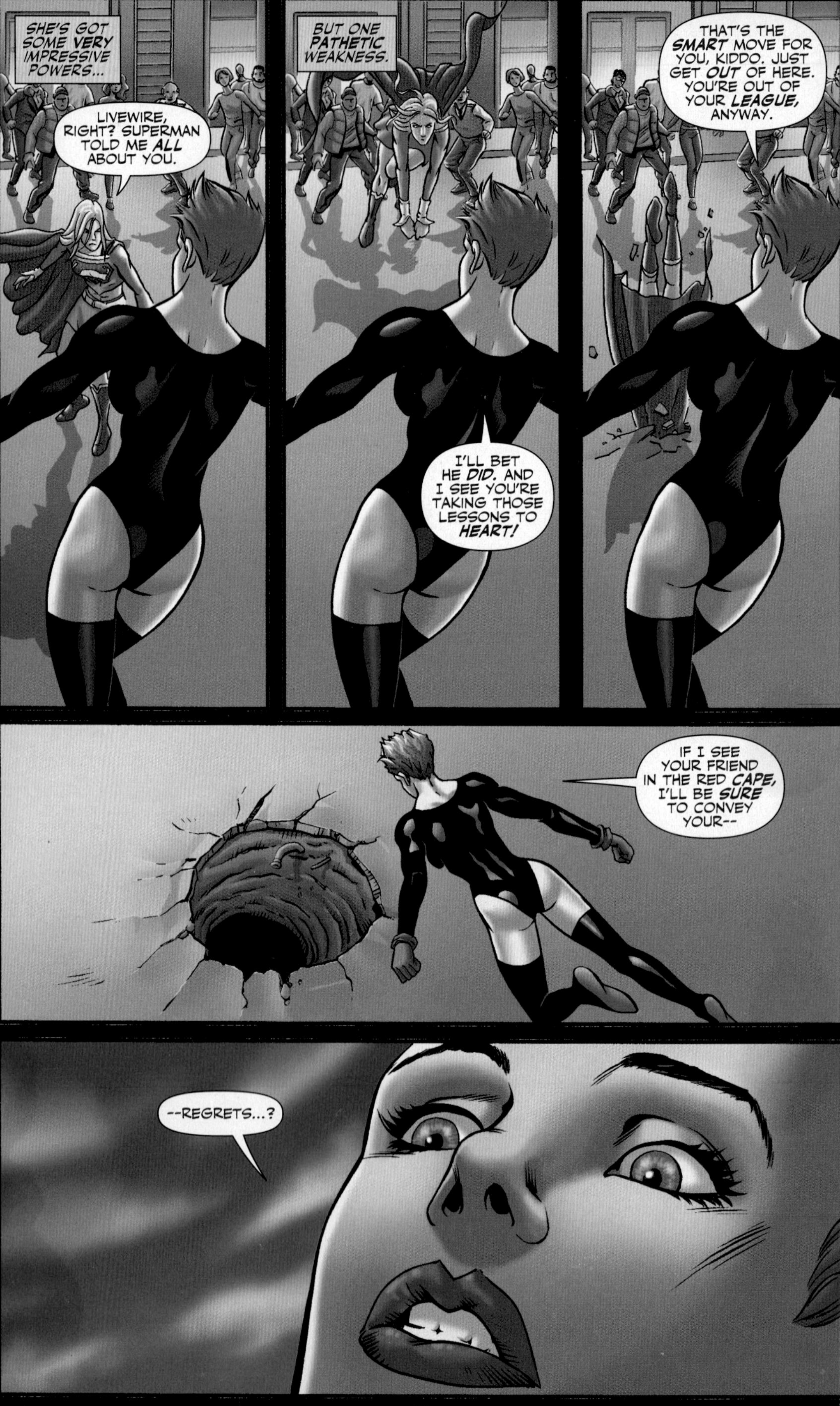
SHE'S GOT SOME VERY IMPRESSIVE POWERS...
LIVEWIRE, RIGHT? SUPERMAN TOLD ME ALL ABOUT YOU.
BUT ONE PATHETIC WEAKNESS.
I'LL BET HE DID. AND I SEE YOU'RE TAKING THOSE LESSONS TO HEART!
THAT'S THE SMART MOVE FOR YOU, KIDDO. JUST GET OUT OF HERE. YOU'RE OUT OF YOUR LEAGUE, ANYWAY.
IF I SEE YOUR FRIEND IN THE RED CAPE, I'LL BE SURE TO CONVEY YOUR--
--REGRETS...?

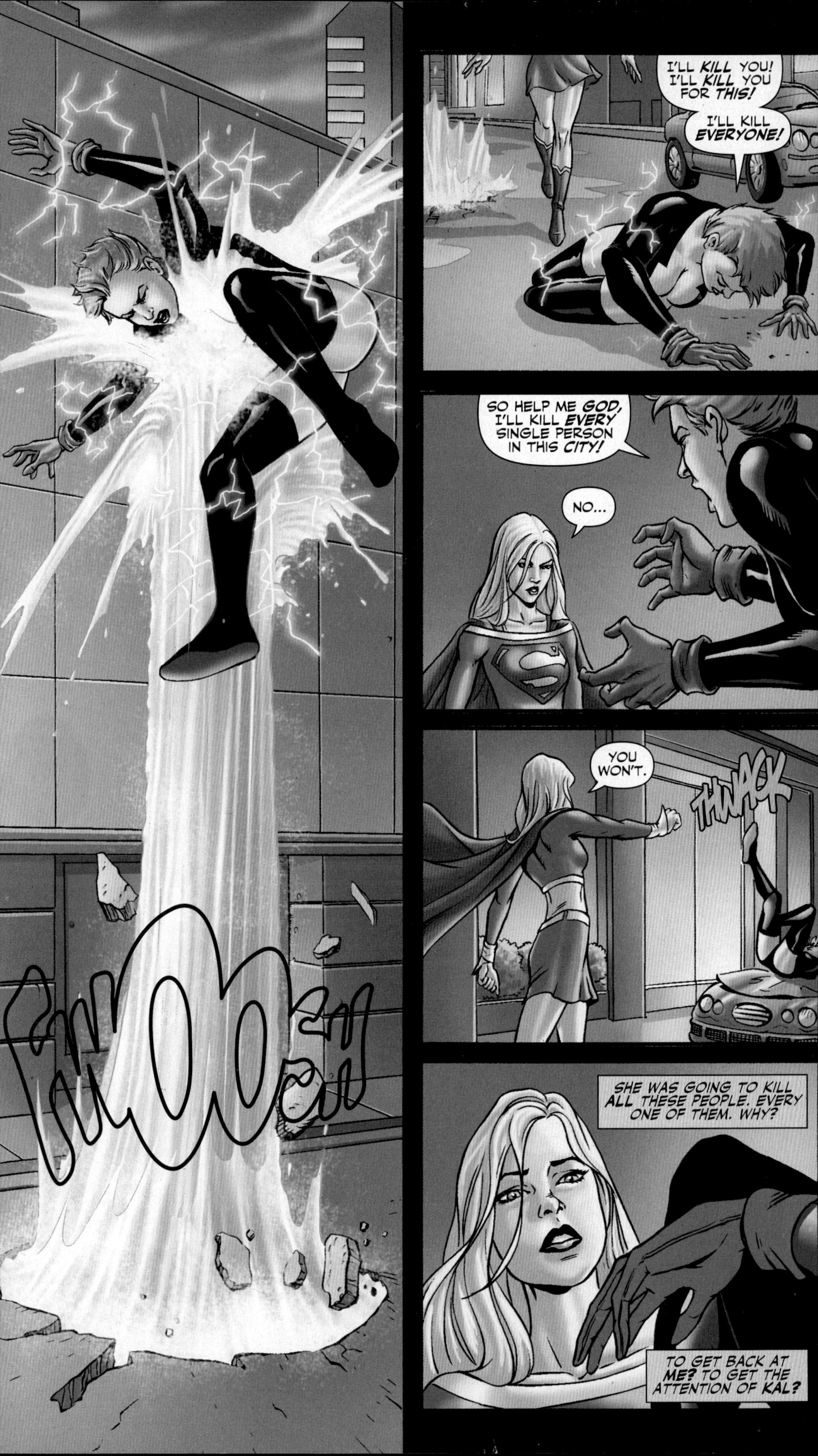
I'LL KILL YOU! I'LL KILL YOU FOR THIS!
I'LL KILL EVERYONE!
SO HELP ME GOD, I'LL KILL EVERY SINGLE PERSON IN THIS CITY!
NO...
YOU WON'T.
THWACK
SHE WAS GOING TO KILL ALL THESE PEOPLE. EVERY ONE OF THEM. WHY?
TO GET BACK AT ME? TO GET THE ATTENTION OF KAL?

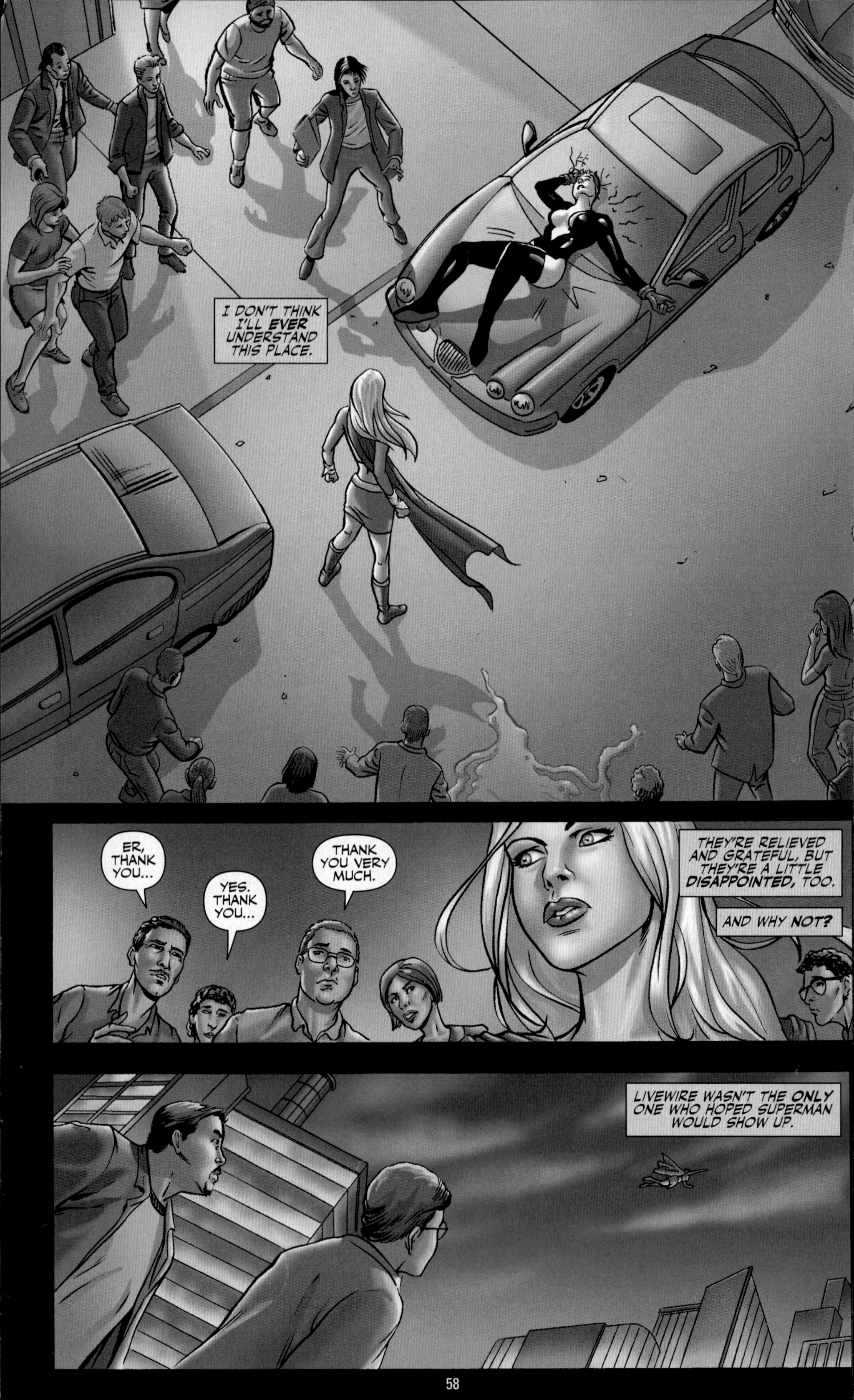
I DON'T THINK I'LL EVER UNDERSTAND THIS PLACE.
ER, THANK YOU...
YES. THANK YOU...
THANK YOU VERY MUCH.
THEY'RE RELIEVED AND GRATEFUL, BUT THEY'RE A LITTLE DISAPPOINTED, TOO.
AND WHY NOT?
LIVEWIRE WASN'T THE ONLY ONE WHO HOPED SUPERMAN WOULD SHOW UP.

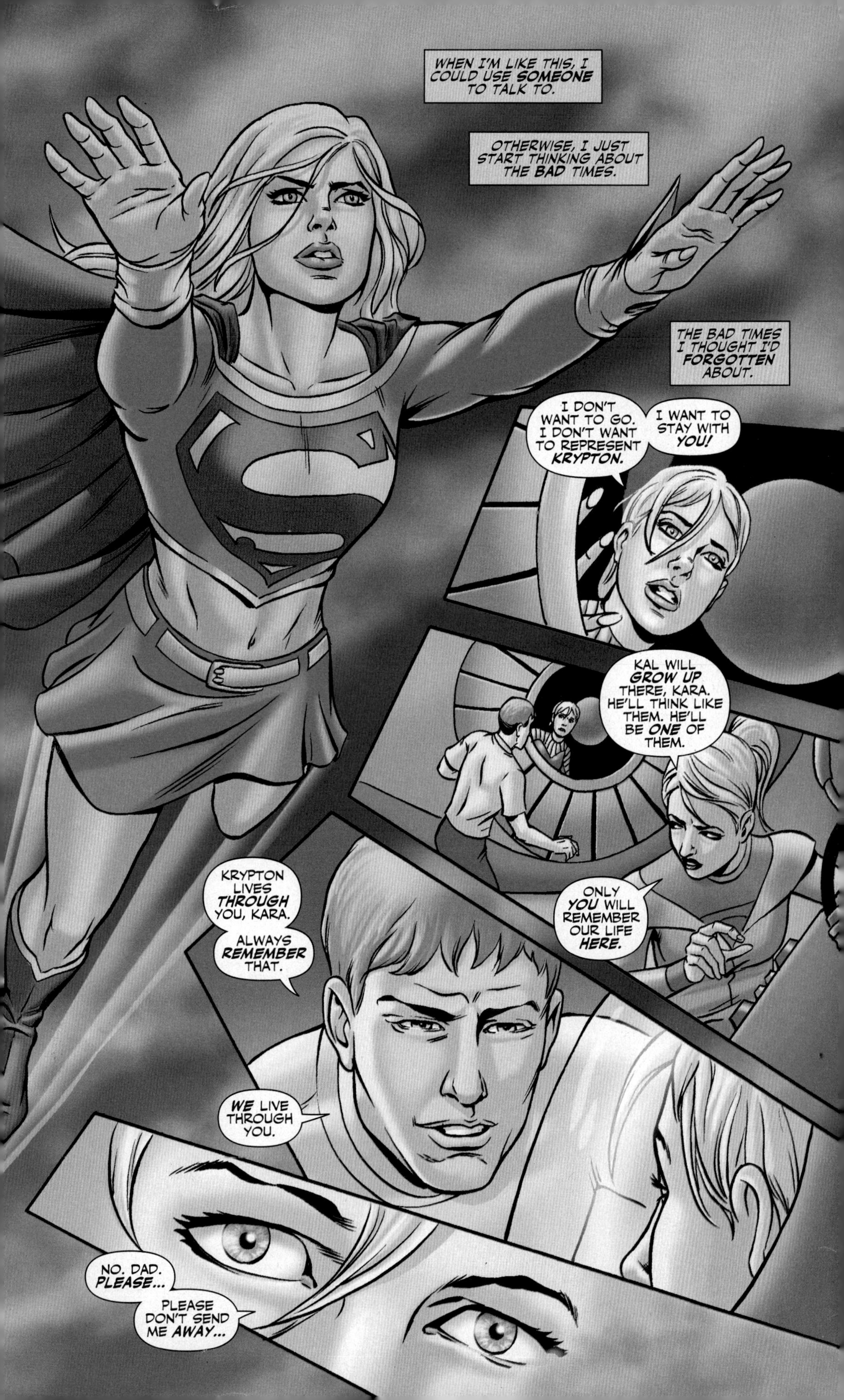
WHEN I'M LIKE THIS, I COULD USE SOMEONE TO TALK TO.
OTHERWISE, I JUST START THINKING ABOUT THE BAD TIMES.
THE BAD TIMES I THOUGHT I'D FORGOTTEN ABOUT.
I DON'T WANT TO GO. I DON'T WANT TO REPRESENT KRYPTON.
I WANT TO STAY WITH YOU!
KAL WILL GROW UP THERE, KARA. HE'LL THINK LIKE THEM. HE'LL BE ONE OF THEM.
ONLY YOU WILL REMEMBER OUR LIFE HERE.
KRYPTON LIVES THROUGH YOU, KARA.
ALWAYS REMEMBER THAT.
WE LIVE THROUGH YOU.
NO. DAD. PLEASE...
PLEASE DON'T SEND ME AWAY...

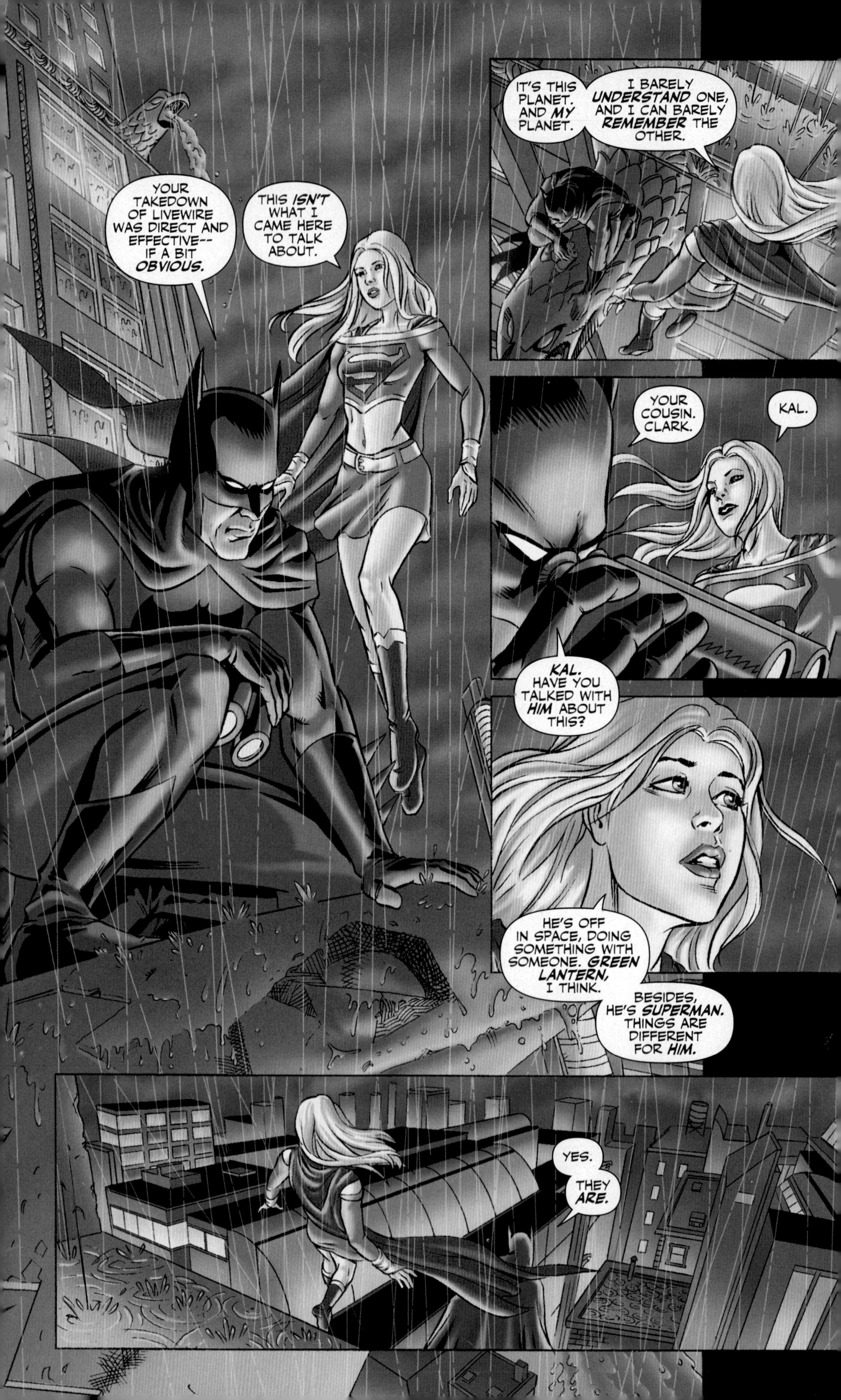
YOUR TAKEDOWN OF LIVEWIRE WAS DIRECT AND EFFECTIVE-- IF A BIT *OBVIOUS.*
THIS *ISN'T* WHAT I CAME HERE TO TALK ABOUT.
IT'S THIS PLANET. AND *MY* PLANET.
I BARELY *UNDERSTAND* ONE, AND I CAN BARELY *REMEMBER* THE OTHER.
YOUR COUSIN. CLARK.
KAL.
KAL. HAVE YOU TALKED WITH *HIM* ABOUT THIS?
HE'S OFF IN SPACE, DOING SOMETHING WITH SOMEONE. *GREEN LANTERN,* I THINK.
BESIDES, HE'S *SUPERMAN.* THINGS ARE DIFFERENT FOR *HIM.*
YES.
THEY *ARE.*

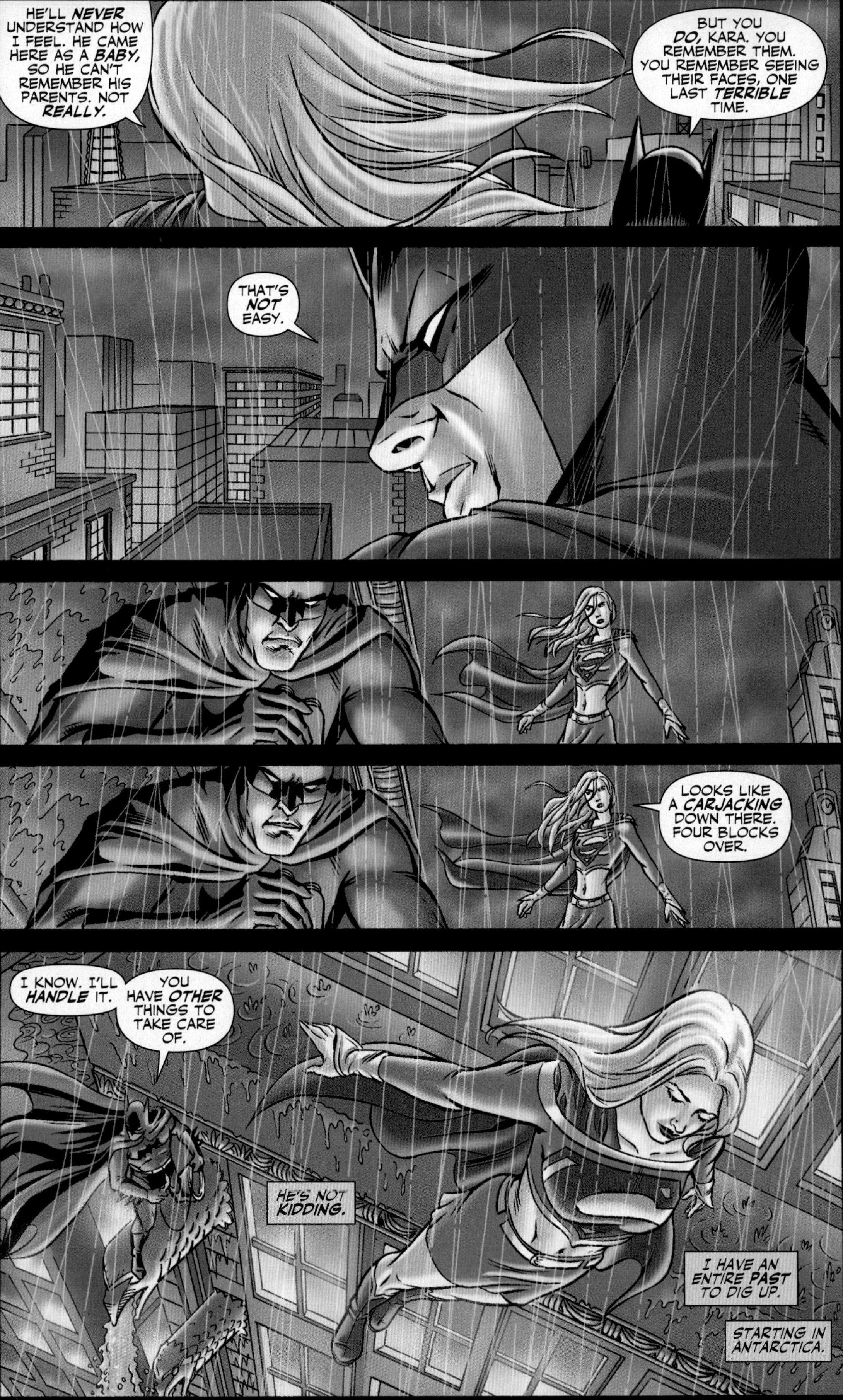
HE'LL NEVER UNDERSTAND HOW I FEEL. HE CAME HERE AS A BABY, SO HE CAN'T REMEMBER HIS PARENTS. NOT REALLY.
BUT YOU DO, KARA. YOU REMEMBER THEM. YOU REMEMBER SEEING THEIR FACES, ONE LAST TERRIBLE TIME.
THAT'S NOT EASY.
LOOKS LIKE A CARJACKING DOWN THERE. FOUR BLOCKS OVER.
I KNOW. I'LL HANDLE IT.
YOU HAVE OTHER THINGS TO TAKE CARE OF.
HE'S NOT KIDDING.
I HAVE AN ENTIRE PAST TO DIG UP.
STARTING IN ANTARCTICA.

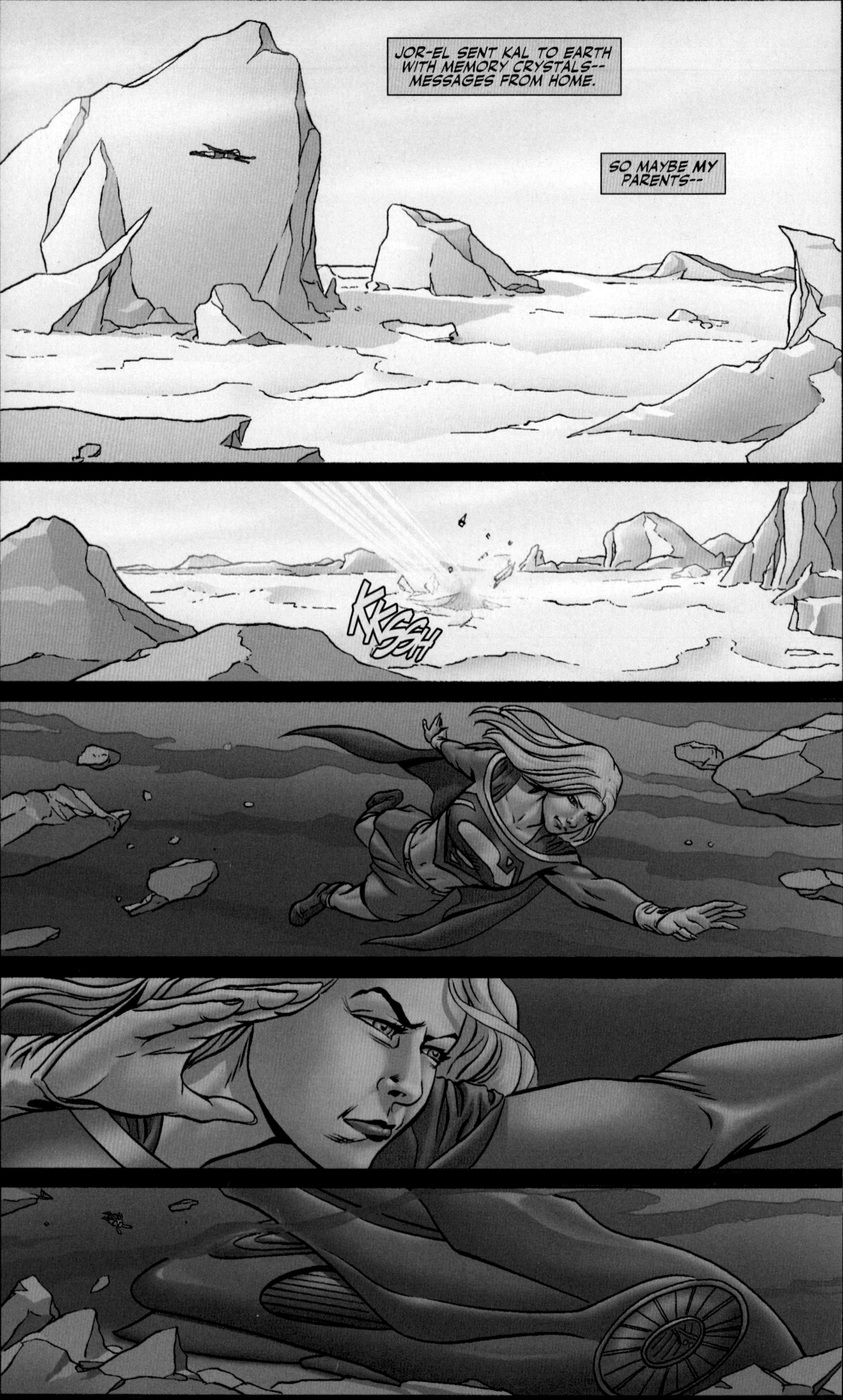
JOR-EL SENT KAL TO EARTH WITH MEMORY CRYSTALS-- MESSAGES FROM HOME.
SO MAYBE MY PARENTS--
KKSSH

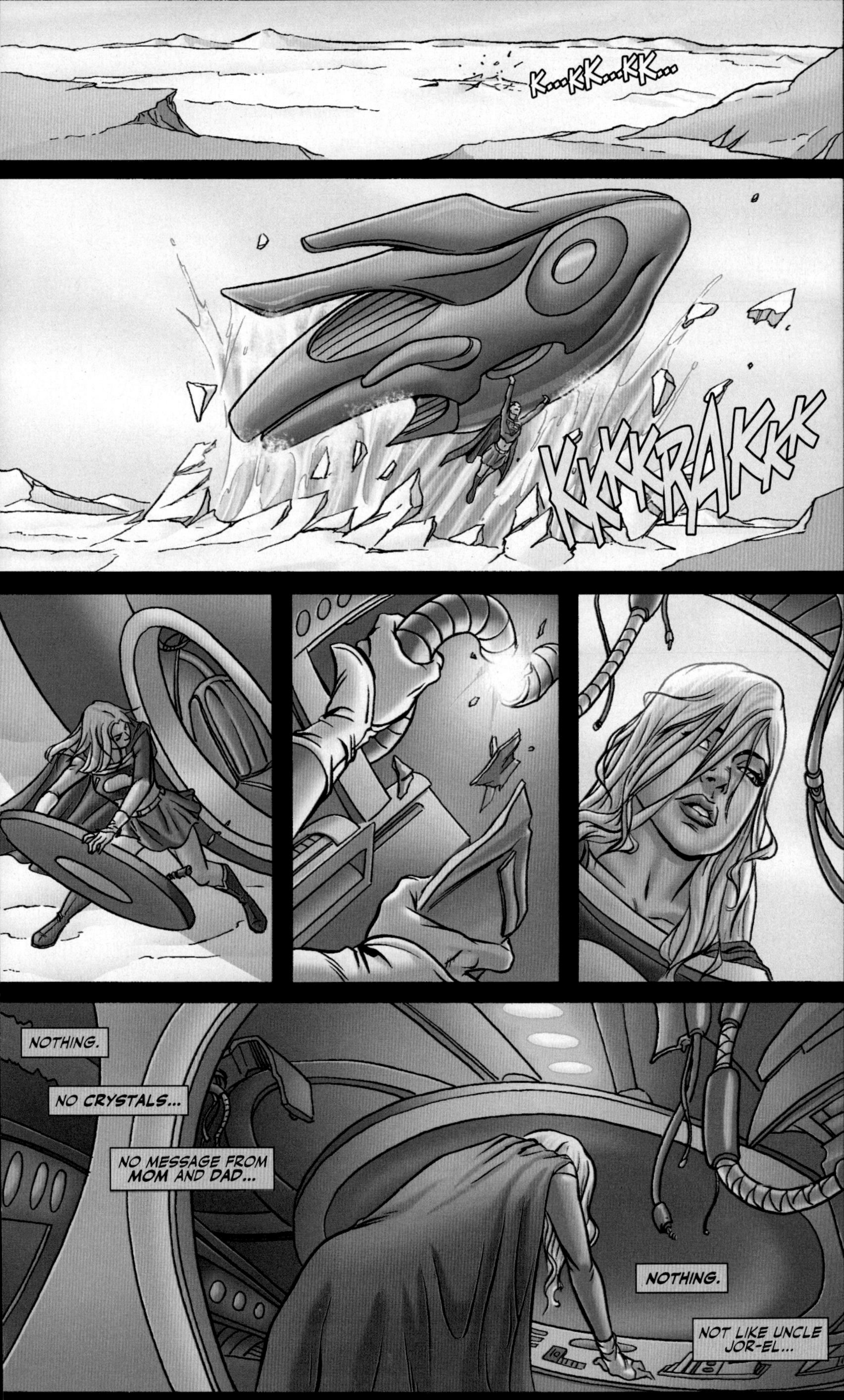

K...KK...KK...
KKKRAKKK
NOTHING.
NO CRYSTALS...
NO MESSAGE FROM MOM AND DAD...
NOTHING.
NOT LIKE UNCLE JOR-EL...

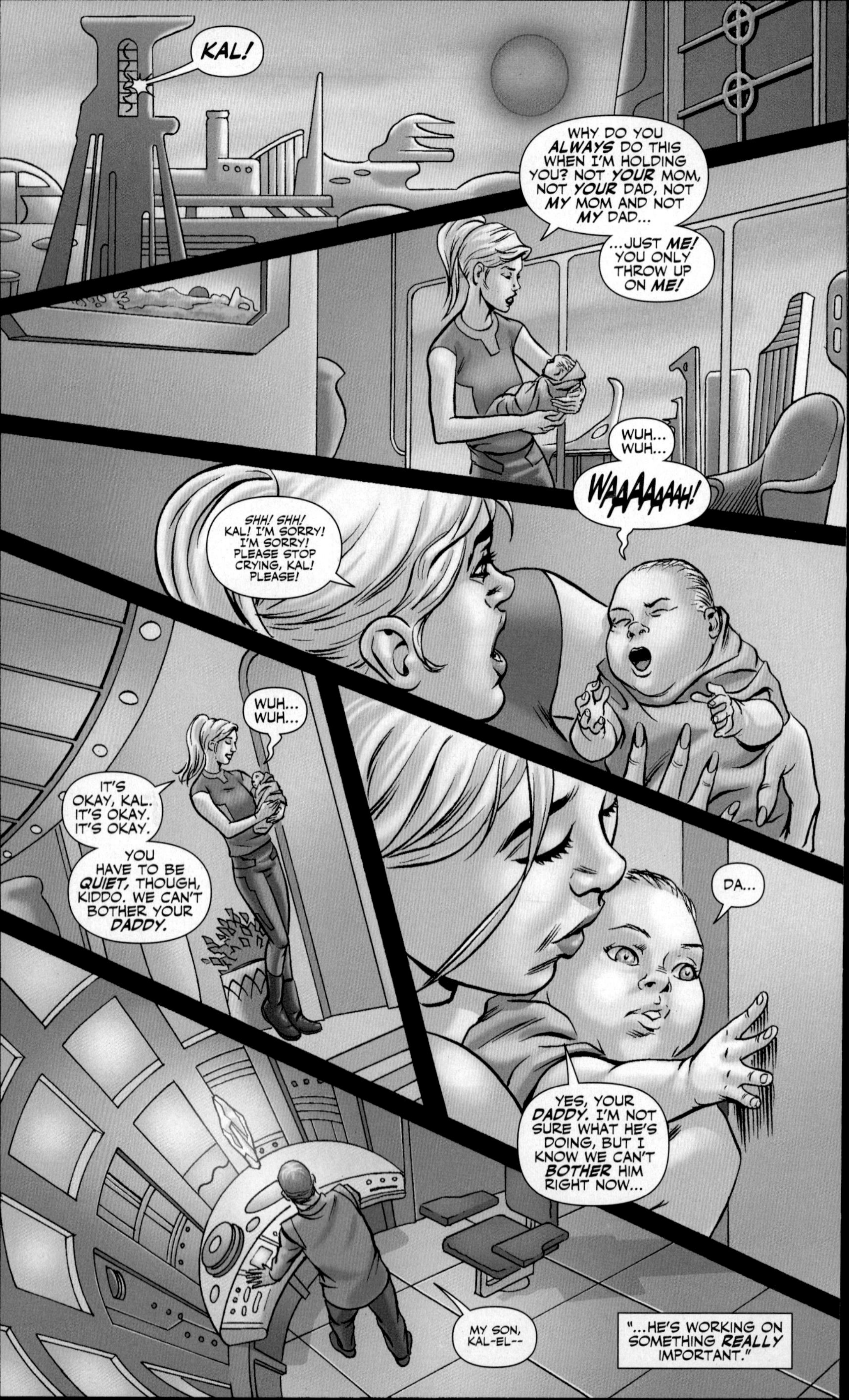

KAL!
WHY DO YOU ALWAYS DO THIS WHEN I'M HOLDING YOU? NOT YOUR MOM, NOT YOUR DAD, NOT MY MOM AND NOT MY DAD...
...JUST ME! YOU ONLY THROW UP ON ME!
WUH... WUH...
WAAAAAAAH!
SHH! SHH! KAL! I'M SORRY! I'M SORRY! PLEASE STOP CRYING, KAL! PLEASE!
WUH... WUH...
IT'S OKAY, KAL. IT'S OKAY. IT'S OKAY.
YOU HAVE TO BE QUIET, THOUGH, KIDDO. WE CAN'T BOTHER YOUR DADDY.
DA...
YES, YOUR DADDY. I'M NOT SURE WHAT HE'S DOING, BUT I KNOW WE CAN'T BOTHER HIM RIGHT NOW...
MY SON, KAL-EL--
"...HE'S WORKING ON SOMETHING REALLY IMPORTANT."

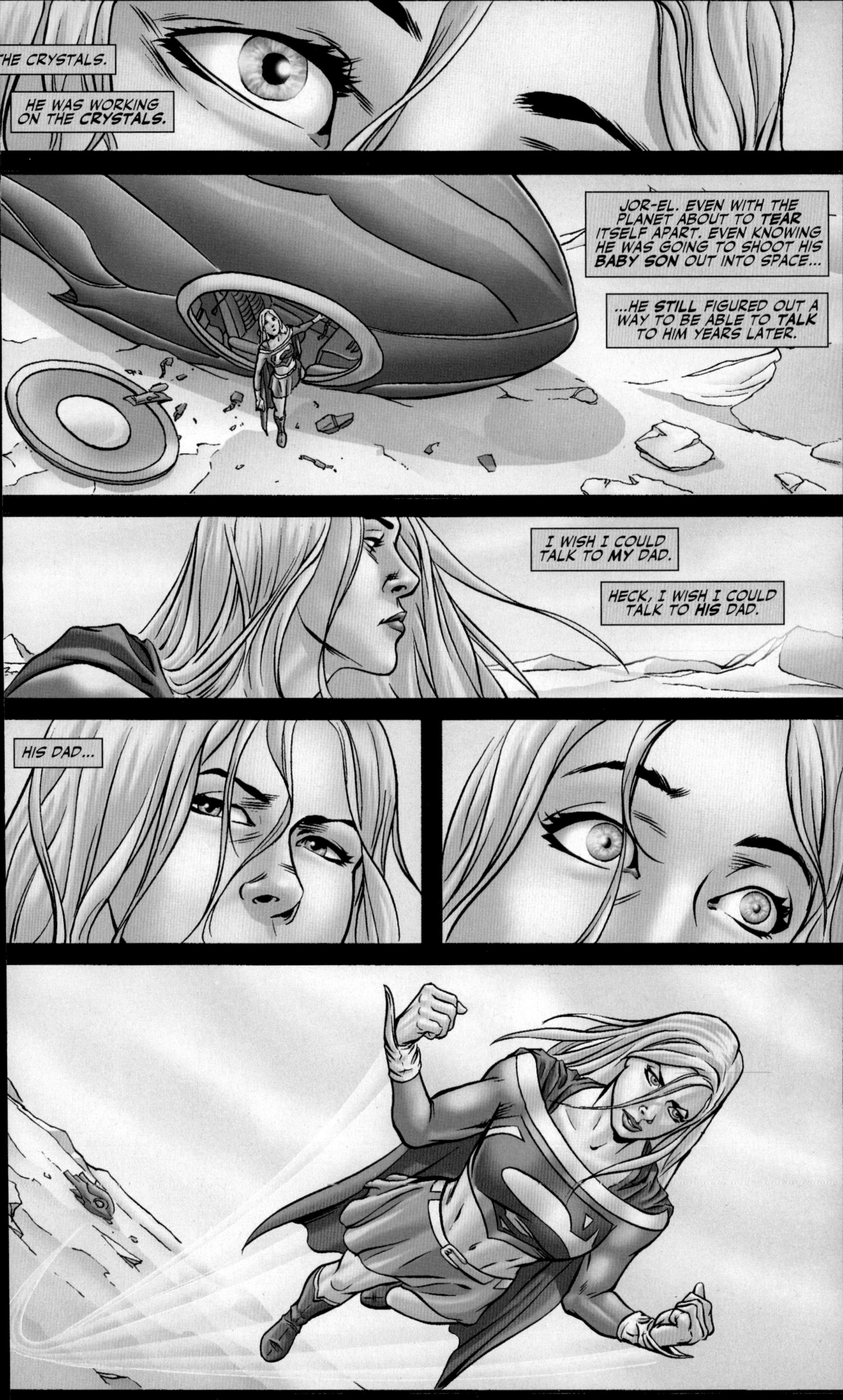
THE CRYSTALS.
HE WAS WORKING ON THE CRYSTALS.
JOR-EL. EVEN WITH THE PLANET ABOUT TO TEAR ITSELF APART. EVEN KNOWING HE WAS GOING TO SHOOT HIS BABY SON OUT INTO SPACE...
...HE STILL FIGURED OUT A WAY TO BE ABLE TO TALK TO HIM YEARS LATER.
I WISH I COULD TALK TO MY DAD.
HECK, I WISH I COULD TALK TO HIS DAD.
HIS DAD...

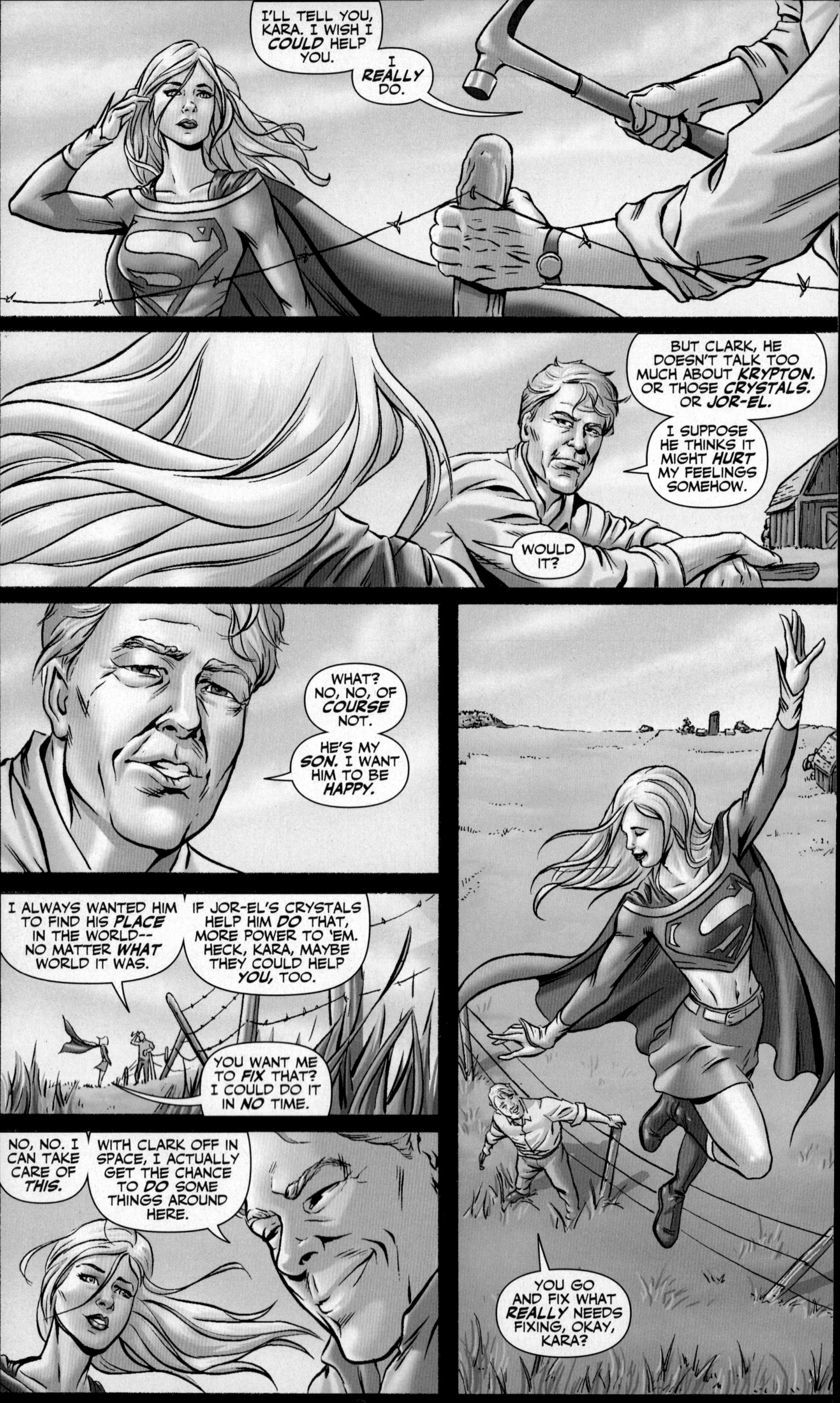
I'LL TELL YOU, KARA. I WISH I COULD HELP YOU.
I REALLY DO.
BUT CLARK, HE DOESN'T TALK TOO MUCH ABOUT KRYPTON. OR THOSE CRYSTALS. OR JOR-EL.
I SUPPOSE HE THINKS IT MIGHT HURT MY FEELINGS SOMEHOW.
WOULD IT?
WHAT? NO, NO, OF COURSE NOT.
HE'S MY SON. I WANT HIM TO BE HAPPY.
I ALWAYS WANTED HIM TO FIND HIS PLACE IN THE WORLD-- NO MATTER WHAT WORLD IT WAS.
IF JOR-EL'S CRYSTALS HELP HIM DO THAT, MORE POWER TO 'EM. HECK, KARA, MAYBE THEY COULD HELP YOU, TOO.
YOU WANT ME TO FIX THAT? I COULD DO IT IN NO TIME.
NO, NO. I CAN TAKE CARE OF THIS.
WITH CLARK OFF IN SPACE, I ACTUALLY GET THE CHANCE TO DO SOME THINGS AROUND HERE.
YOU GO AND FIX WHAT REALLY NEEDS FIXING, OKAY, KARA?

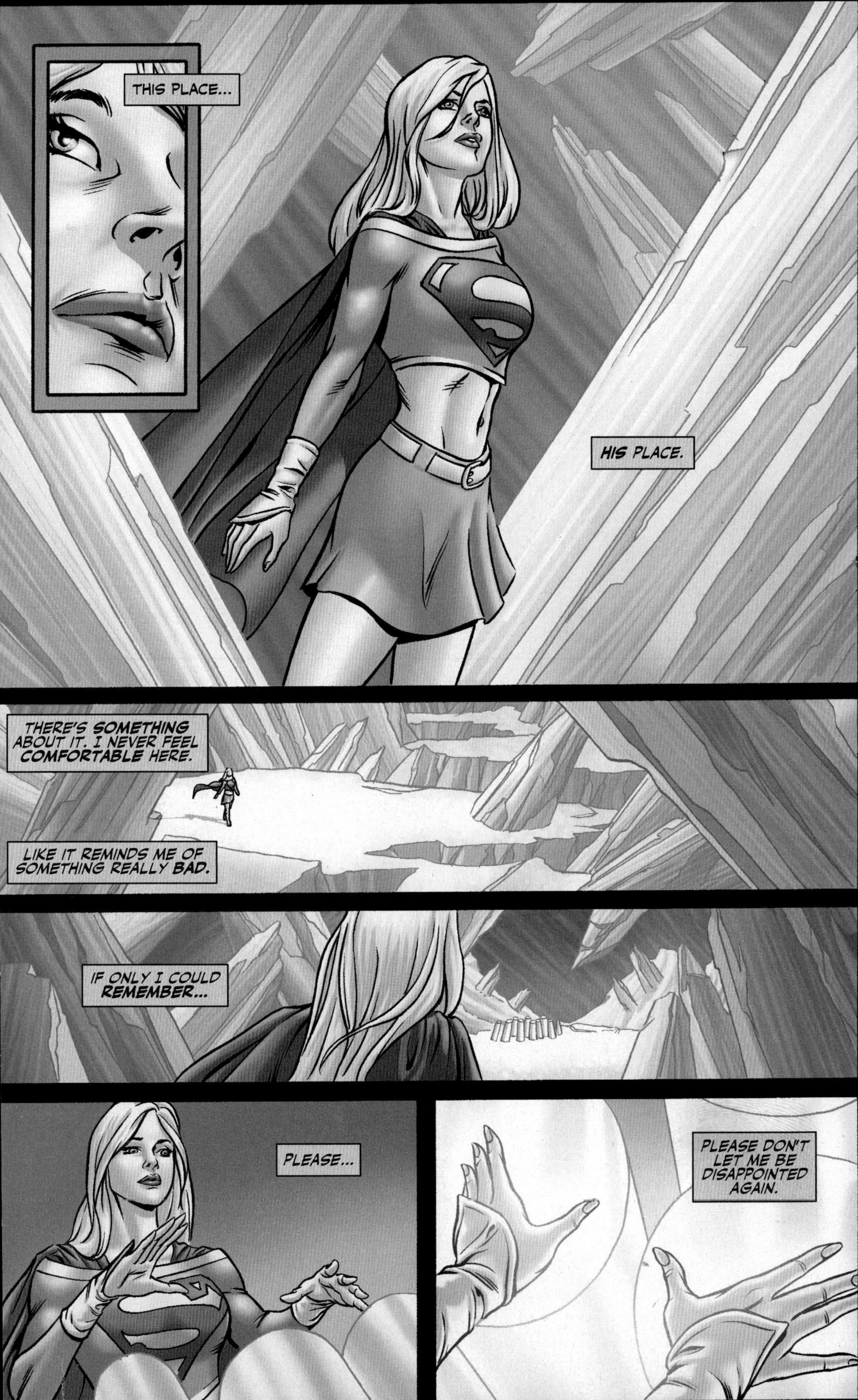
THIS PLACE...
HIS PLACE.
THERE'S SOMETHING ABOUT IT. I NEVER FEEL COMFORTABLE HERE.
LIKE IT REMINDS ME OF SOMETHING REALLY BAD.
IF ONLY I COULD REMEMBER...
PLEASE...
PLEASE DON'T LET ME BE DISAPPOINTED AGAIN.

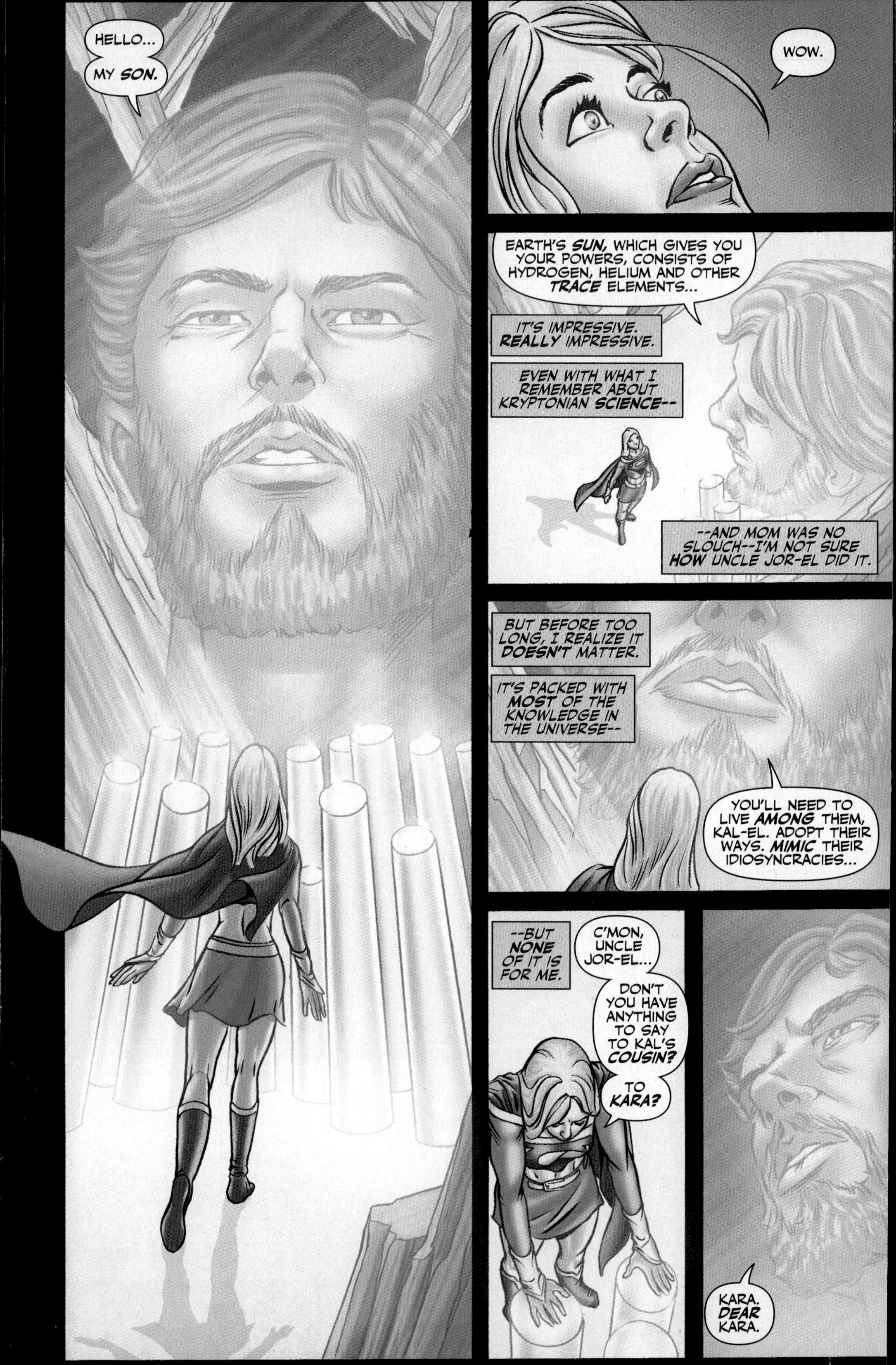

HELLO...
MY SON.
WOW.
EARTH'S SUN, WHICH GIVES YOU YOUR POWERS, CONSISTS OF HYDROGEN, HELIUM AND OTHER TRACE ELEMENTS...
IT'S IMPRESSIVE. REALLY IMPRESSIVE.
EVEN WITH WHAT I REMEMBER ABOUT KRYPTONIAN SCIENCE--
--AND MOM WAS NO SLOUCH--I'M NOT SURE HOW UNCLE JOR-EL DID IT.
BUT BEFORE TOO LONG, I REALIZE IT DOESN'T MATTER.
IT'S PACKED WITH MOST OF THE KNOWLEDGE IN THE UNIVERSE--
YOU'LL NEED TO LIVE AMONG THEM, KAL-EL. ADOPT THEIR WAYS. MIMIC THEIR IDIOSYNCRACIES...
--BUT NONE OF IT IS FOR ME.
C'MON, UNCLE JOR-EL...
DON'T YOU HAVE ANYTHING TO SAY TO KAL'S COUSIN?
TO KARA?
KARA. DEAR KARA.

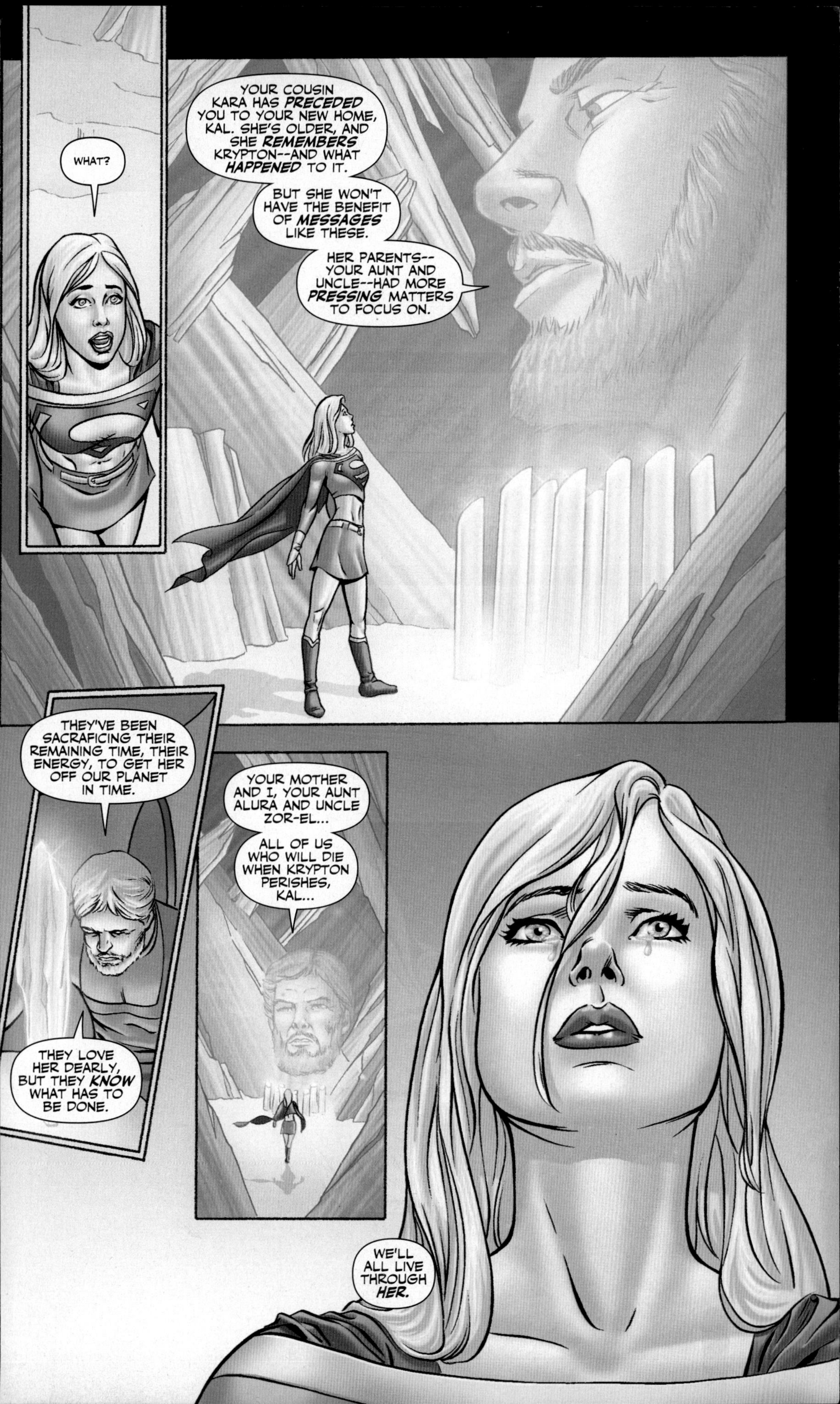

WHAT?
YOUR COUSIN KARA HAS PRECEDED YOU TO YOUR NEW HOME, KAL. SHE'S OLDER, AND SHE REMEMBERS KRYPTON--AND WHAT HAPPENED TO IT.
BUT SHE WON'T HAVE THE BENEFIT OF MESSAGES LIKE THESE.
HER PARENTS--YOUR AUNT AND UNCLE--HAD MORE PRESSING MATTERS TO FOCUS ON.
THEY'VE BEEN SACRAFICING THEIR REMAINING TIME, THEIR ENERGY, TO GET HER OFF OUR PLANET IN TIME.
THEY LOVE HER DEARLY, BUT THEY KNOW WHAT HAS TO BE DONE.
YOUR MOTHER AND I, YOUR AUNT ALURA AND UNCLE ZOR-EL...
ALL OF US WHO WILL DIE WHEN KRYPTON PERISHES, KAL...
WE'LL ALL LIVE THROUGH HER.

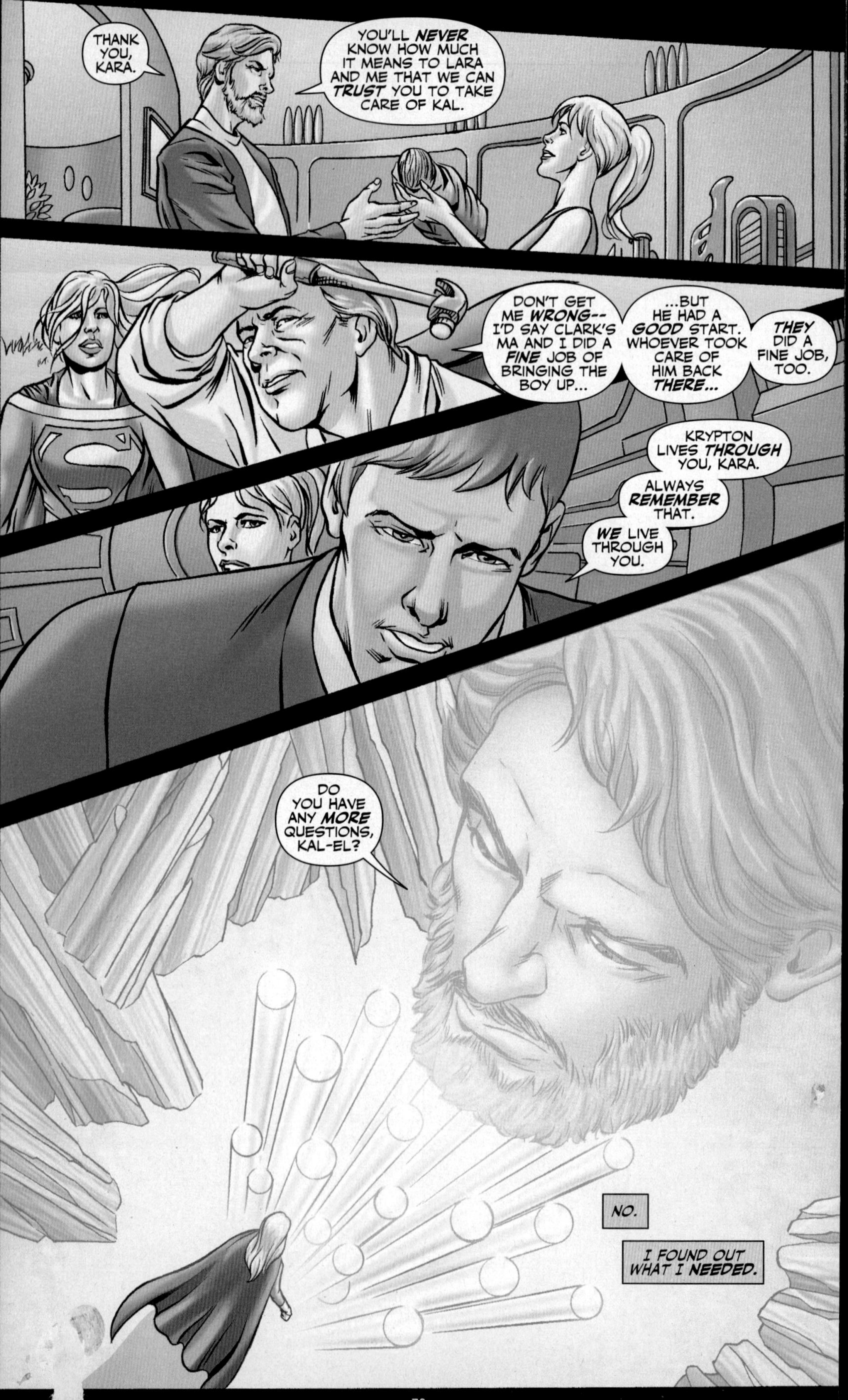
THANK YOU, KARA.
YOU'LL NEVER KNOW HOW MUCH IT MEANS TO LARA AND ME THAT WE CAN TRUST YOU TO TAKE CARE OF KAL.
DON'T GET ME WRONG-- I'D SAY CLARK'S MA AND I DID A FINE JOB OF BRINGING THE BOY UP...
...BUT HE HAD A GOOD START. WHOEVER TOOK CARE OF HIM BACK THERE...
THEY DID A FINE JOB, TOO.
KRYPTON LIVES THROUGH YOU, KARA.
ALWAYS REMEMBER THAT.
WE LIVE THROUGH YOU.
DO YOU HAVE ANY MORE QUESTIONS, KAL-EL?
NO.
I FOUND OUT WHAT I NEEDED.

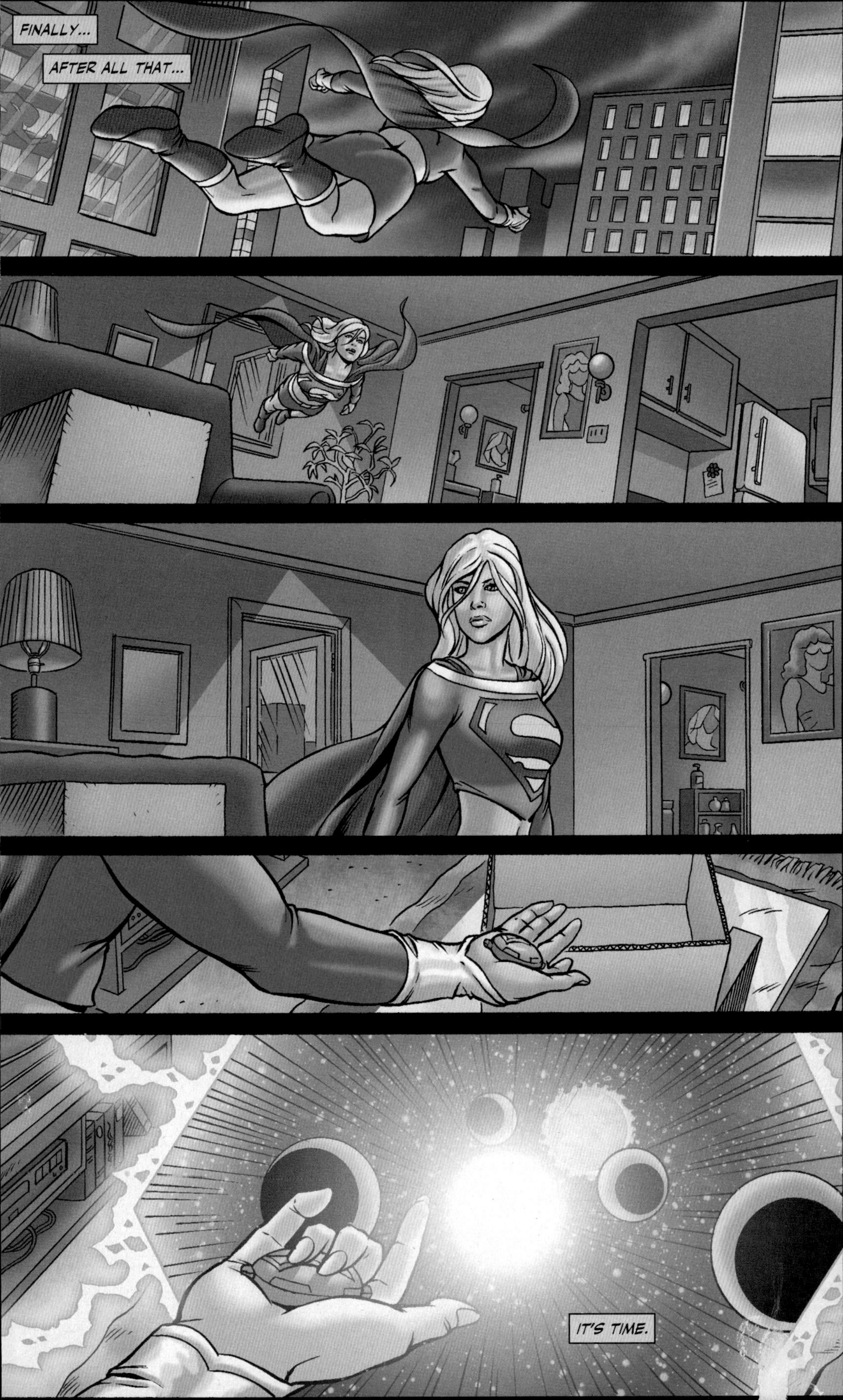
FINALLY...
AFTER ALL THAT...
IT'S TIME.

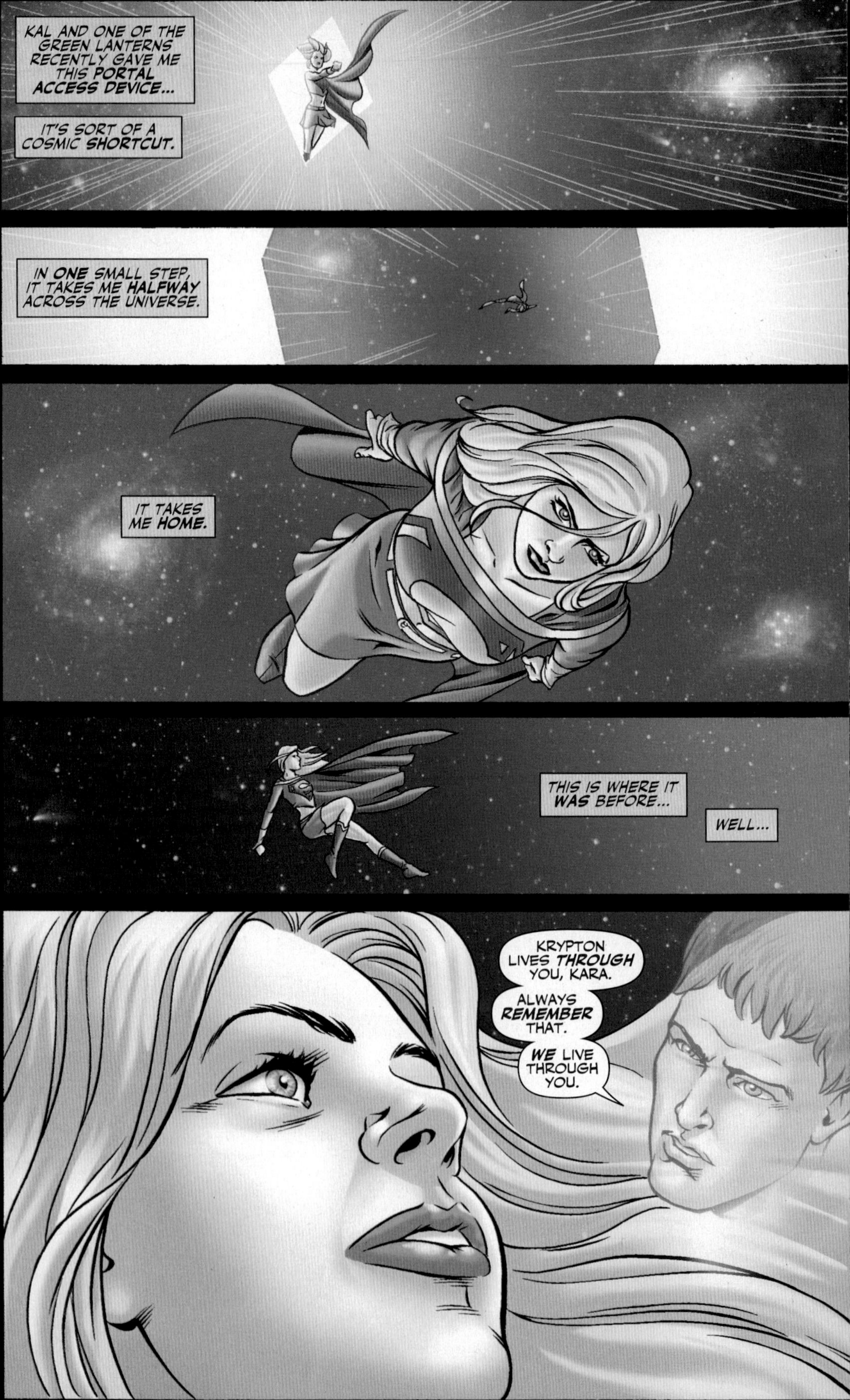
KAL AND ONE OF THE GREEN LANTERNS RECENTLY GAVE ME THIS PORTAL ACCESS DEVICE...
IT'S SORT OF A COSMIC SHORTCUT.
IN ONE SMALL STEP, IT TAKES ME HALFWAY ACROSS THE UNIVERSE.
IT TAKES ME HOME.
THIS IS WHERE IT WAS BEFORE...
WELL...
KRYPTON LIVES THROUGH YOU, KARA.
ALWAYS REMEMBER THAT.
WE LIVE THROUGH YOU.

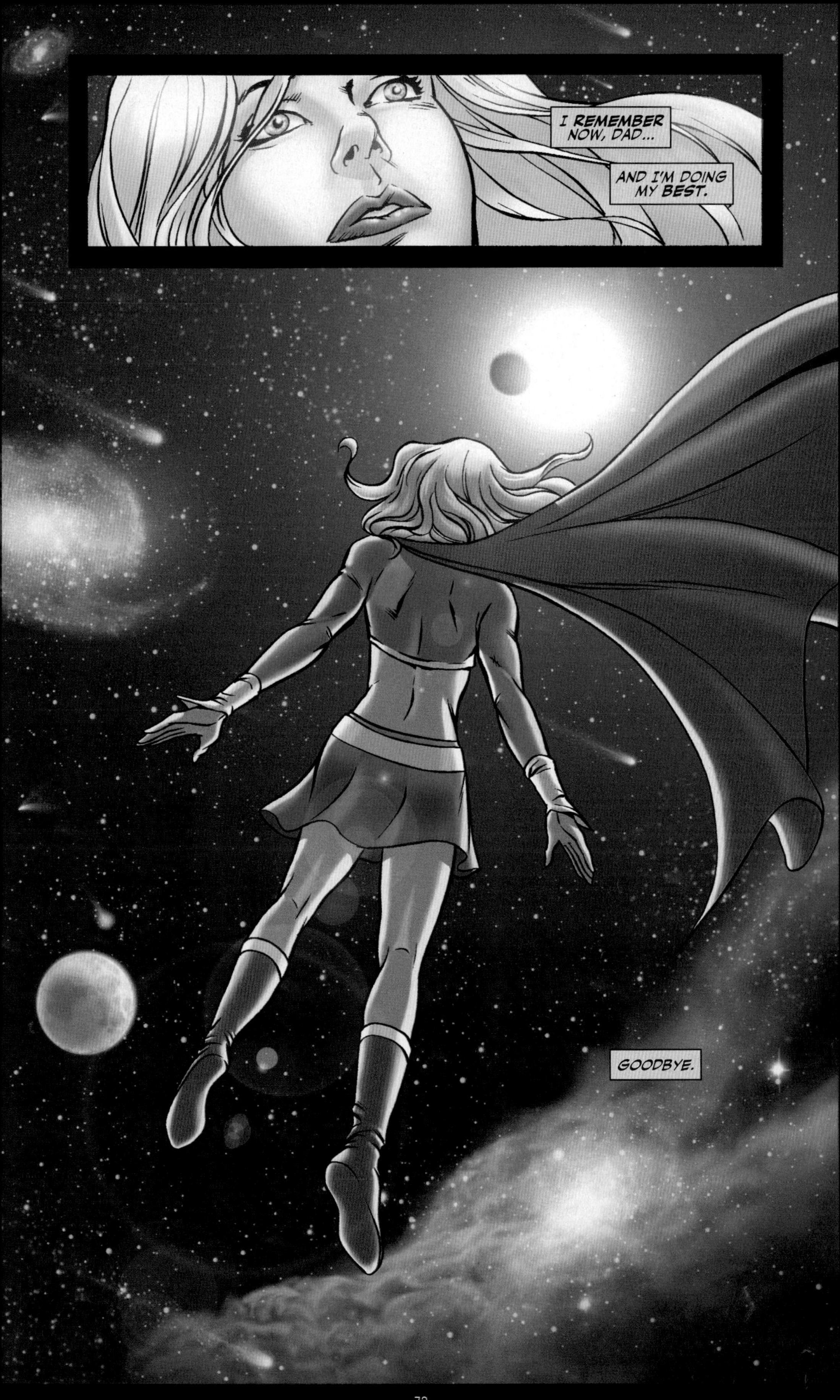
I REMEMBER NOW, DAD...
AND I'M DOING MY BEST.
GOODBYE.

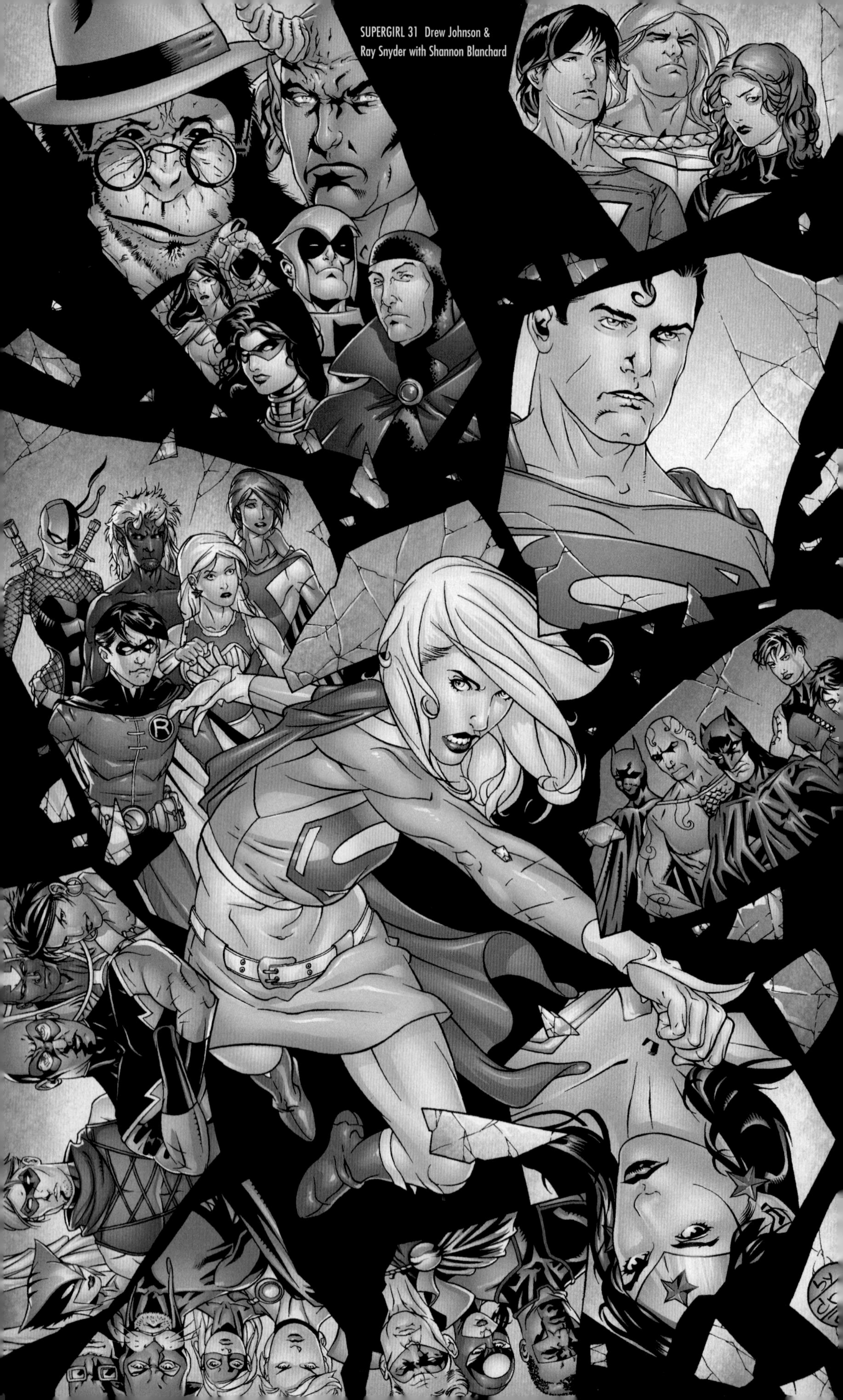
SUPERGIRL 31 Drew Johnson &
Ray Snyder with Shannon Blanchard

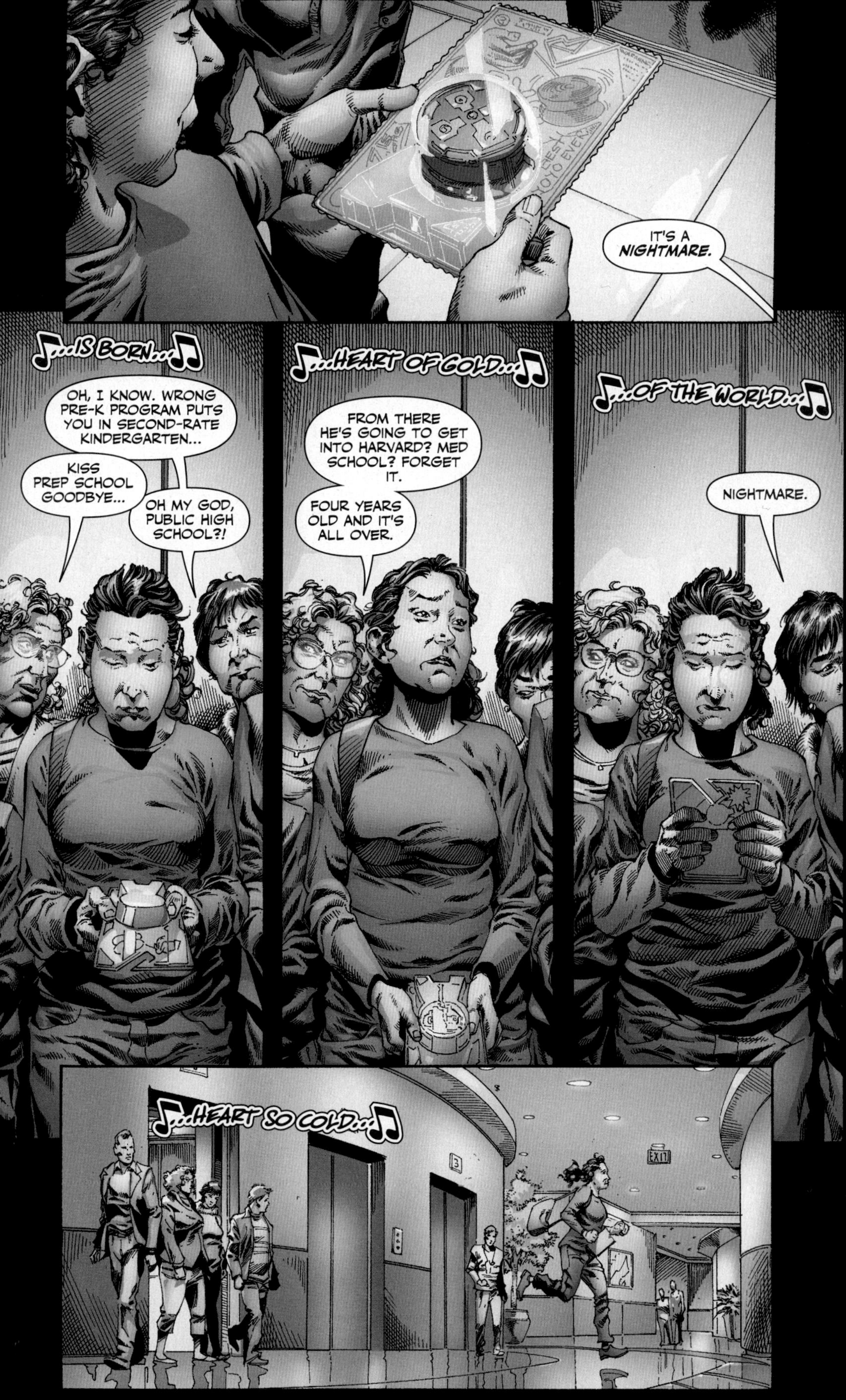
IT'S A NIGHTMARE.
...IS BORN...
OH, I KNOW. WRONG PRE-K PROGRAM PUTS YOU IN SECOND-RATE KINDERGARTEN...
KISS PREP SCHOOL GOODBYE...
OH MY GOD, PUBLIC HIGH SCHOOL?!
...HEART OF GOLD...
FROM THERE HE'S GOING TO GET INTO HARVARD? MED SCHOOL? FORGET IT.
FOUR YEARS OLD AND IT'S ALL OVER.
...OF THE WORLD...
NIGHTMARE.
...HEART SO COLD...
3
EXIT

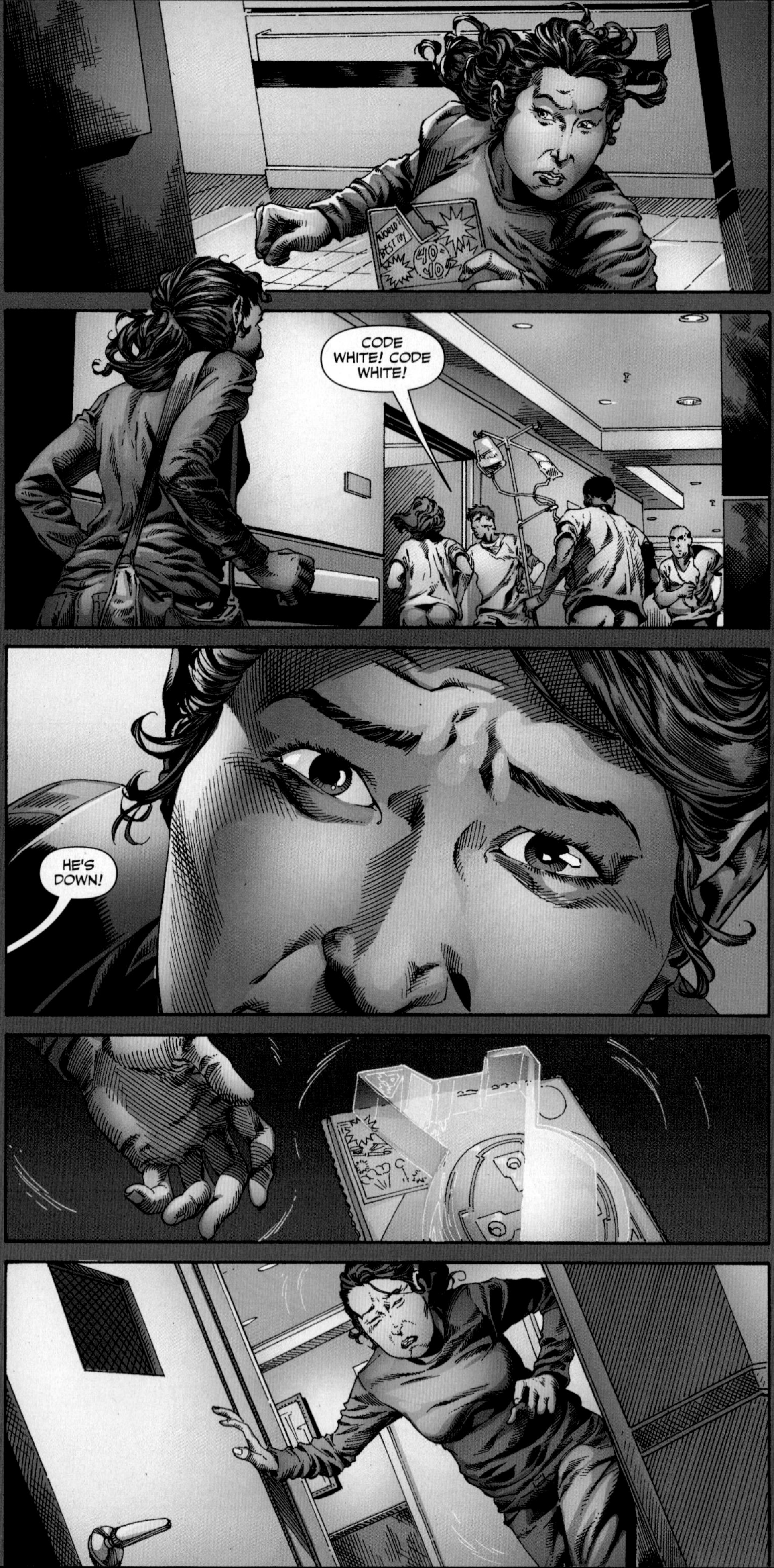
CODE WHITE! CODE WHITE!
HE'S DOWN!

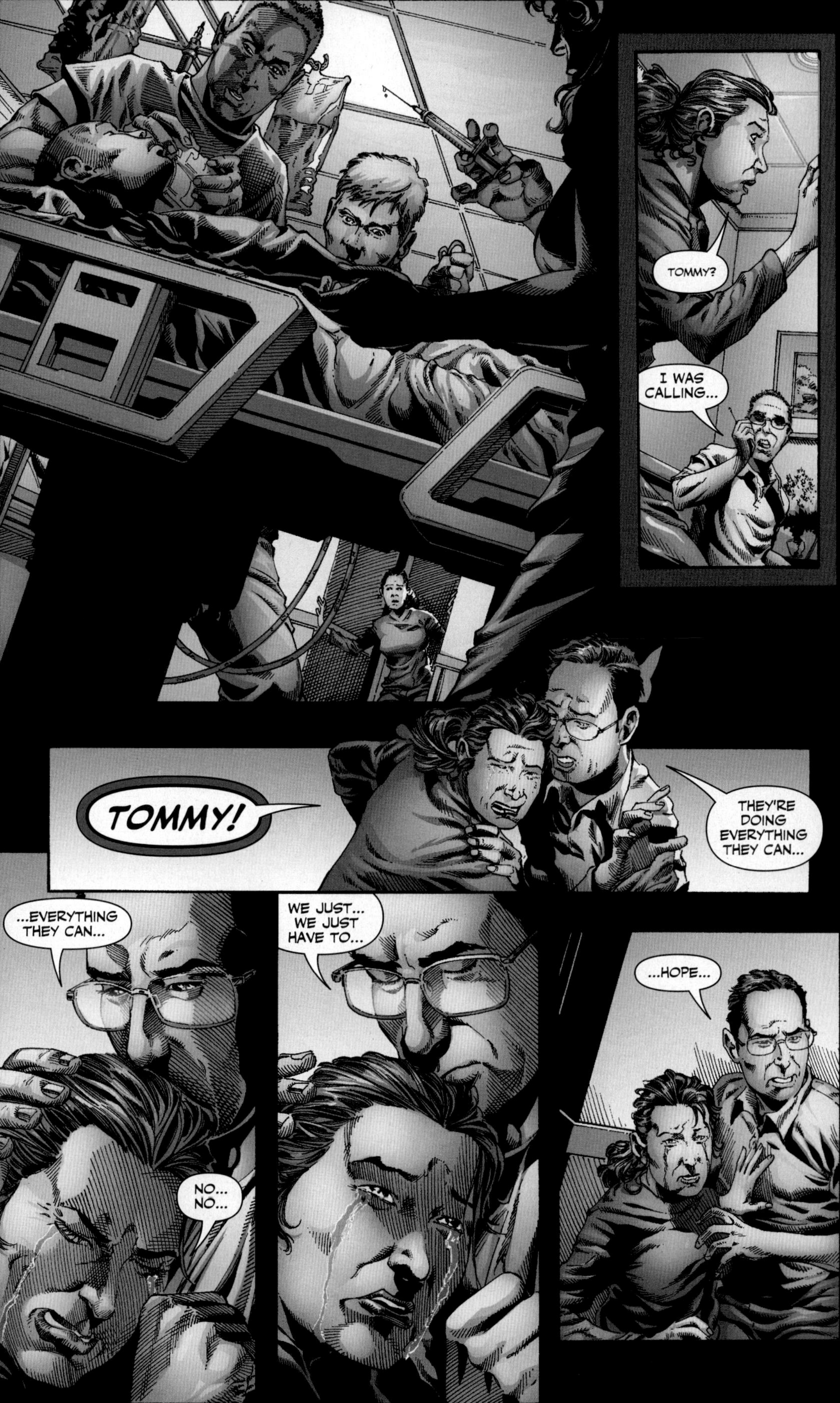

TOMMY?
I WAS CALLING...
TOMMY!
THEY'RE DOING EVERYTHING THEY CAN...
...EVERYTHING THEY CAN...
NO... NO...
WE JUST... WE JUST HAVE TO...
...HOPE...

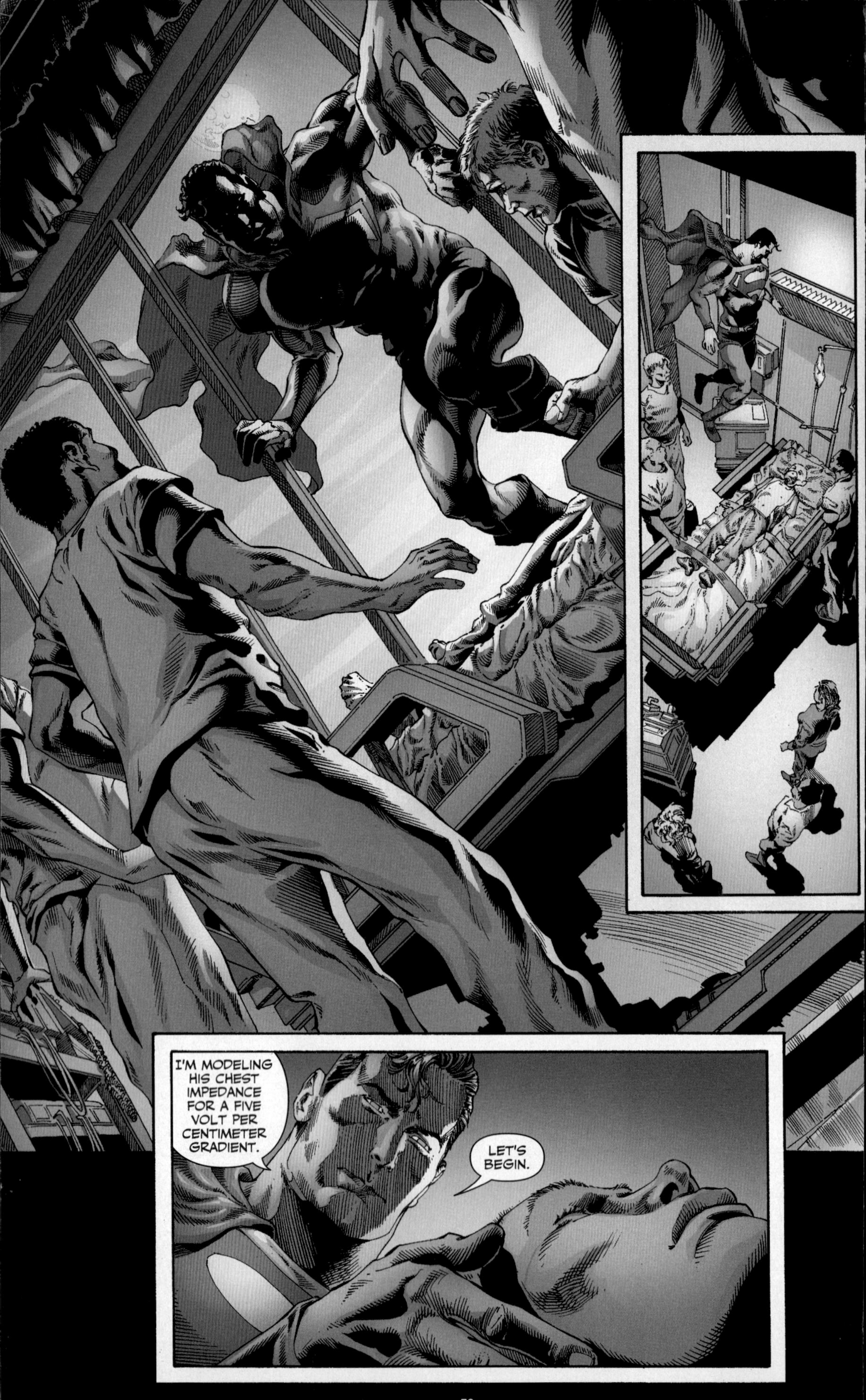
I'M MODELING HIS CHEST IMPEDANCE FOR A FIVE VOLT PER CENTIMETER GRADIENT.
LET'S BEGIN.

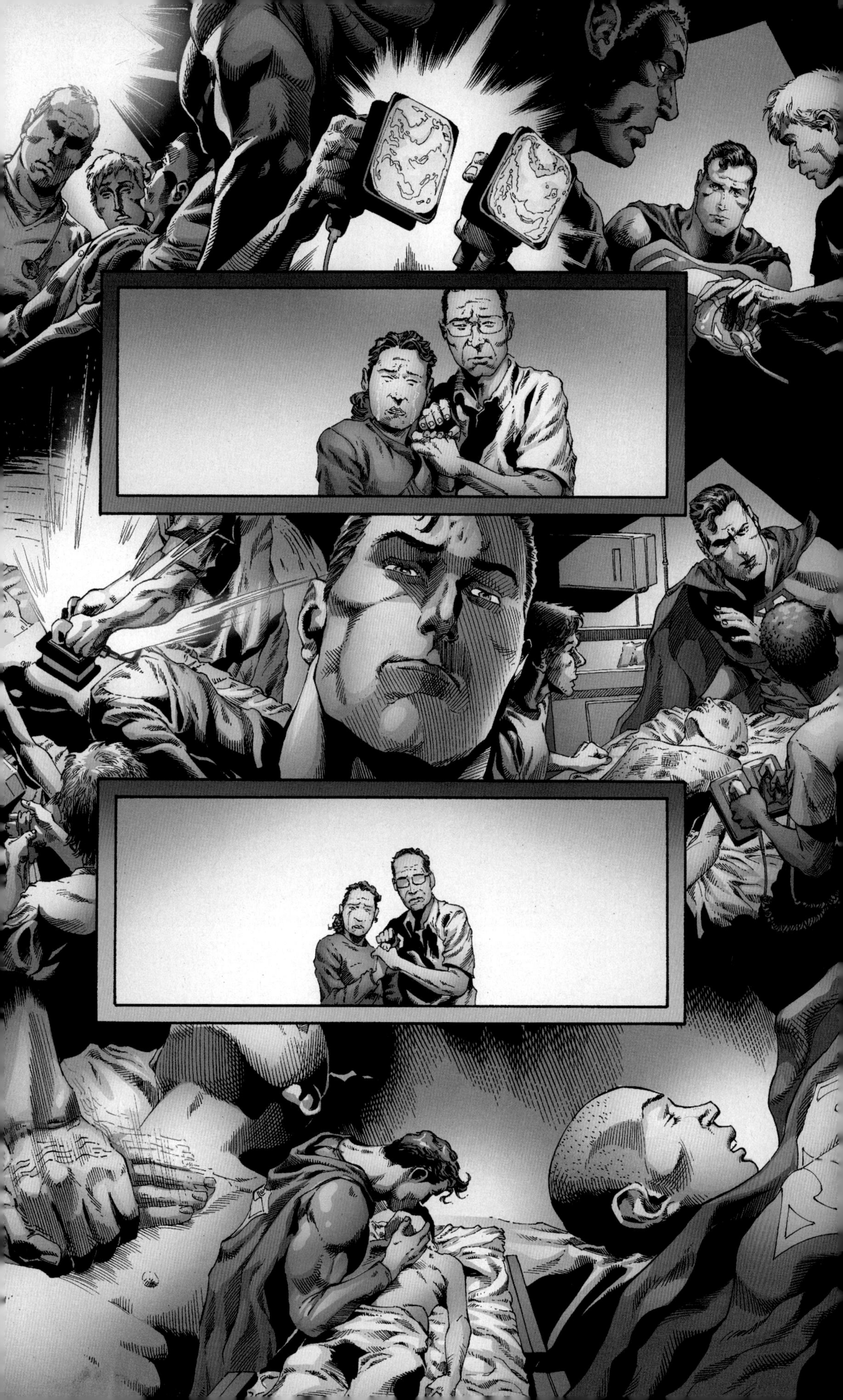

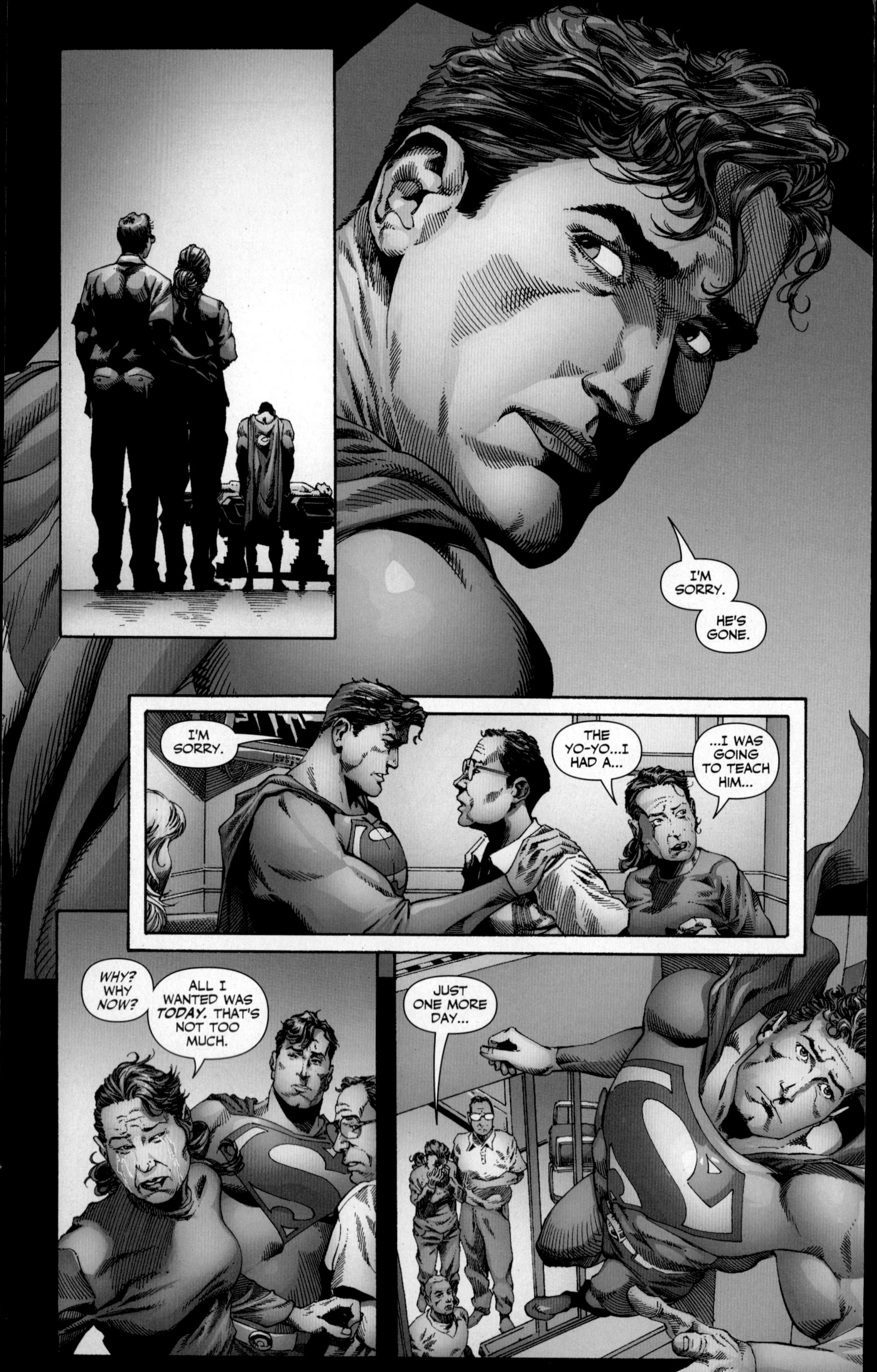
I'M SORRY.
HE'S GONE.
I'M SORRY.
THE YO-YO...I HAD A...
...I WAS GOING TO TEACH HIM...
WHY? WHY NOW?
ALL I WANTED WAS TODAY. THAT'S NOT TOO MUCH.
JUST ONE MORE DAY...

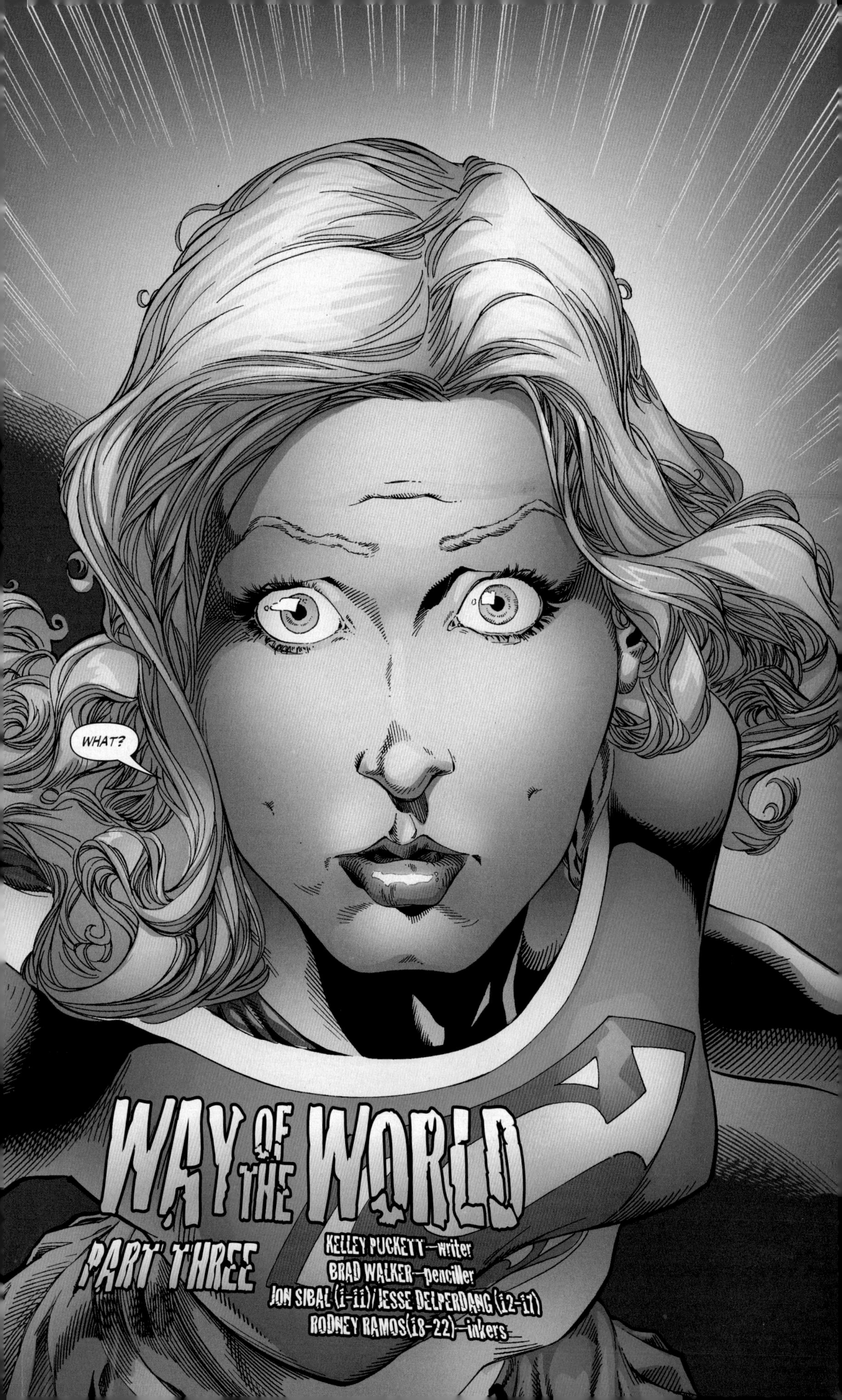
WHAT?
WAY OF THE WORLD
PART THREE
KELLEY PUCKETT—writer
BRAD WALKER—penciller
JON SIBAL (1-11)/JESSE DELPERDANG (12-17)
RODNEY RAMOS(18-22)—inkers

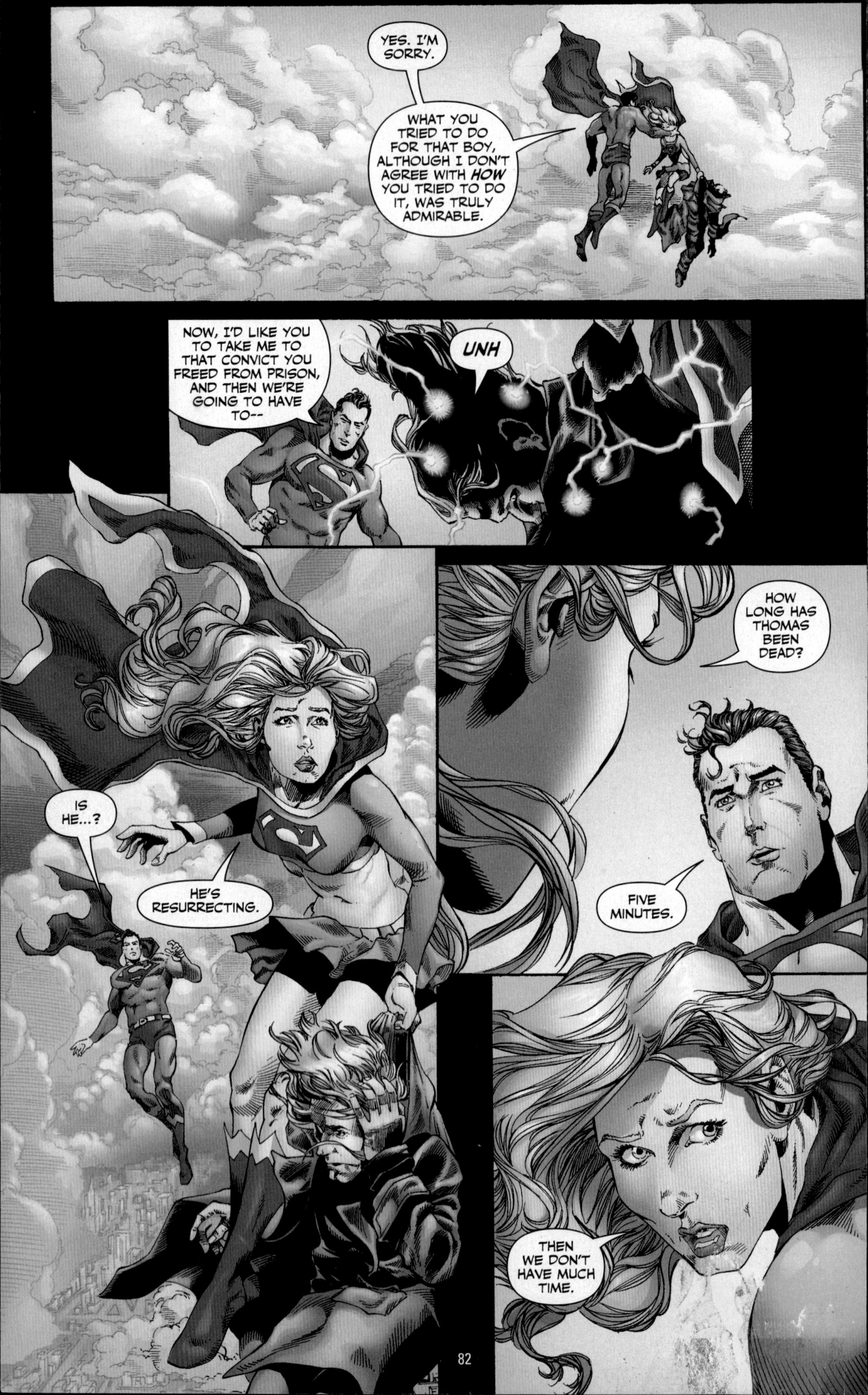
YES. I'M SORRY.
WHAT YOU TRIED TO DO FOR THAT BOY, ALTHOUGH I DON'T AGREE WITH *HOW* YOU TRIED TO DO IT, WAS TRULY ADMIRABLE.
NOW, I'D LIKE YOU TO TAKE ME TO THAT CONVICT YOU FREED FROM PRISON, AND THEN WE'RE GOING TO HAVE TO--
UNH
IS HE...?
HE'S RESURRECTING.
HOW LONG HAS THOMAS BEEN DEAD?
FIVE MINUTES.
THEN WE DON'T HAVE MUCH TIME.

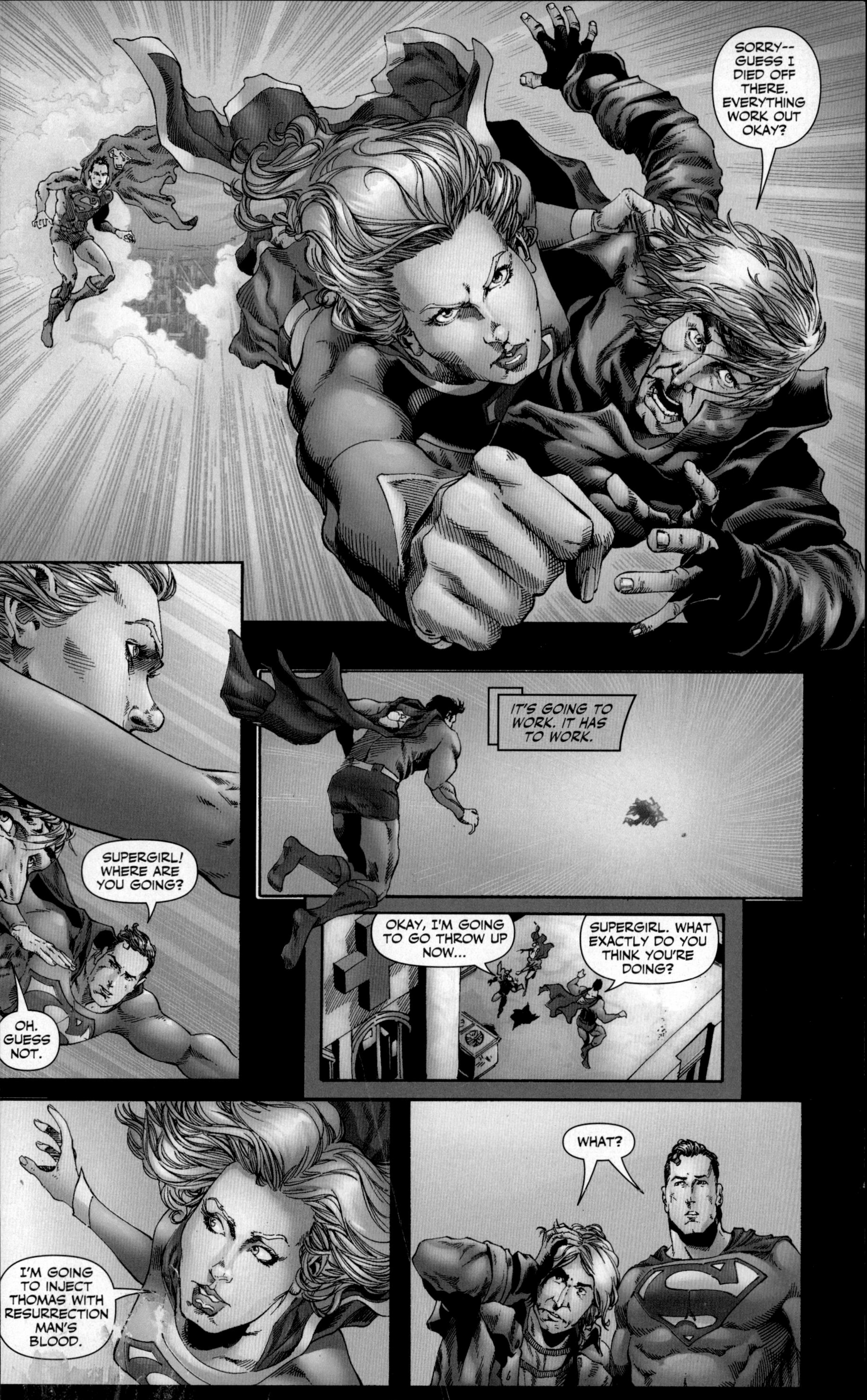
SORRY--
GUESS I
DIED OFF
THERE.
EVERYTHING
WORK OUT
OKAY?
SUPERGIRL!
WHERE ARE
YOU GOING?
OH.
GUESS
NOT.
IT'S GOING TO
WORK. IT HAS
TO WORK.
OKAY, I'M GOING
TO GO THROW UP
NOW...
SUPERGIRL. WHAT
EXACTLY DO YOU
THINK YOU'RE
DOING?
I'M GOING
TO INJECT
THOMAS WITH
RESURRECTION
MAN'S
BLOOD.
WHAT?

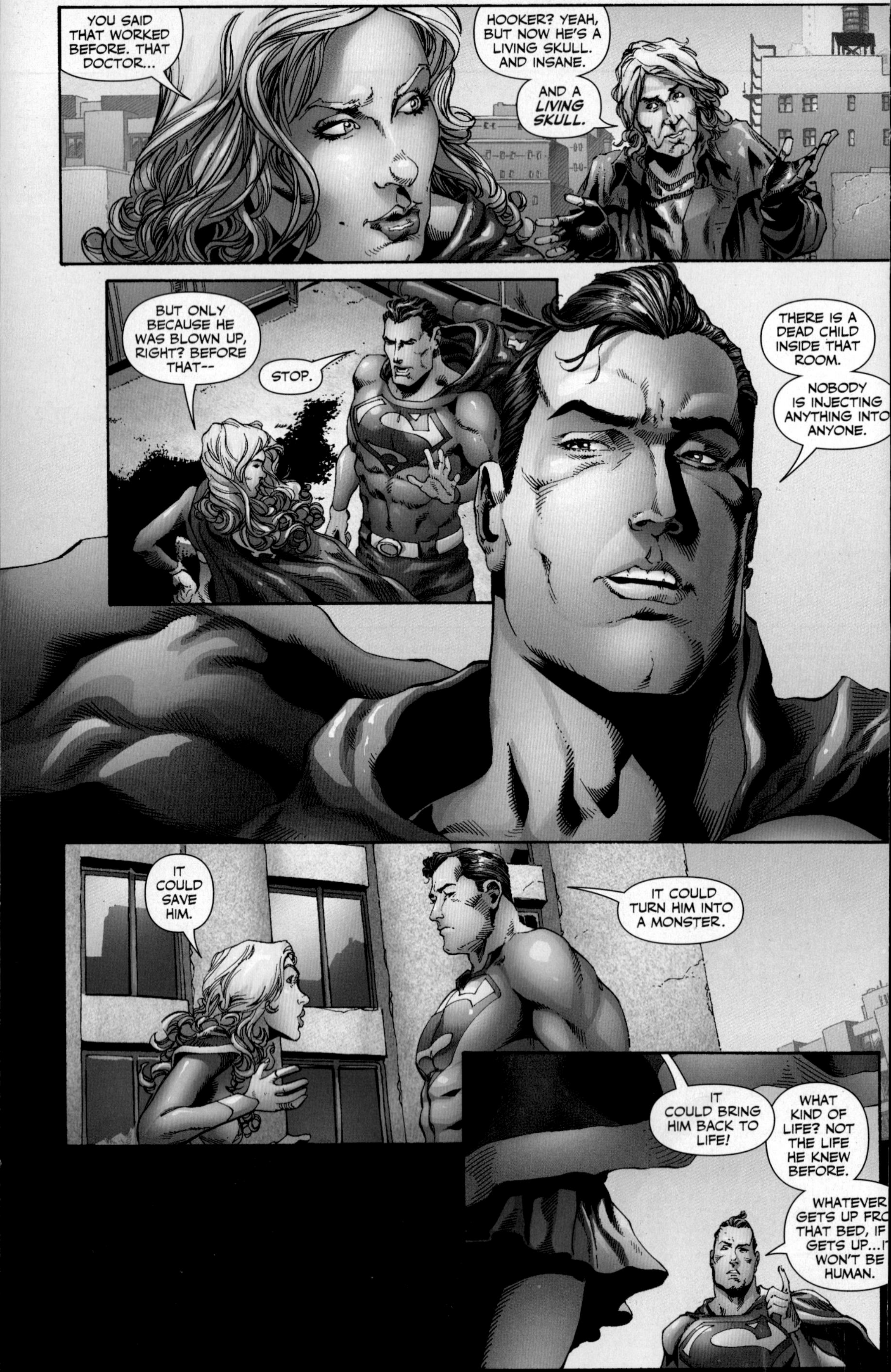
YOU SAID THAT WORKED BEFORE. THAT DOCTOR...
HOOKER? YEAH, BUT NOW HE'S A LIVING SKULL. AND INSANE.
AND A *LIVING SKULL.*
BUT ONLY BECAUSE HE WAS BLOWN UP, RIGHT? BEFORE THAT--
STOP.
THERE IS A DEAD CHILD INSIDE THAT ROOM.
NOBODY IS INJECTING ANYTHING INTO ANYONE.
IT COULD SAVE HIM.
IT COULD TURN HIM INTO A MONSTER.
IT COULD BRING HIM BACK TO LIFE!
WHAT KIND OF LIFE? NOT THE LIFE HE KNEW BEFORE.
WHATEVER GETS UP FRO THAT BED, IF GETS UP...I WON'T BE HUMAN.

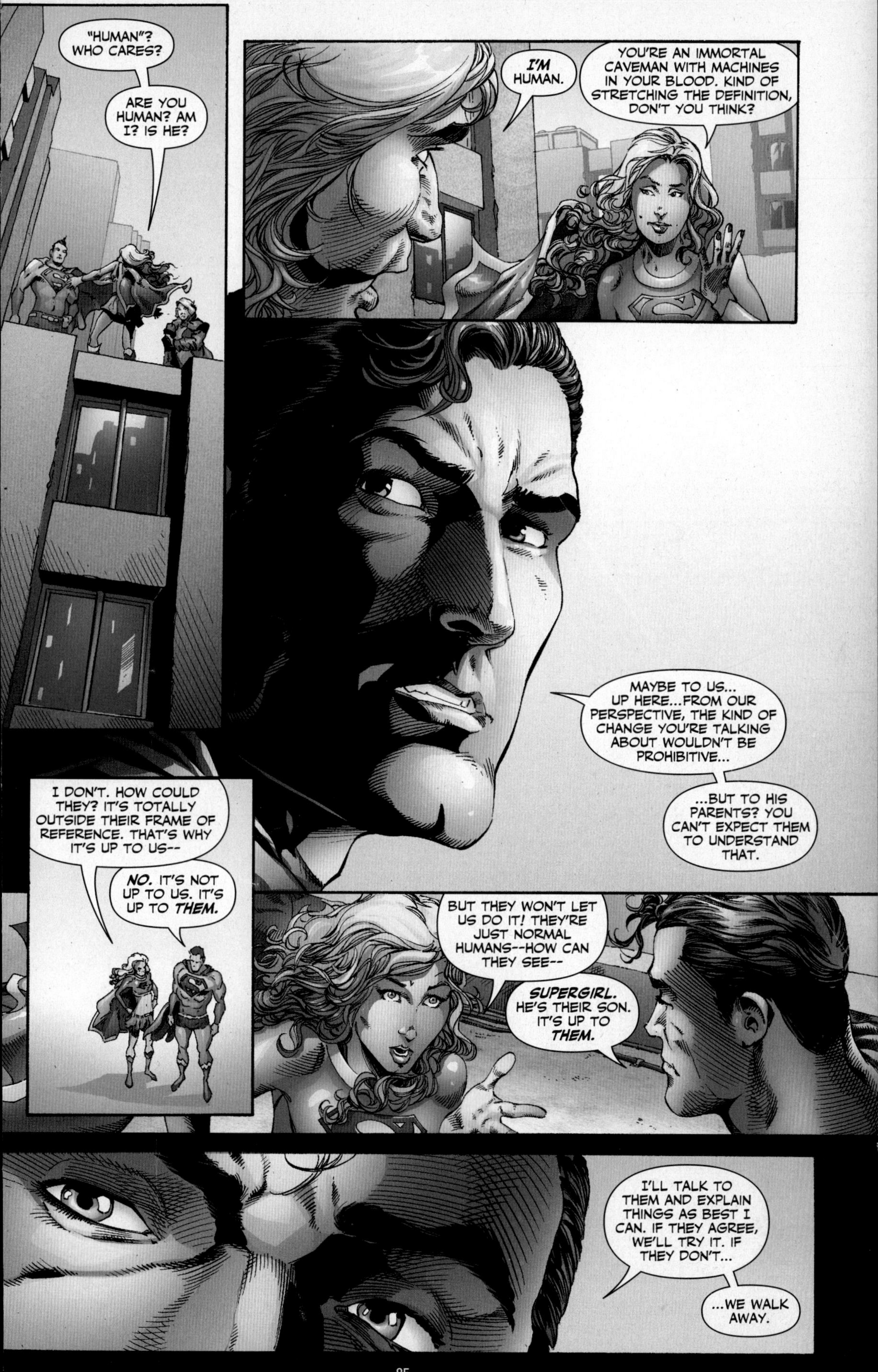
"HUMAN"? WHO CARES?
ARE YOU HUMAN? AM I? IS HE?
I'M HUMAN.
YOU'RE AN IMMORTAL CAVEMAN WITH MACHINES IN YOUR BLOOD. KIND OF STRETCHING THE DEFINITION, DON'T YOU THINK?
MAYBE TO US... UP HERE...FROM OUR PERSPECTIVE, THE KIND OF CHANGE YOU'RE TALKING ABOUT WOULDN'T BE PROHIBITIVE...
...BUT TO HIS PARENTS? YOU CAN'T EXPECT THEM TO UNDERSTAND THAT.
I DON'T. HOW COULD THEY? IT'S TOTALLY OUTSIDE THEIR FRAME OF REFERENCE. THAT'S WHY IT'S UP TO US--
NO. IT'S NOT UP TO US. IT'S UP TO THEM.
BUT THEY WON'T LET US DO IT! THEY'RE JUST NORMAL HUMANS--HOW CAN THEY SEE--
SUPERGIRL. HE'S THEIR SON. IT'S UP TO THEM.
I'LL TALK TO THEM AND EXPLAIN THINGS AS BEST I CAN. IF THEY AGREE, WE'LL TRY IT. IF THEY DON'T...
...WE WALK AWAY.

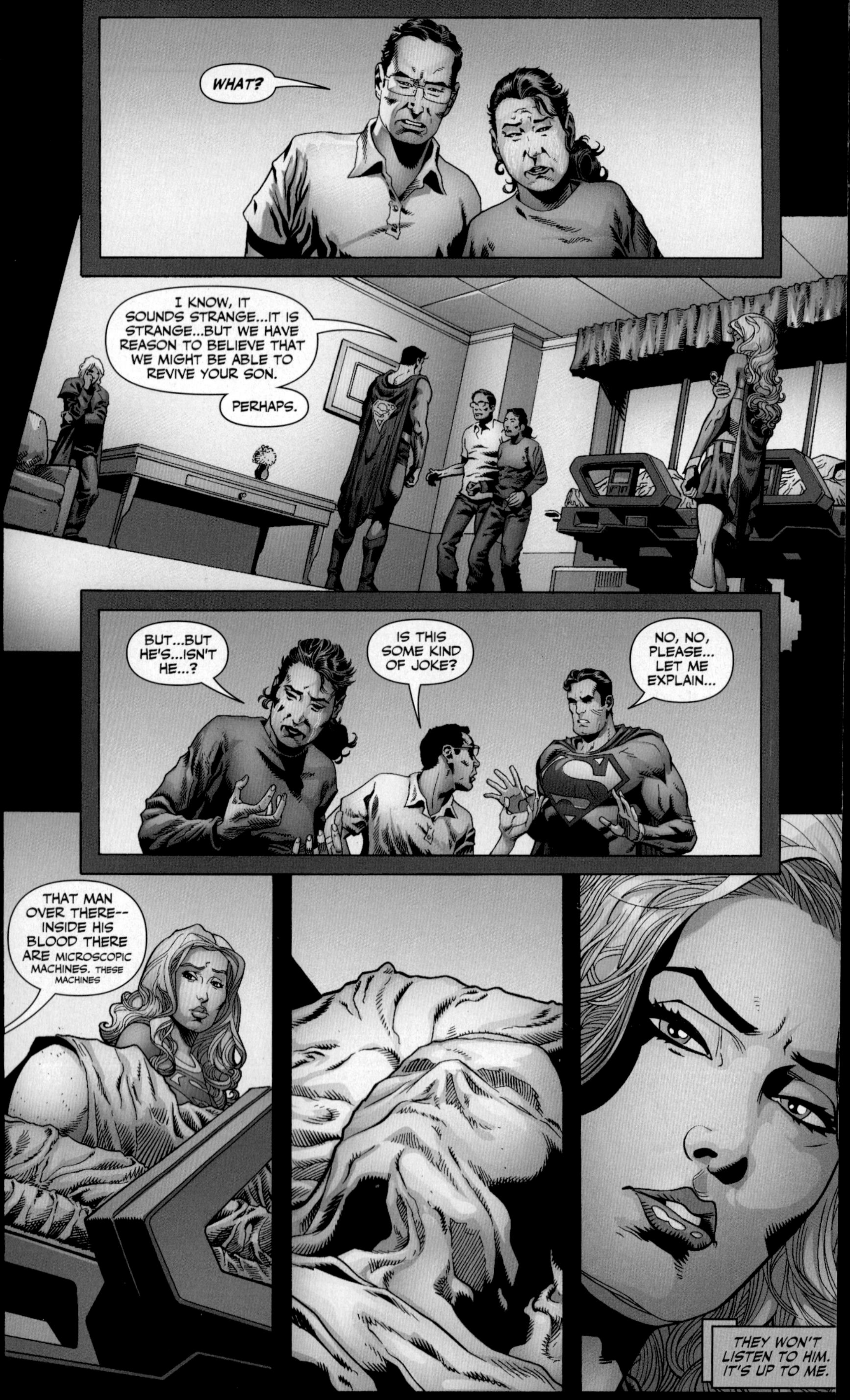
WHAT?
I KNOW, IT SOUNDS STRANGE...IT IS STRANGE...BUT WE HAVE REASON TO BELIEVE THAT WE MIGHT BE ABLE TO REVIVE YOUR SON.
PERHAPS.
BUT...BUT HE'S...ISN'T HE...?
IS THIS SOME KIND OF JOKE?
NO, NO, PLEASE... LET ME EXPLAIN...
THAT MAN OVER THERE-- INSIDE HIS BLOOD THERE ARE MICROSCOPIC MACHINES. THESE MACHINES
THEY WON'T LISTEN TO HIM. IT'S UP TO ME.

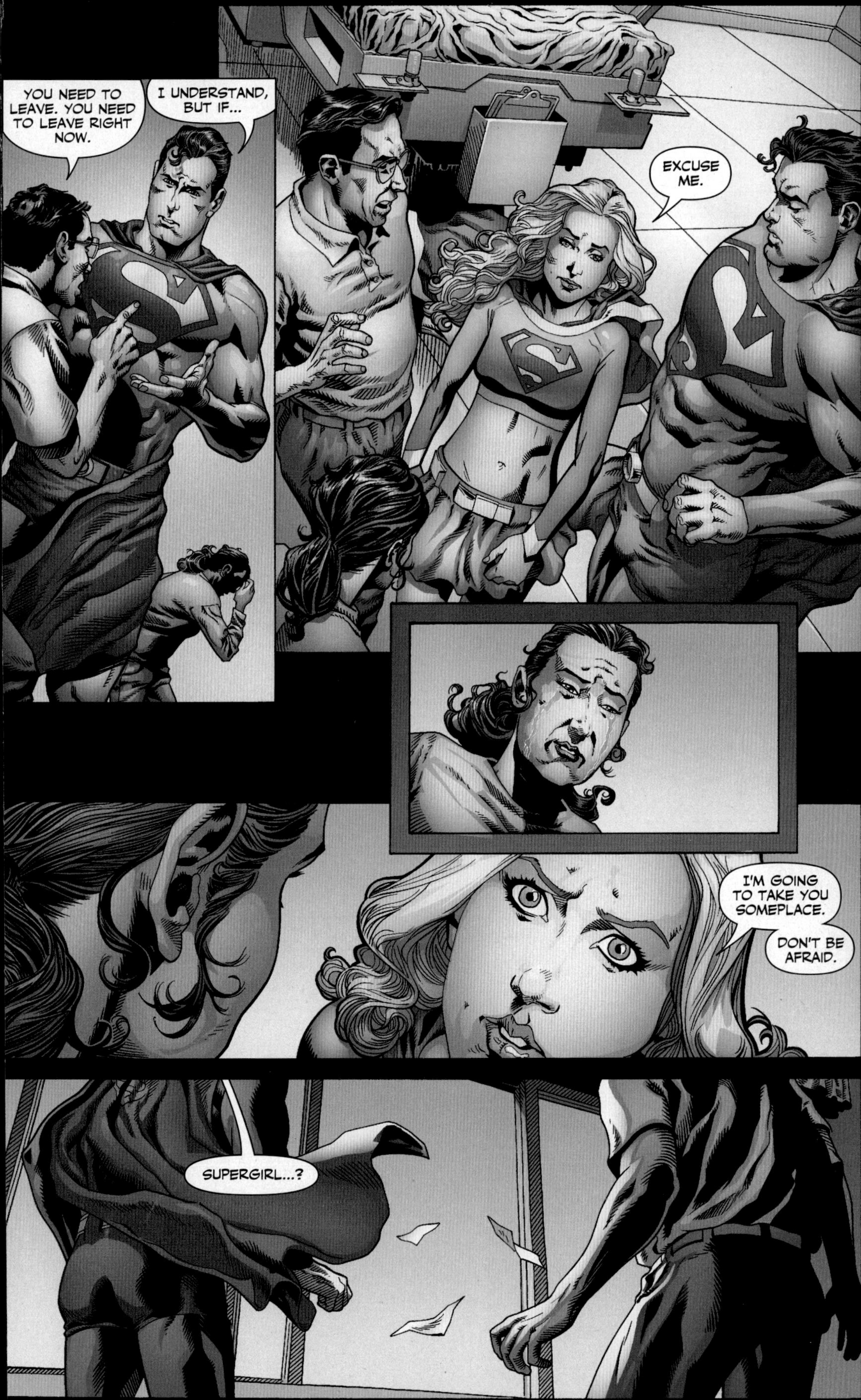
YOU NEED TO LEAVE. YOU NEED TO LEAVE RIGHT NOW.
I UNDERSTAND, BUT IF...
EXCUSE ME.
I'M GOING TO TAKE YOU SOMEPLACE.
DON'T BE AFRAID.
SUPERGIRL...?

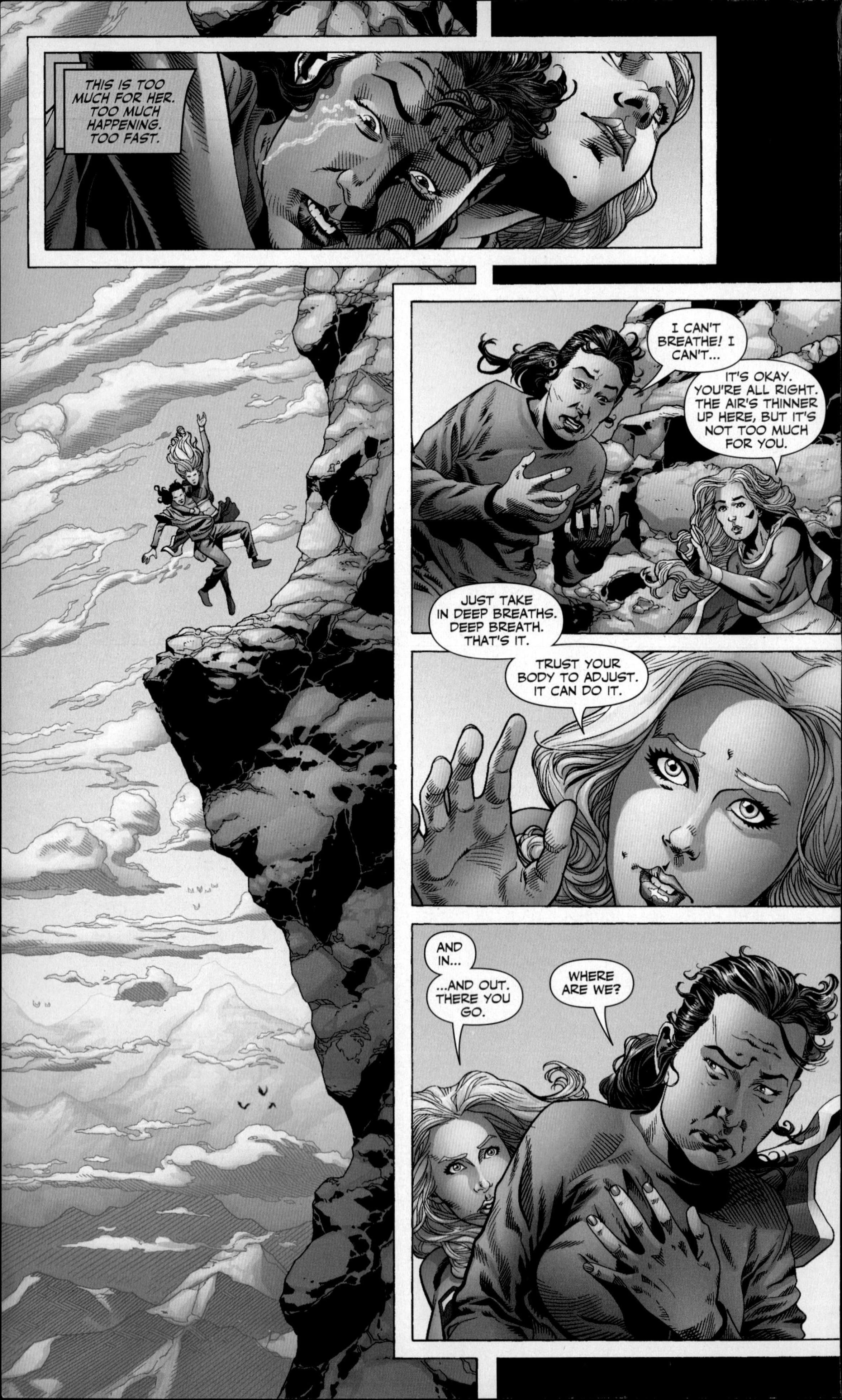
THIS IS TOO MUCH FOR HER. TOO MUCH HAPPENING. TOO FAST.
I CAN'T BREATHE! I CAN'T...
IT'S OKAY. YOU'RE ALL RIGHT. THE AIR'S THINNER UP HERE, BUT IT'S NOT TOO MUCH FOR YOU.
JUST TAKE IN DEEP BREATHS. DEEP BREATH. THAT'S IT.
TRUST YOUR BODY TO ADJUST. IT CAN DO IT.
AND IN...
...AND OUT. THERE YOU GO.
WHERE ARE WE?

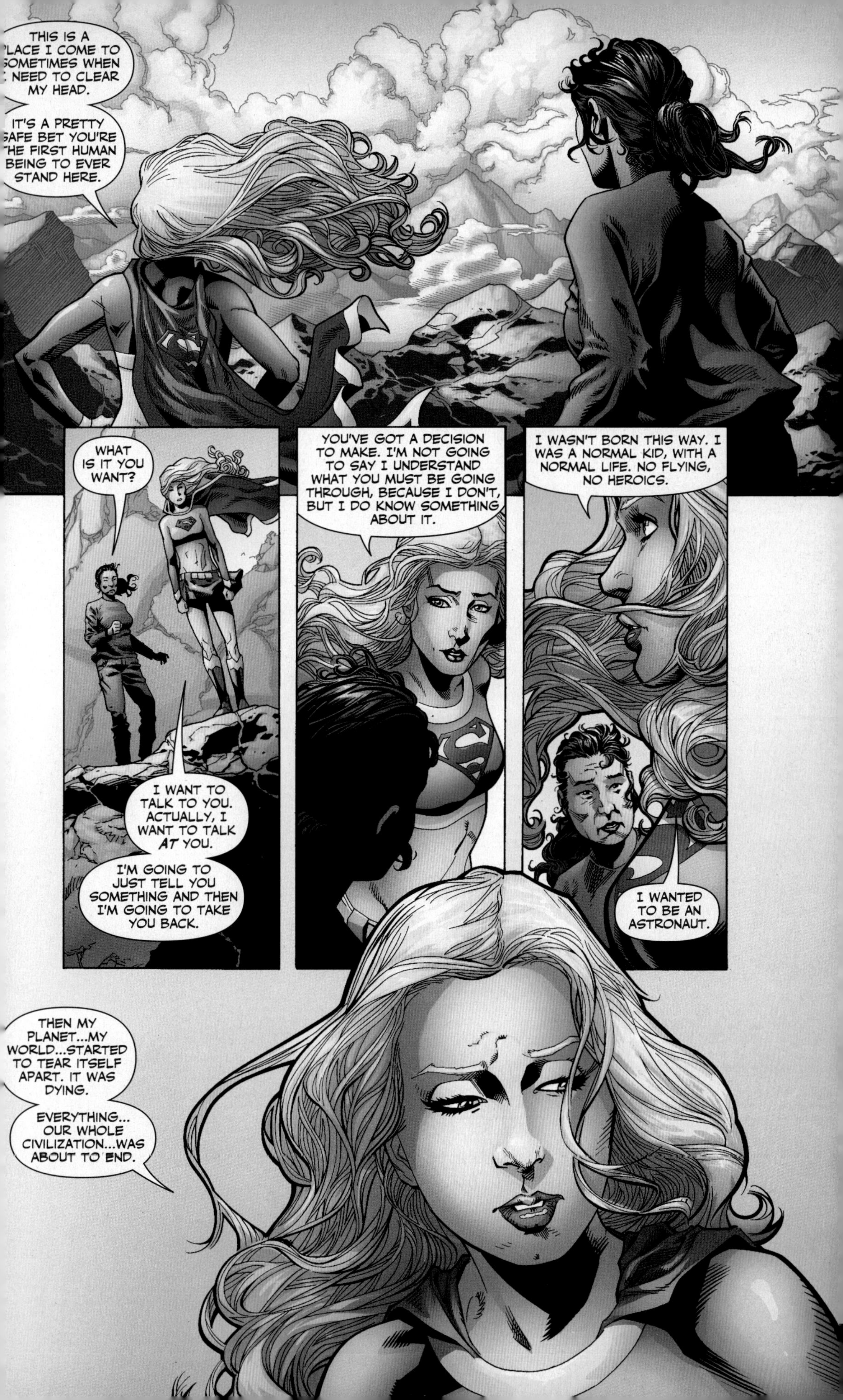
THIS IS A PLACE I COME TO SOMETIMES WHEN I NEED TO CLEAR MY HEAD.
IT'S A PRETTY SAFE BET YOU'RE THE FIRST HUMAN BEING TO EVER STAND HERE.
WHAT IS IT YOU WANT?
I WANT TO TALK TO YOU. ACTUALLY, I WANT TO TALK AT YOU.
I'M GOING TO JUST TELL YOU SOMETHING AND THEN I'M GOING TO TAKE YOU BACK.
YOU'VE GOT A DECISION TO MAKE. I'M NOT GOING TO SAY I UNDERSTAND WHAT YOU MUST BE GOING THROUGH, BECAUSE I DON'T, BUT I DO KNOW SOMETHING ABOUT IT.
I WASN'T BORN THIS WAY. I WAS A NORMAL KID, WITH A NORMAL LIFE. NO FLYING, NO HEROICS.
I WANTED TO BE AN ASTRONAUT.
THEN MY PLANET...MY WORLD...STARTED TO TEAR ITSELF APART. IT WAS DYING.
EVERYTHING... OUR WHOLE CIVILIZATION...WAS ABOUT TO END.

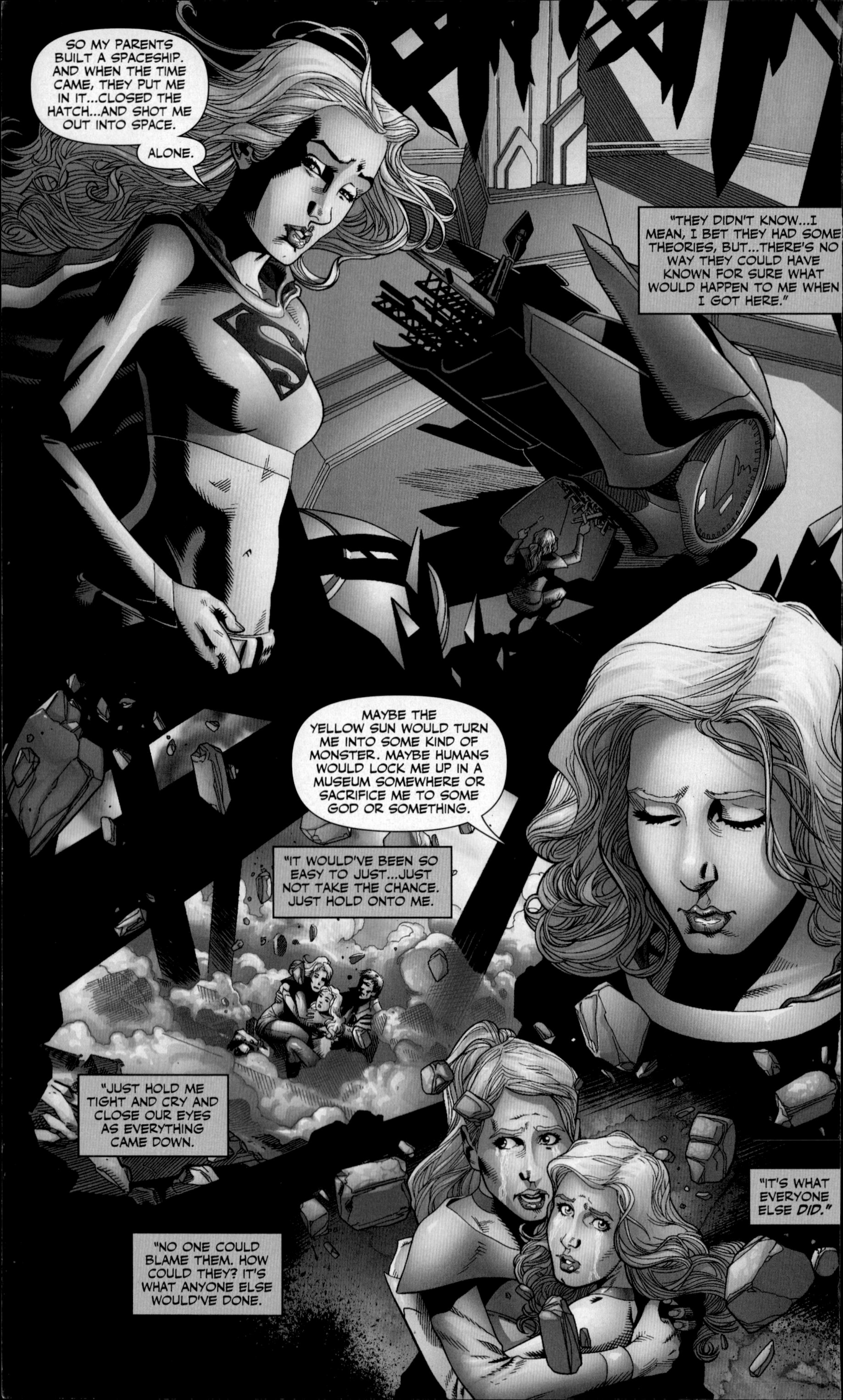
SO MY PARENTS BUILT A SPACESHIP. AND WHEN THE TIME CAME, THEY PUT ME IN IT...CLOSED THE HATCH...AND SHOT ME OUT INTO SPACE.
ALONE.
"THEY DIDN'T KNOW...I MEAN, I BET THEY HAD SOME THEORIES, BUT...THERE'S NO WAY THEY COULD HAVE KNOWN FOR SURE WHAT WOULD HAPPEN TO ME WHEN I GOT HERE."
MAYBE THE YELLOW SUN WOULD TURN ME INTO SOME KIND OF MONSTER. MAYBE HUMANS WOULD LOCK ME UP IN A MUSEUM SOMEWHERE OR SACRIFICE ME TO SOME GOD OR SOMETHING.
"IT WOULD'VE BEEN SO EASY TO JUST...JUST NOT TAKE THE CHANCE. JUST HOLD ONTO ME.
"JUST HOLD ME TIGHT AND CRY AND CLOSE OUR EYES AS EVERYTHING CAME DOWN.
"NO ONE COULD BLAME THEM. HOW COULD THEY? IT'S WHAT ANYONE ELSE WOULD'VE DONE.
"IT'S WHAT EVERYONE ELSE *DID.*"

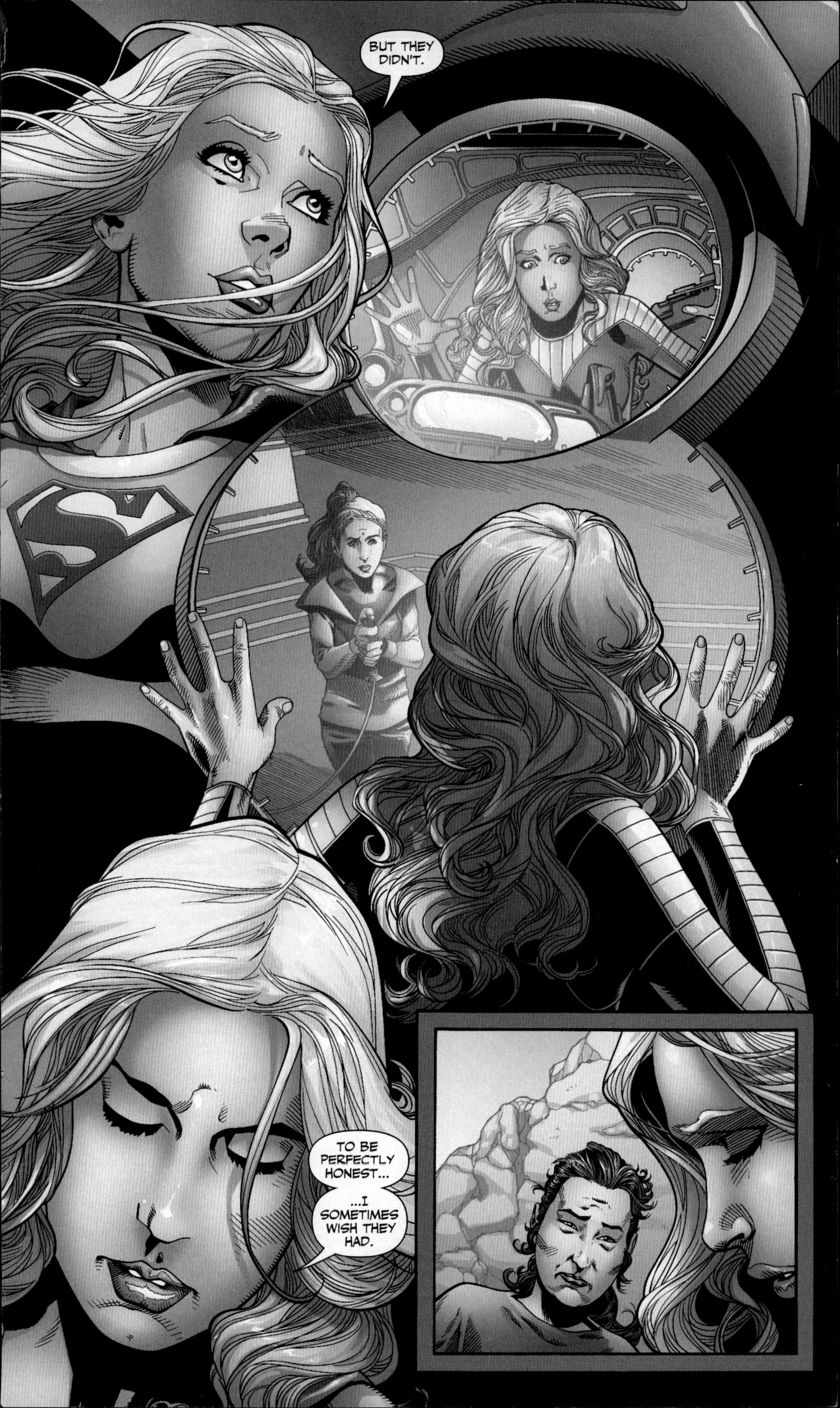

BUT THEY DIDN'T.
TO BE PERFECTLY HONEST...
...I SOMETIMES WISH THEY HAD.

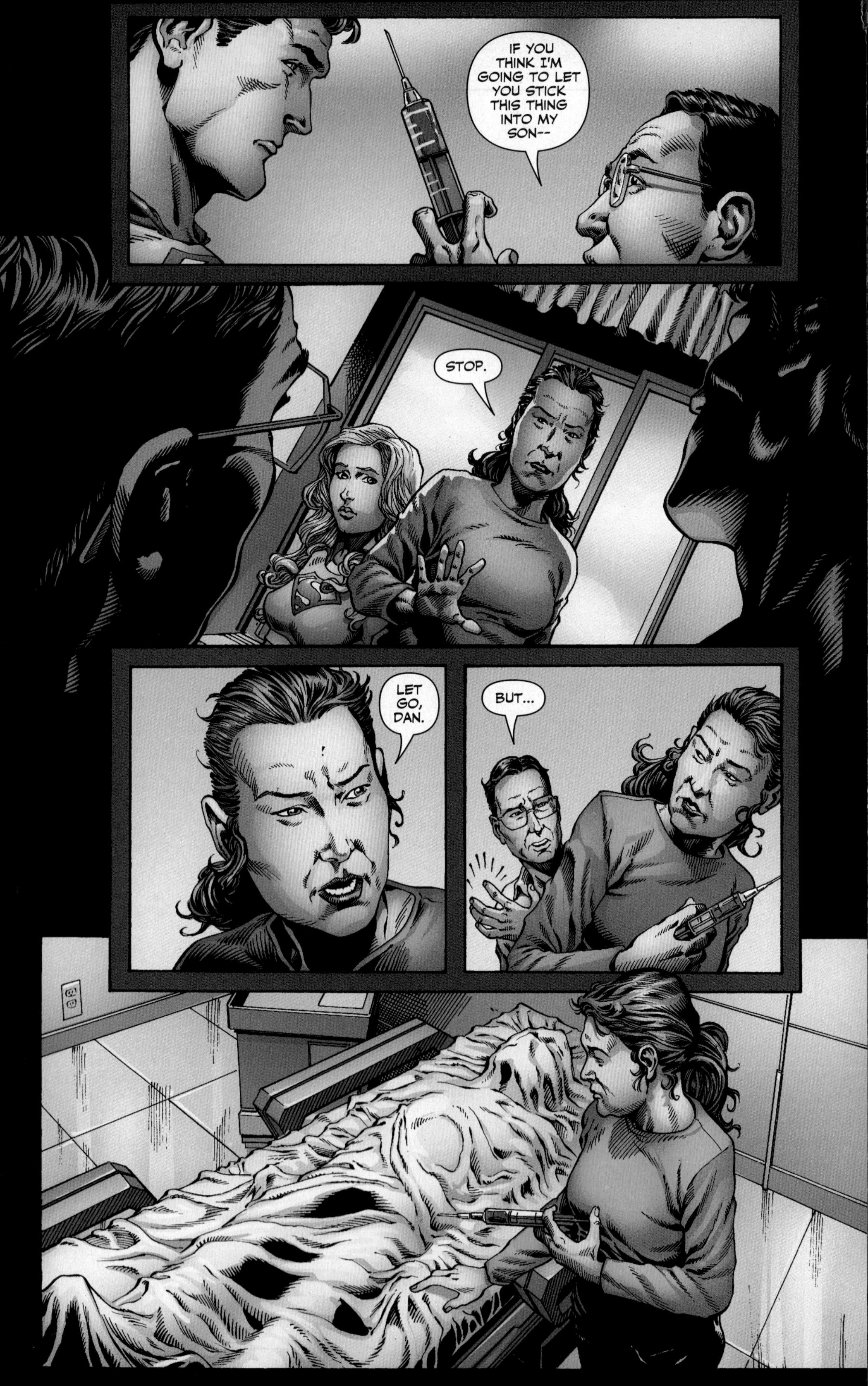
IF YOU THINK I'M GOING TO LET YOU STICK THIS THING INTO MY SON--
STOP.
LET GO, DAN.
BUT...

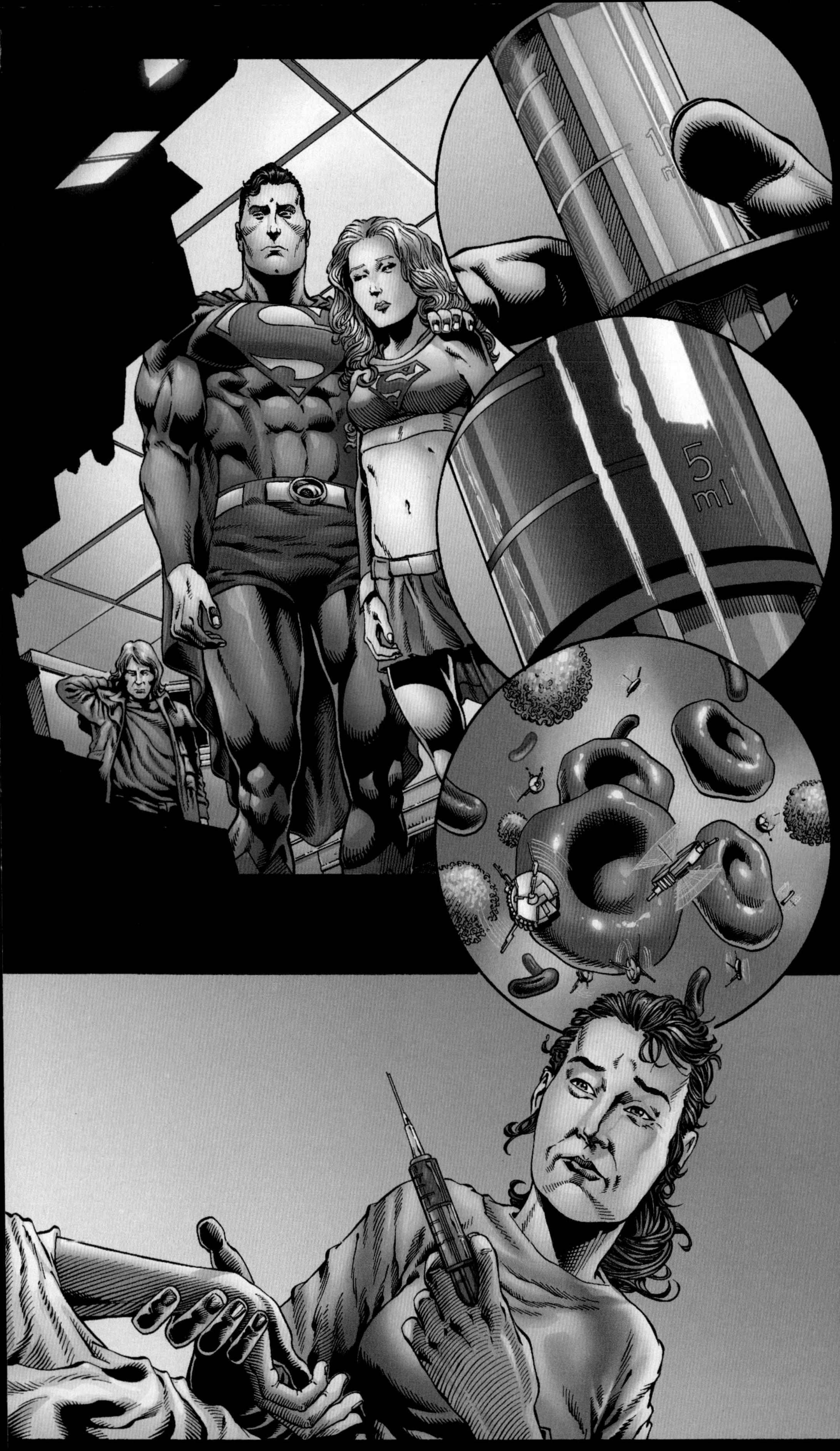
5 ml

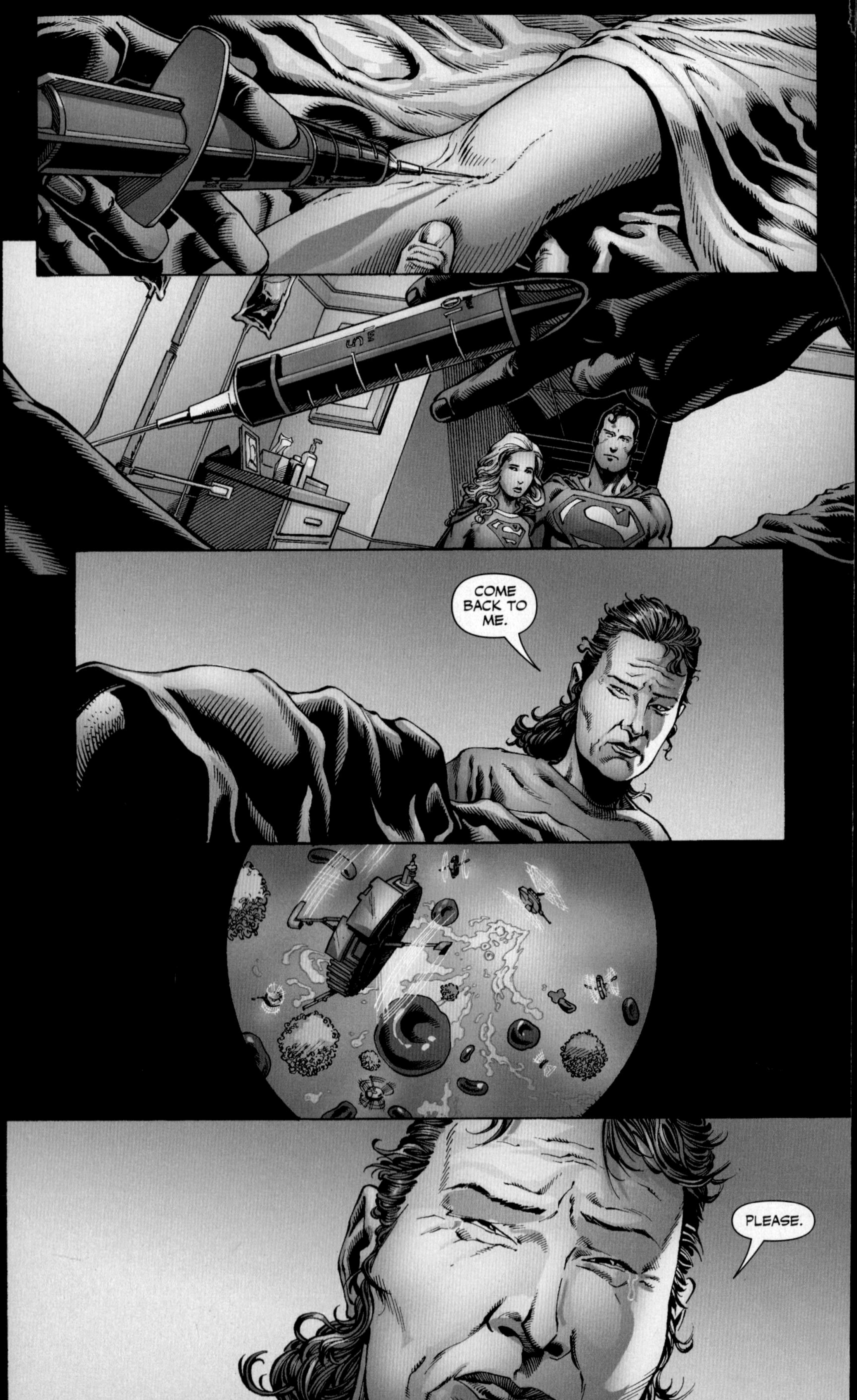

COME BACK TO ME.
PLEASE.

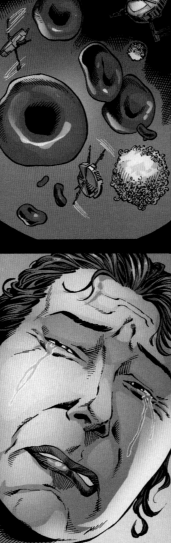
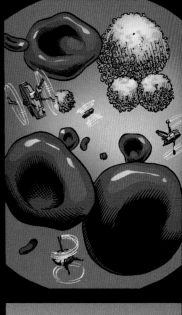

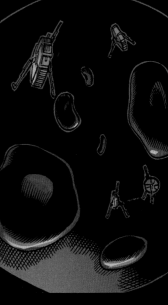

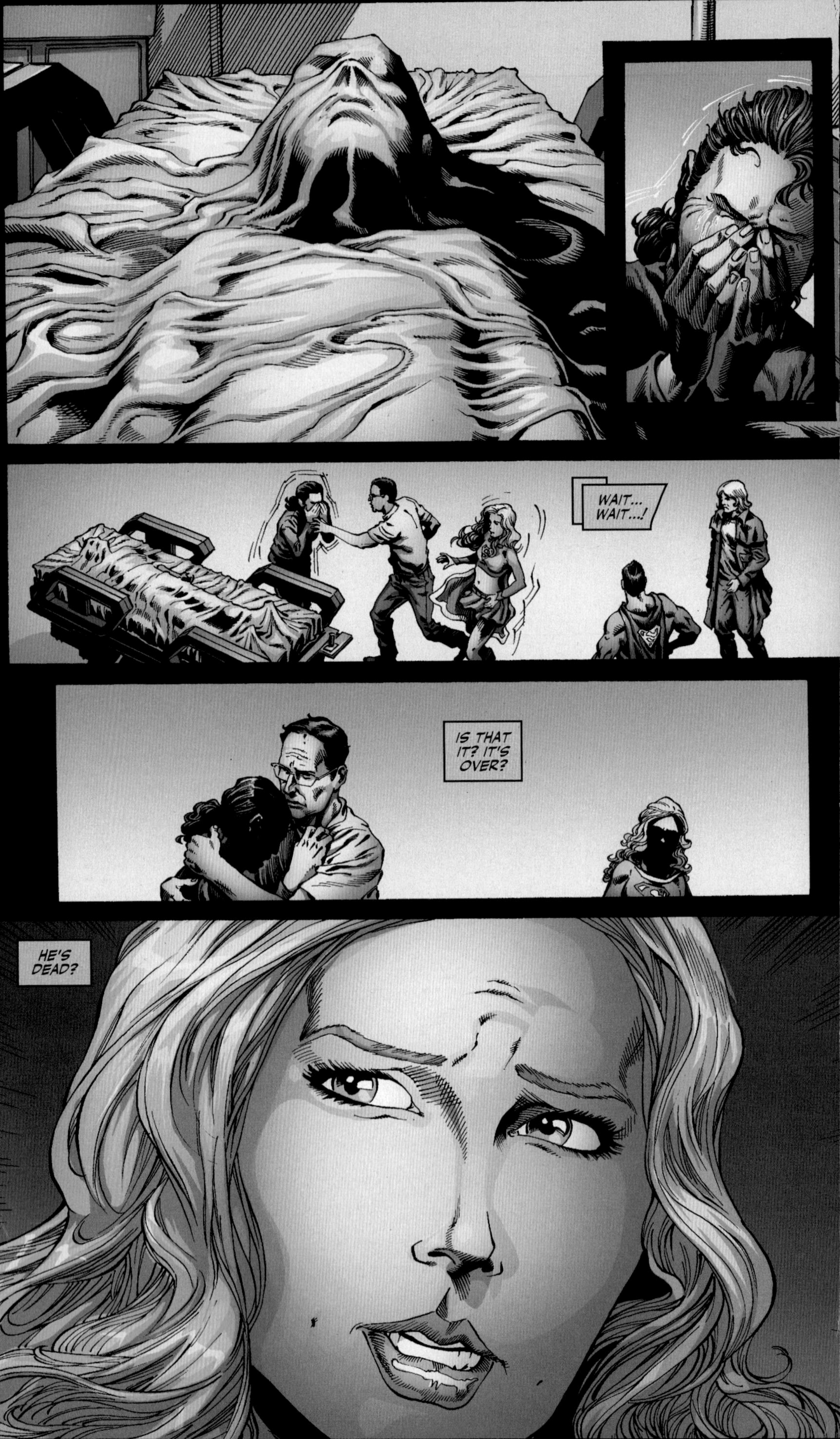
WAIT... WAIT...!
IS THAT IT? IT'S OVER?
HE'S DEAD?

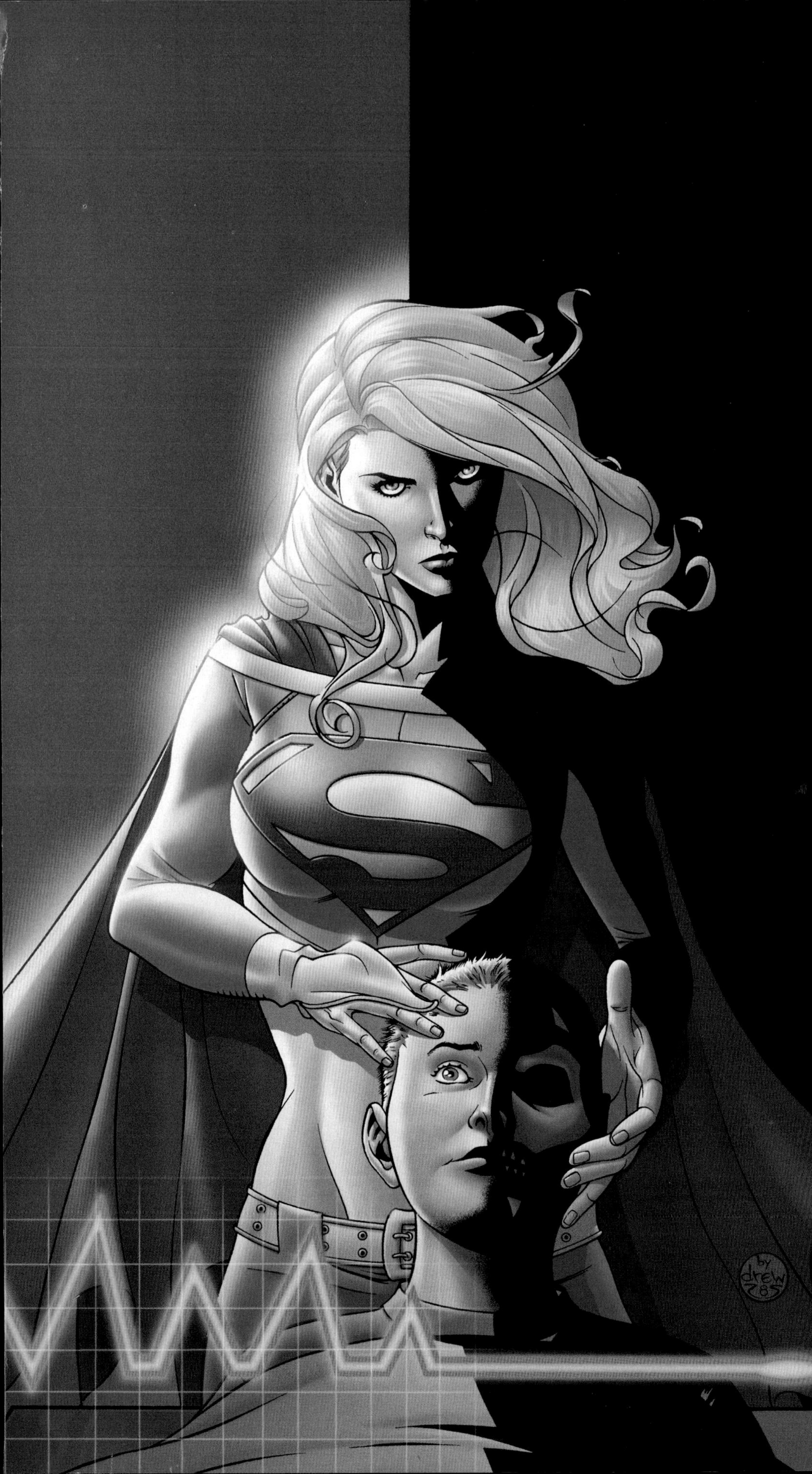

SUPERGIRL 32 Drew Johnson & Ray Snyder with Shannon Blanchard

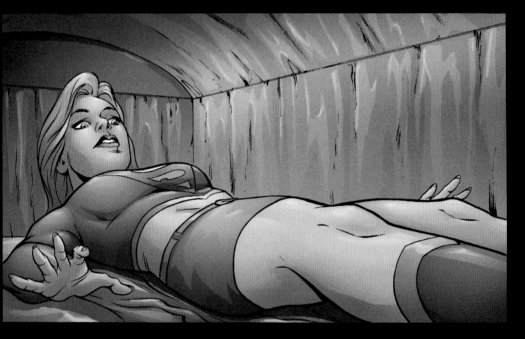

NO.

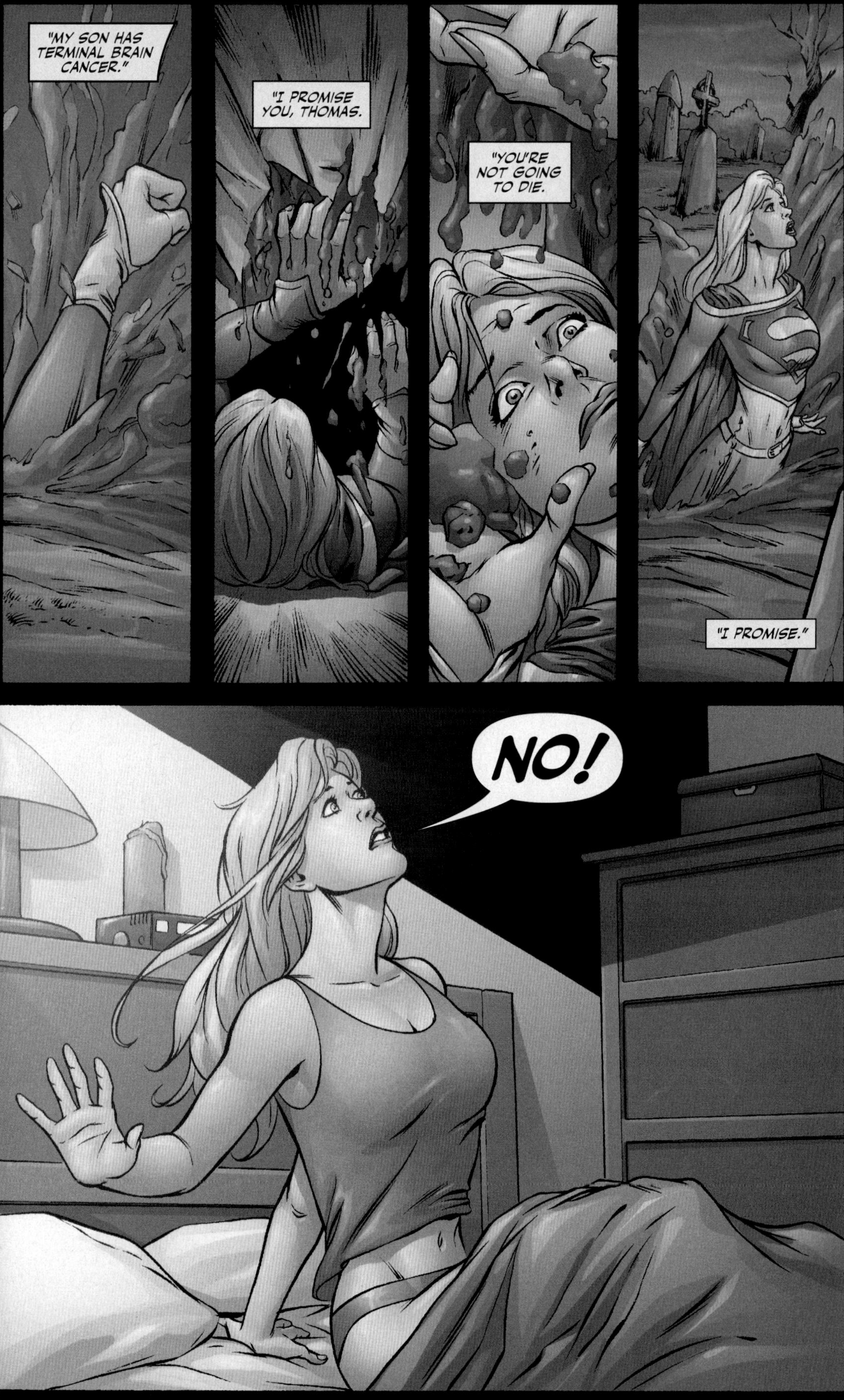
"MY SON HAS TERMINAL BRAIN CANCER."
"I PROMISE YOU, THOMAS.
"YOU'RE NOT GOING TO DIE.
"I PROMISE."
NO!

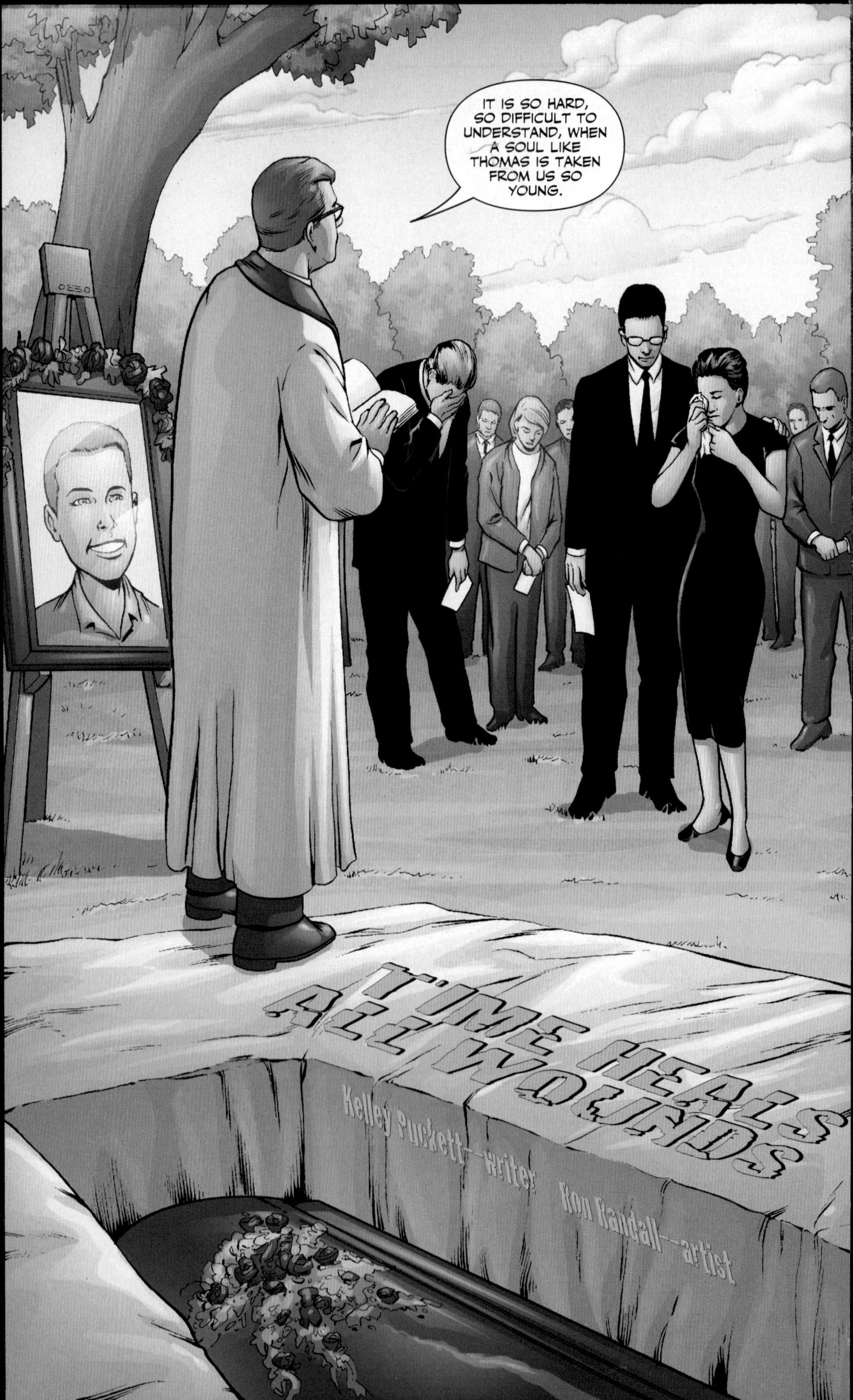
IT IS SO HARD, SO DIFFICULT TO UNDERSTAND, WHEN A SOUL LIKE THOMAS IS TAKEN FROM US SO YOUNG.
TIME HEALS ALL WOUNDS
Kelley Puckett--writer
Ron Randall--artist

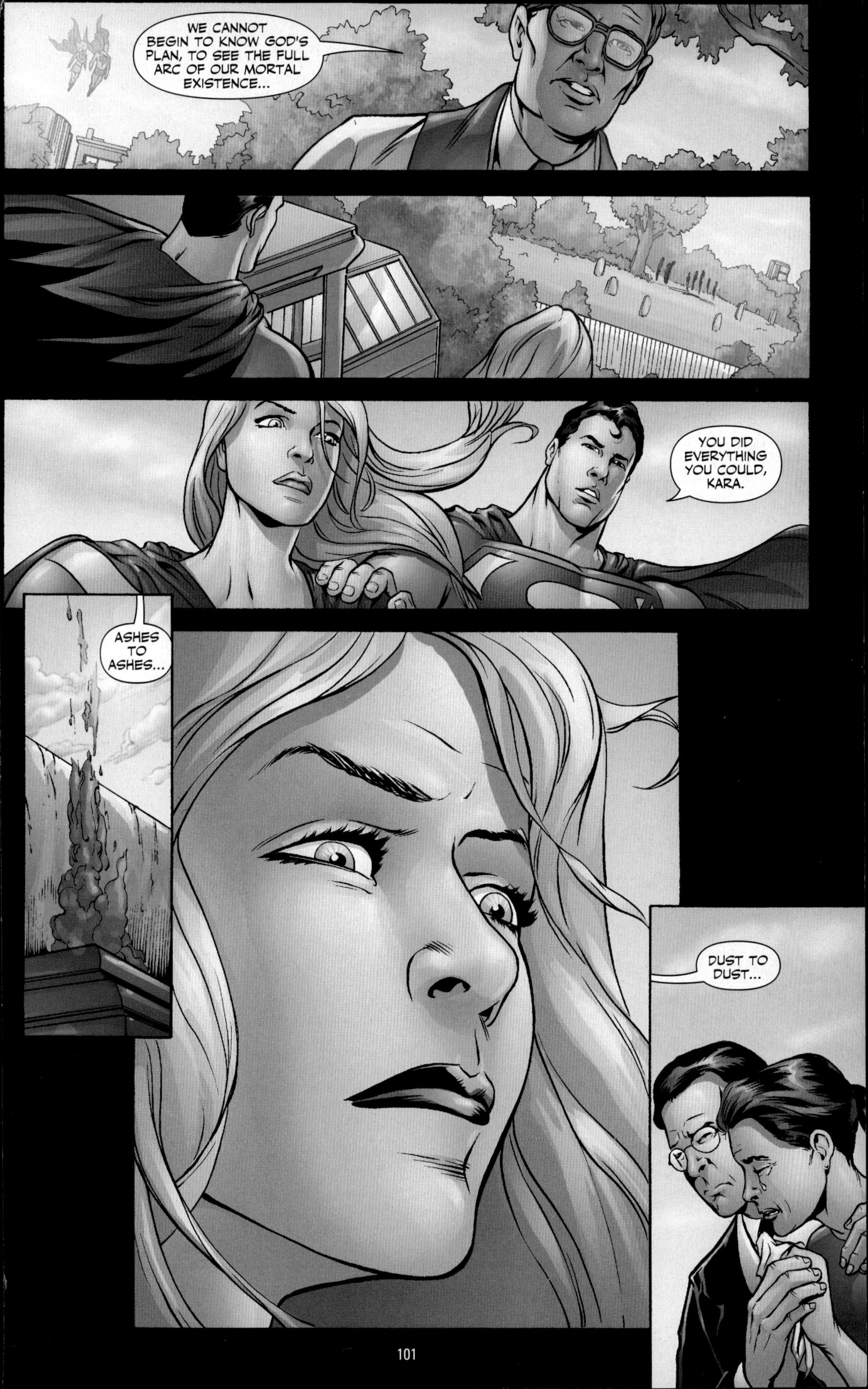
WE CANNOT BEGIN TO KNOW GOD'S PLAN, TO SEE THE FULL ARC OF OUR MORTAL EXISTENCE...
YOU DID EVERYTHING YOU COULD, KARA.
ASHES TO ASHES...
DUST TO DUST...

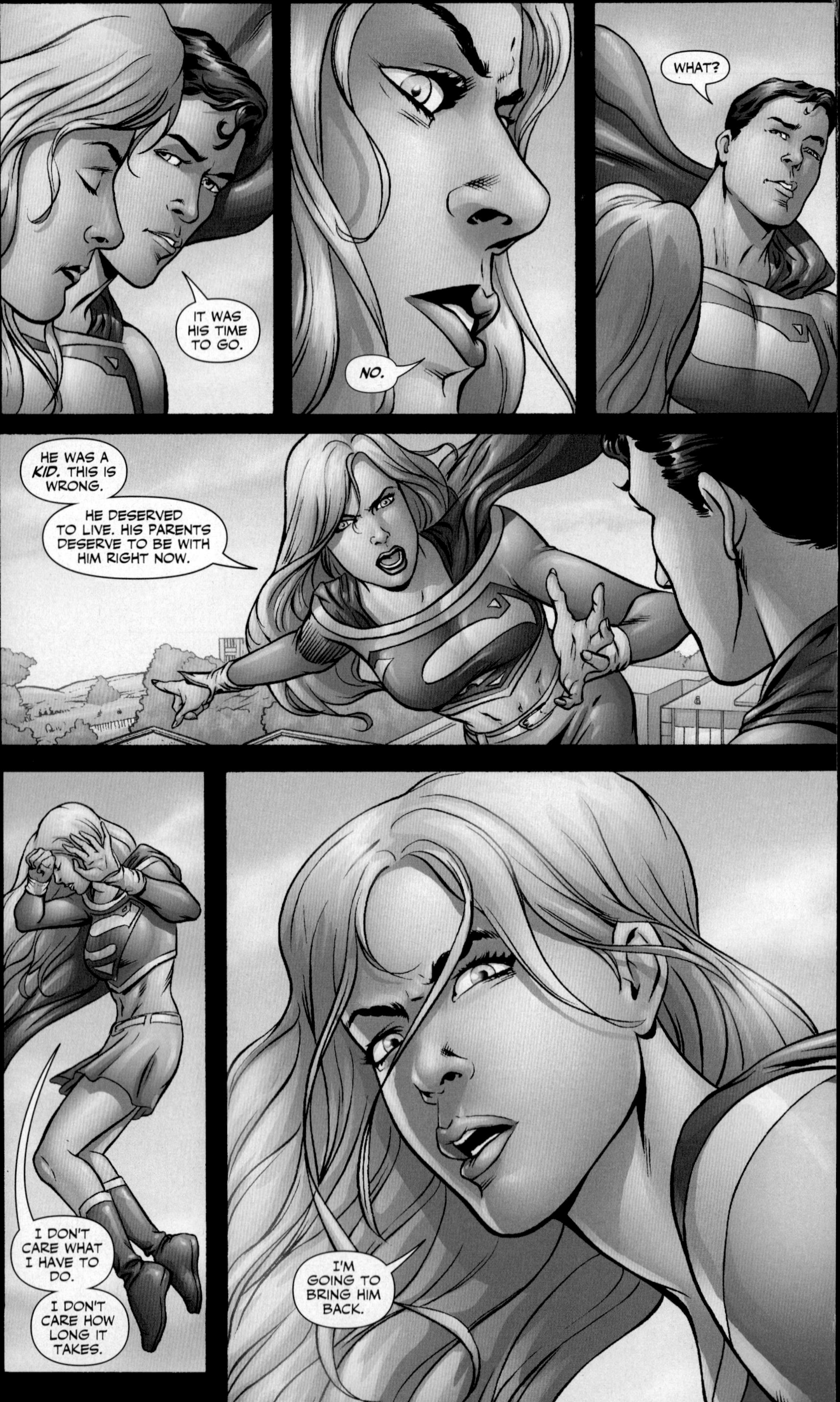
IT WAS HIS TIME TO GO.
NO.
WHAT?
HE WAS A *KID.* THIS IS WRONG.
HE DESERVED TO LIVE. HIS PARENTS DESERVE TO BE WITH HIM RIGHT NOW.
I DON'T CARE WHAT I HAVE TO DO.
I DON'T CARE HOW LONG IT TAKES.
I'M GOING TO BRING HIM BACK.

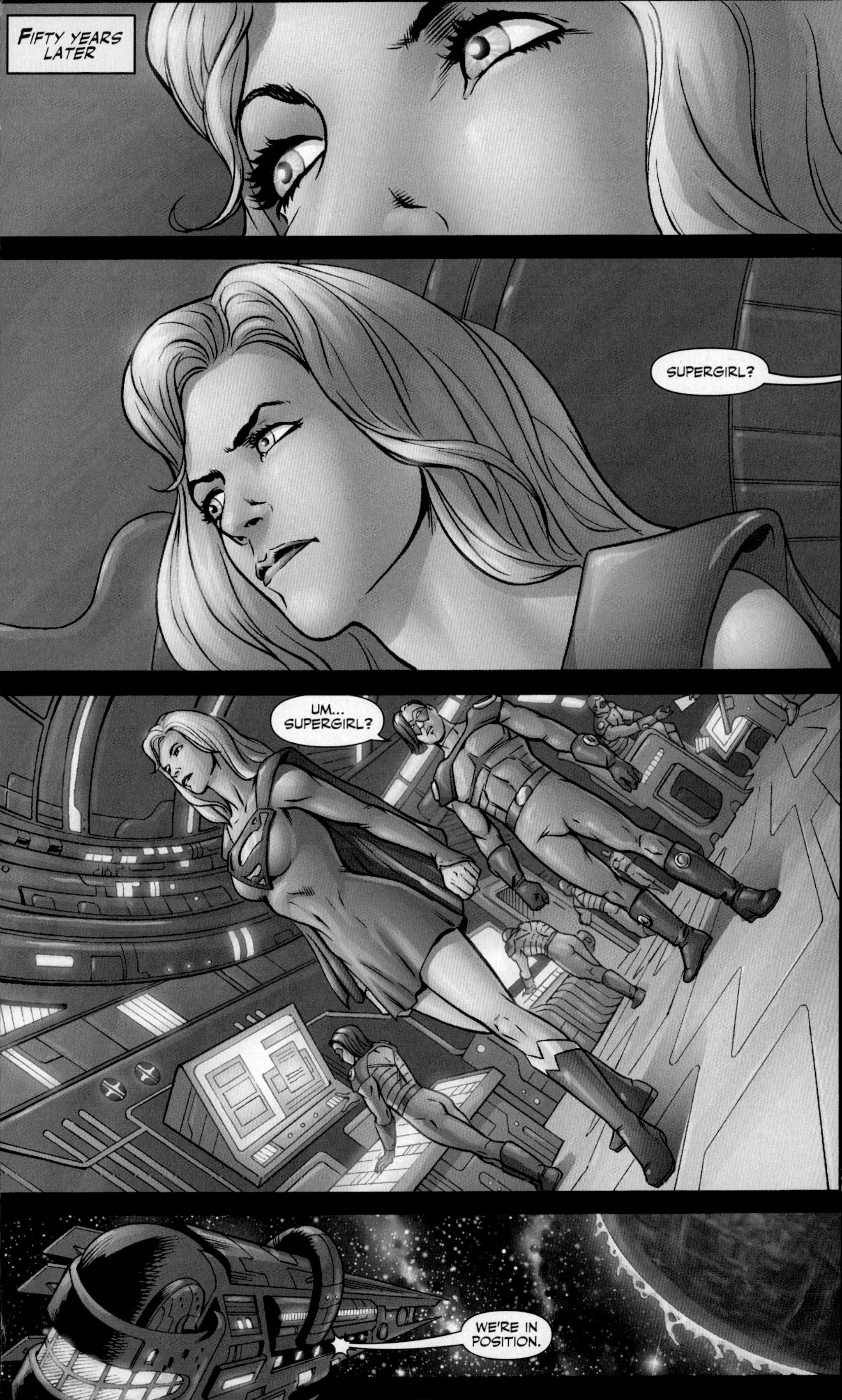
FIFTY YEARS LATER
SUPERGIRL?
UM... SUPERGIRL?
WE'RE IN POSITION.

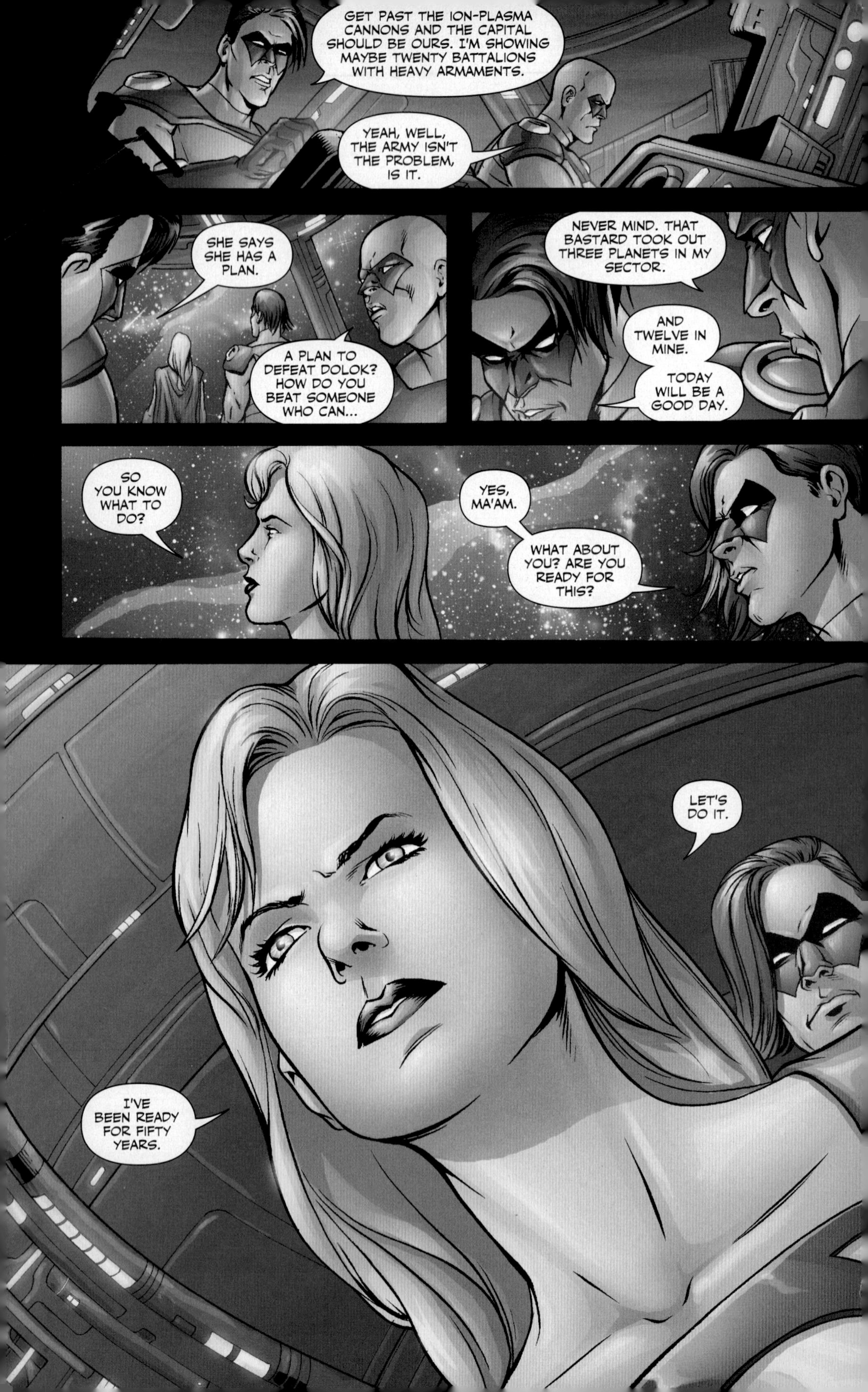
GET PAST THE ION-PLASMA CANNONS AND THE CAPITAL SHOULD BE OURS. I'M SHOWING MAYBE TWENTY BATTALIONS WITH HEAVY ARMAMENTS.
YEAH, WELL, THE ARMY ISN'T THE PROBLEM, IS IT.
SHE SAYS SHE HAS A PLAN.
A PLAN TO DEFEAT DOLOK? HOW DO YOU BEAT SOMEONE WHO CAN...
NEVER MIND. THAT BASTARD TOOK OUT THREE PLANETS IN MY SECTOR.
AND TWELVE IN MINE.
TODAY WILL BE A GOOD DAY.
SO YOU KNOW WHAT TO DO?
YES, MA'AM.
WHAT ABOUT YOU? ARE YOU READY FOR THIS?
LET'S DO IT.
I'VE BEEN READY FOR FIFTY YEARS.

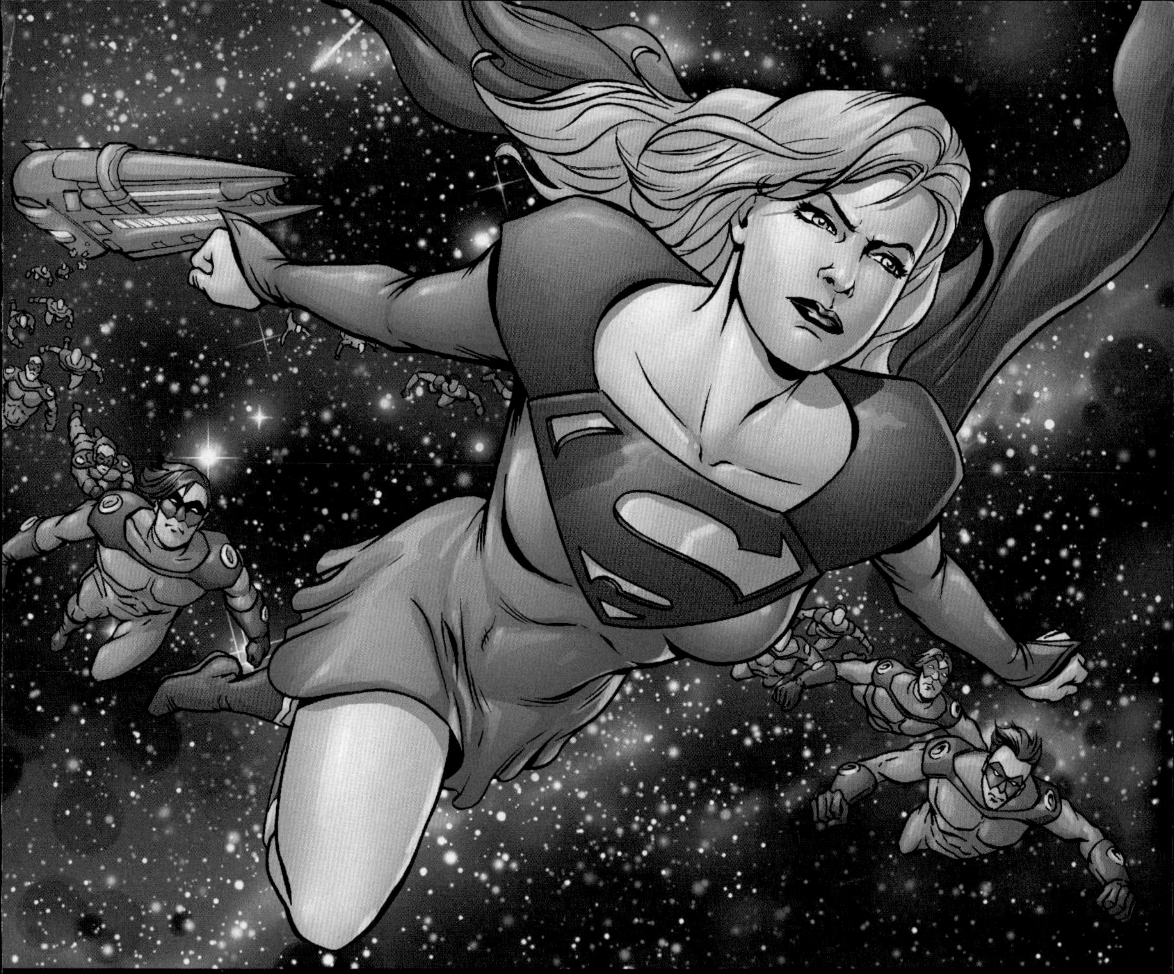
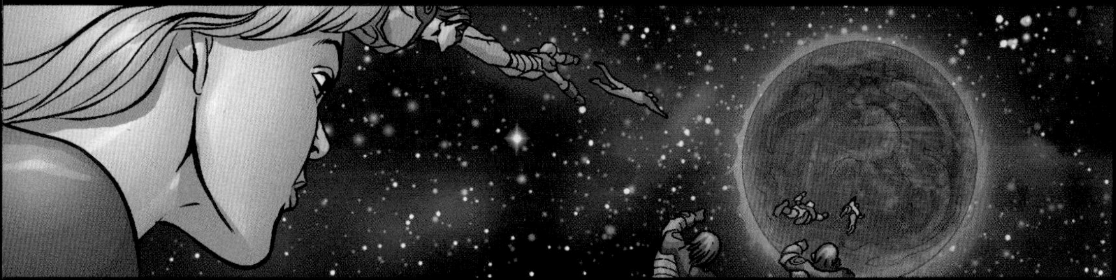
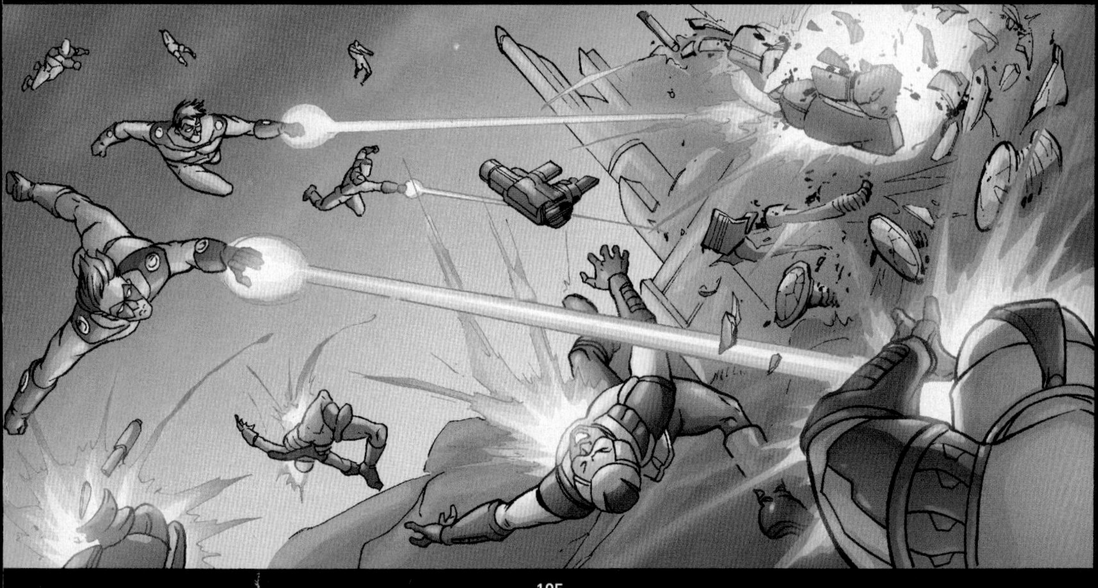

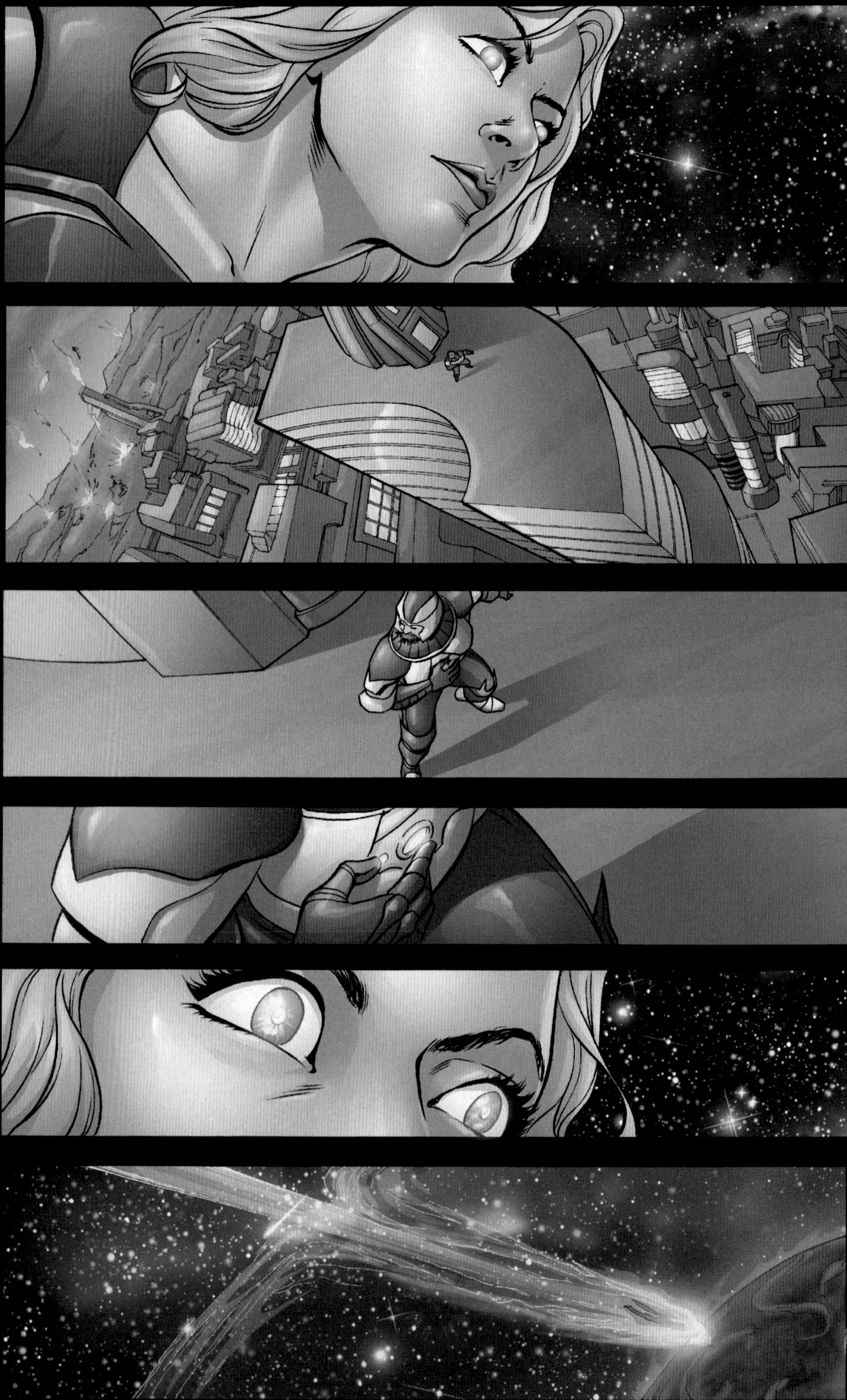

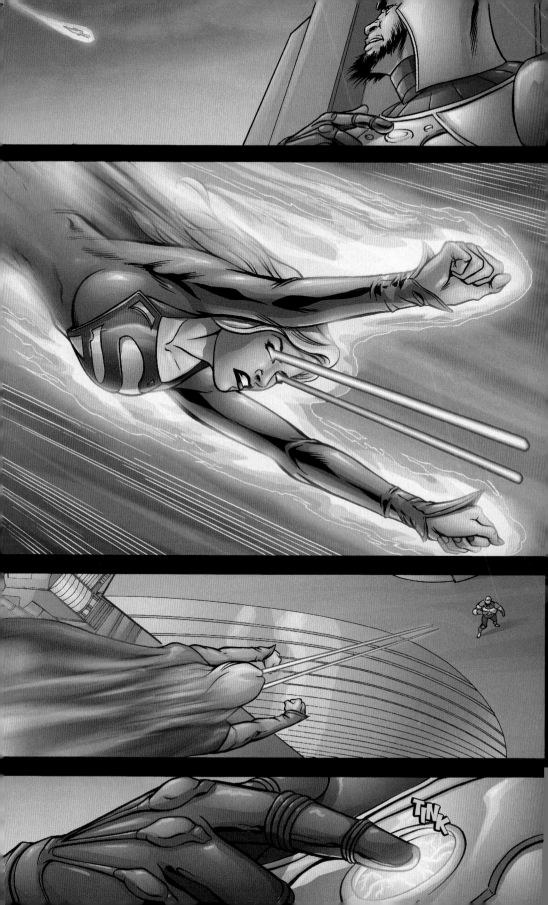

TINK

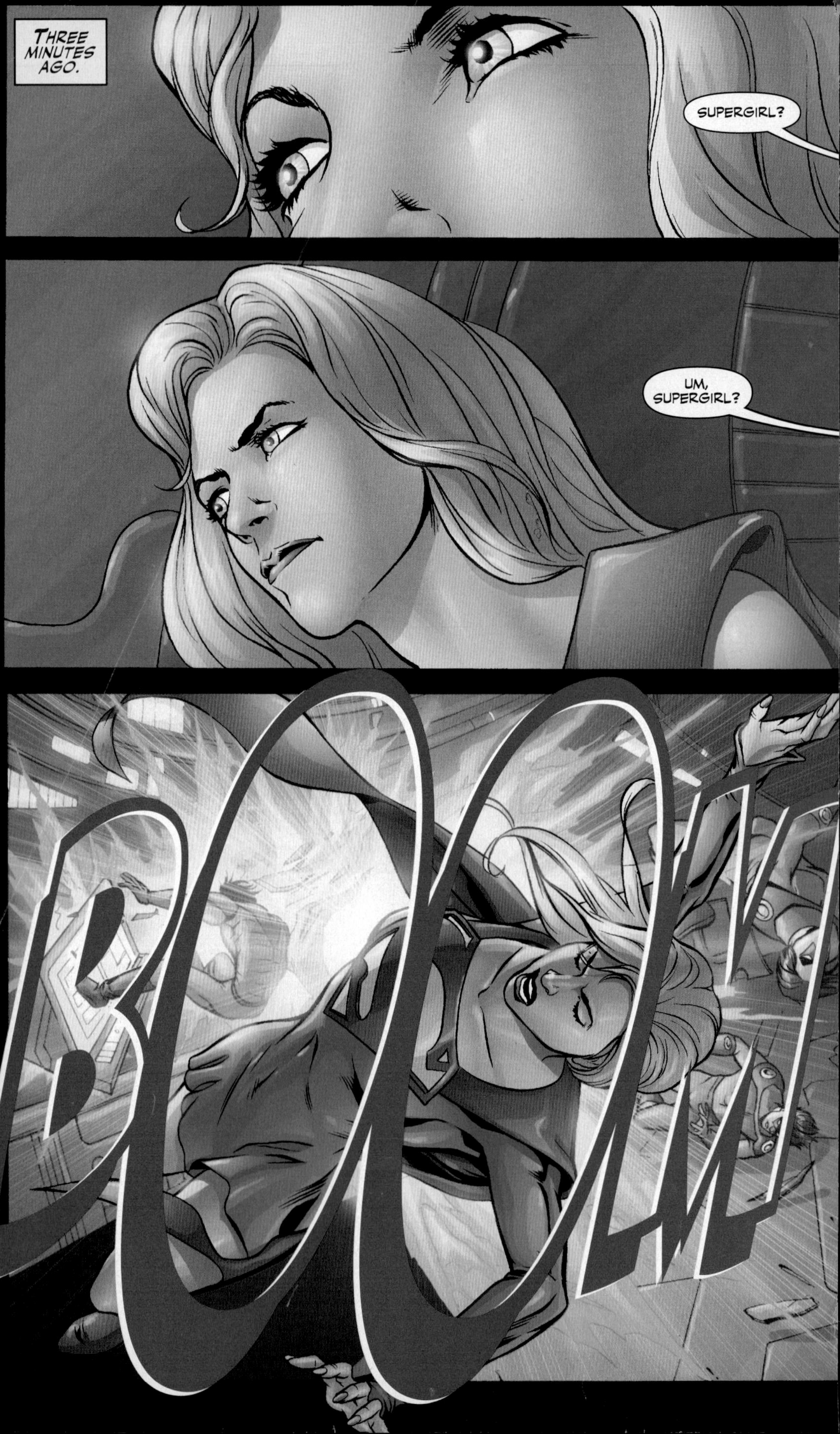
THREE MINUTES AGO.
SUPERGIRL?
UM, SUPERGIRL?
BOOM!

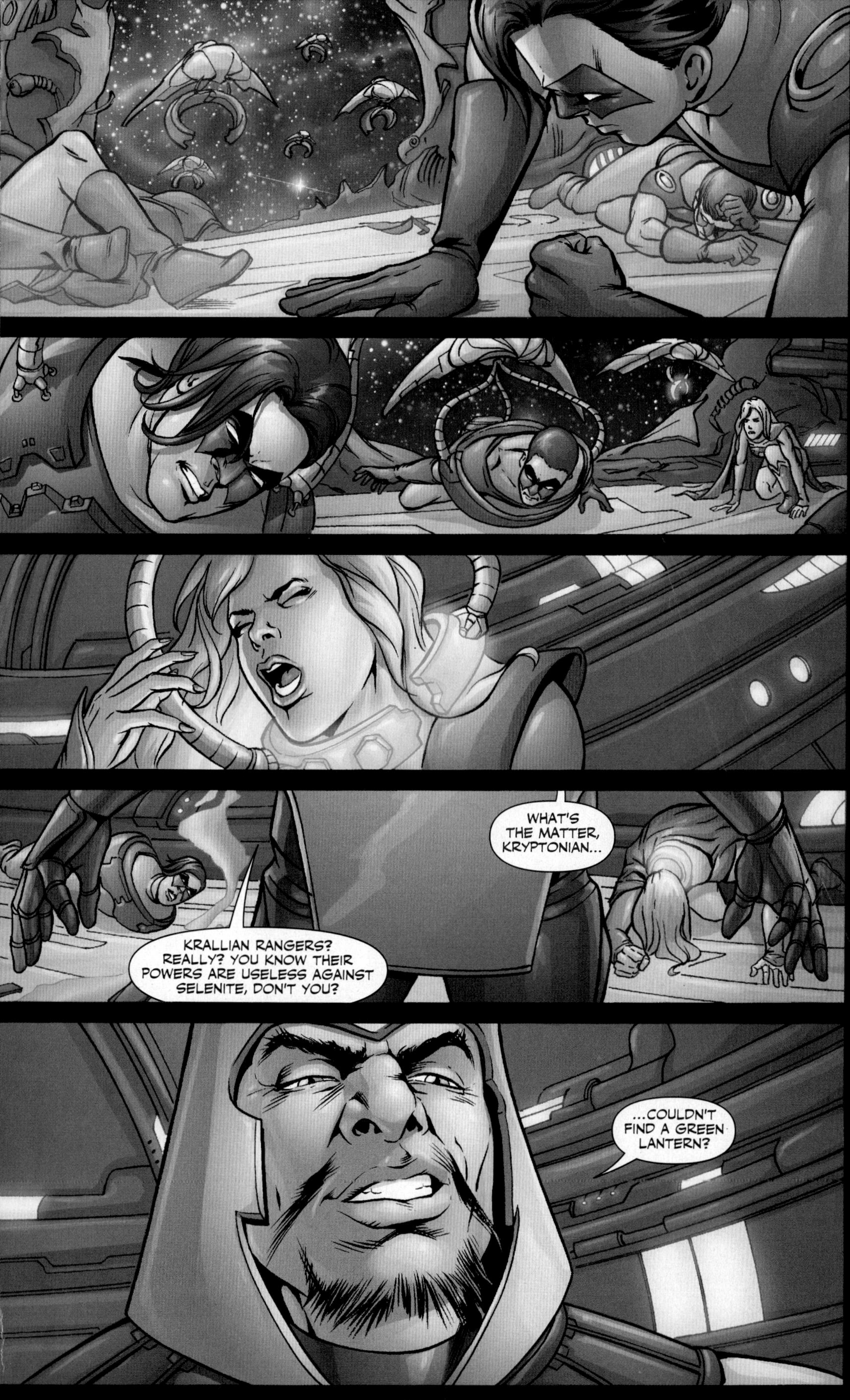
WHAT'S THE MATTER, KRYPTONIAN...
KRALLIAN RANGERS? REALLY? YOU KNOW THEIR POWERS ARE USELESS AGAINST SELENITE, DON'T YOU?
...COULDN'T FIND A GREEN LANTERN?

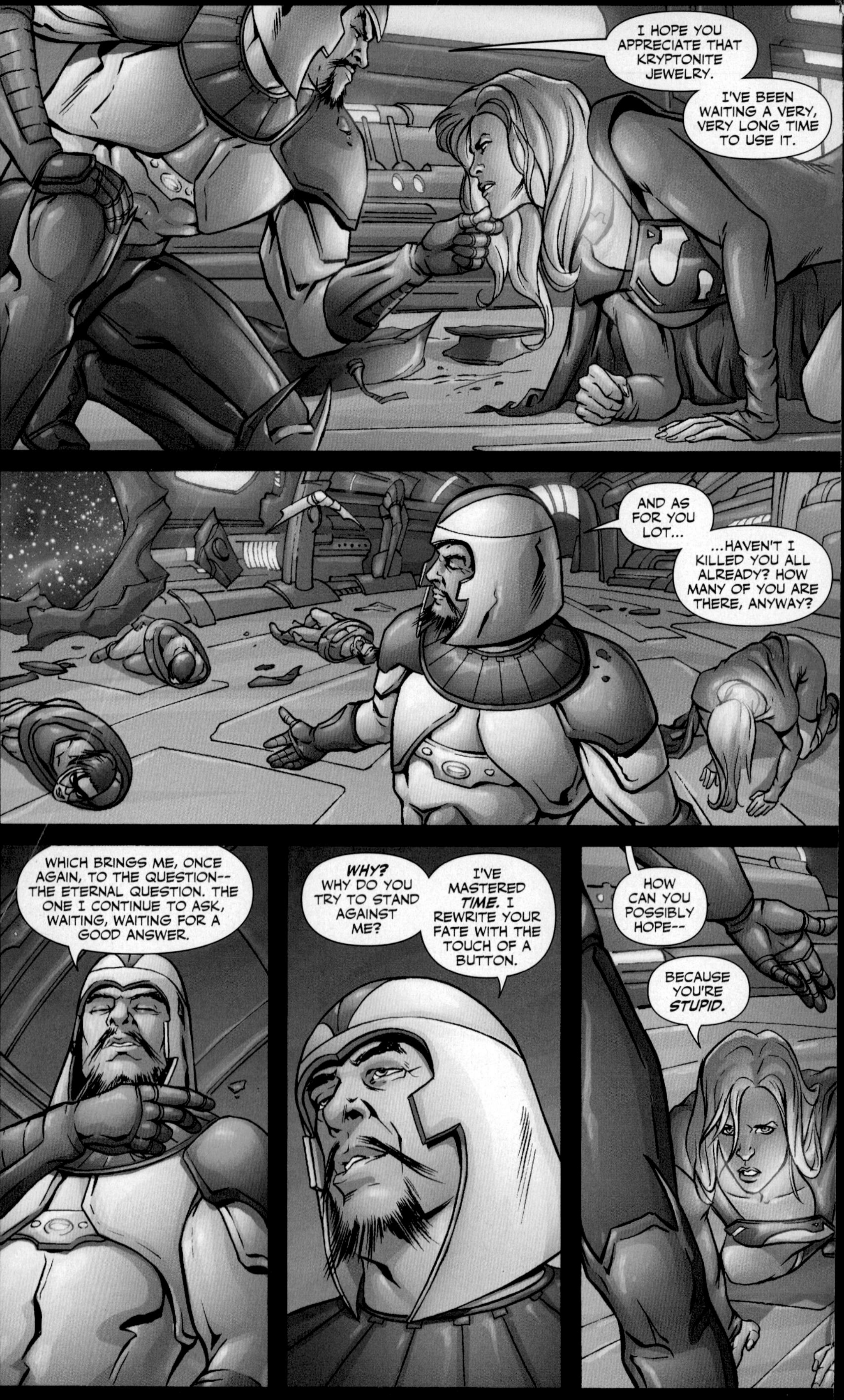
I HOPE YOU APPRECIATE THAT KRYPTONITE JEWELRY.
I'VE BEEN WAITING A VERY, VERY LONG TIME TO USE IT.
AND AS FOR YOU LOT...
...HAVEN'T I KILLED YOU ALL ALREADY? HOW MANY OF YOU ARE THERE, ANYWAY?
WHICH BRINGS ME, ONCE AGAIN, TO THE QUESTION-- THE ETERNAL QUESTION. THE ONE I CONTINUE TO ASK, WAITING, WAITING FOR A GOOD ANSWER.
WHY? WHY DO YOU TRY TO STAND AGAINST ME?
I'VE MASTERED *TIME.* I REWRITE YOUR FATE WITH THE TOUCH OF A BUTTON.
HOW CAN YOU POSSIBLY HOPE--
BECAUSE YOU'RE *STUPID.*

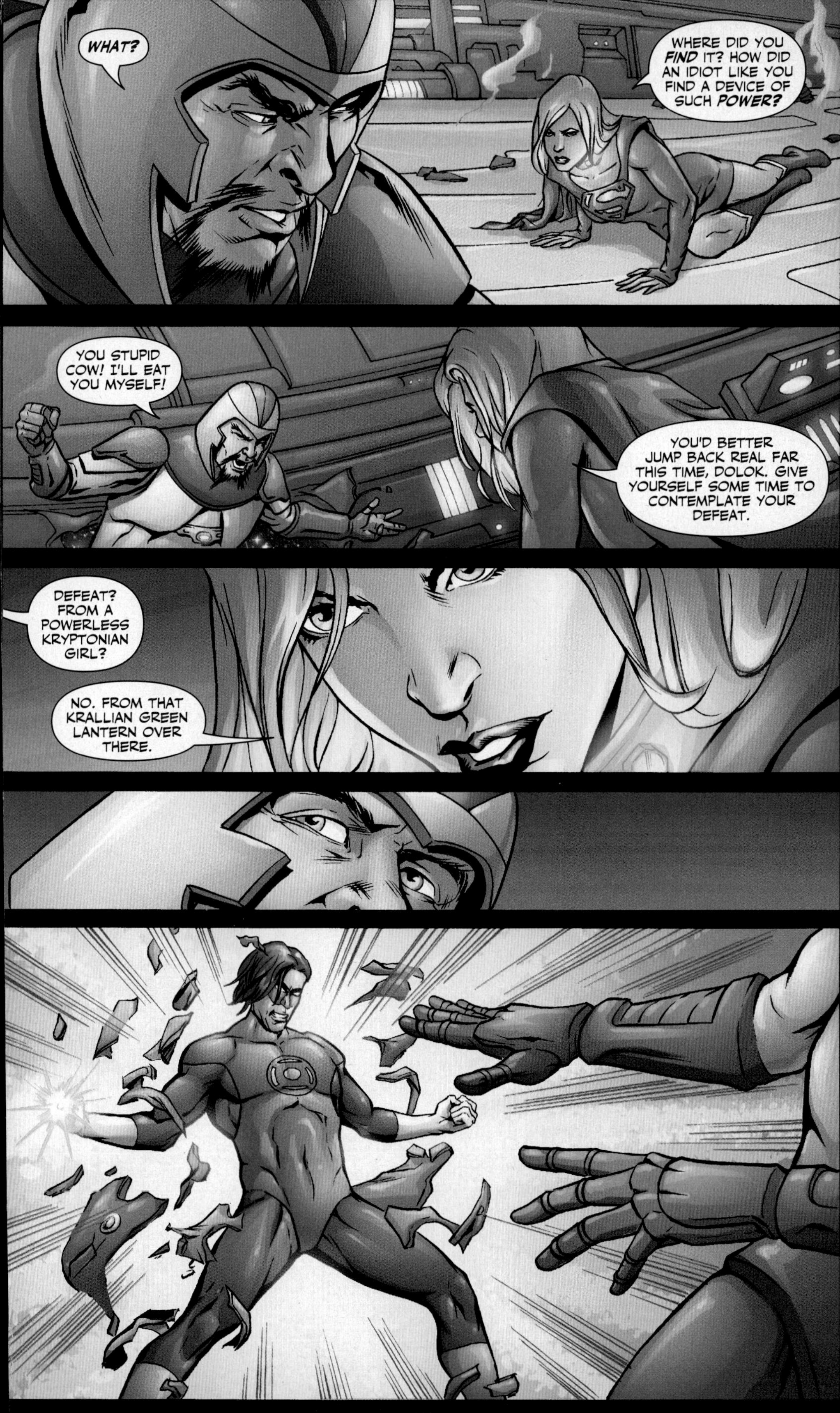
WHAT?
WHERE DID YOU FIND IT? HOW DID AN IDIOT LIKE YOU FIND A DEVICE OF SUCH POWER?
YOU STUPID COW! I'LL EAT YOU MYSELF!
YOU'D BETTER JUMP BACK REAL FAR THIS TIME, DOLOK. GIVE YOURSELF SOME TIME TO CONTEMPLATE YOUR DEFEAT.
DEFEAT? FROM A POWERLESS KRYPTONIAN GIRL?
NO. FROM THAT KRALLIAN GREEN LANTERN OVER THERE.

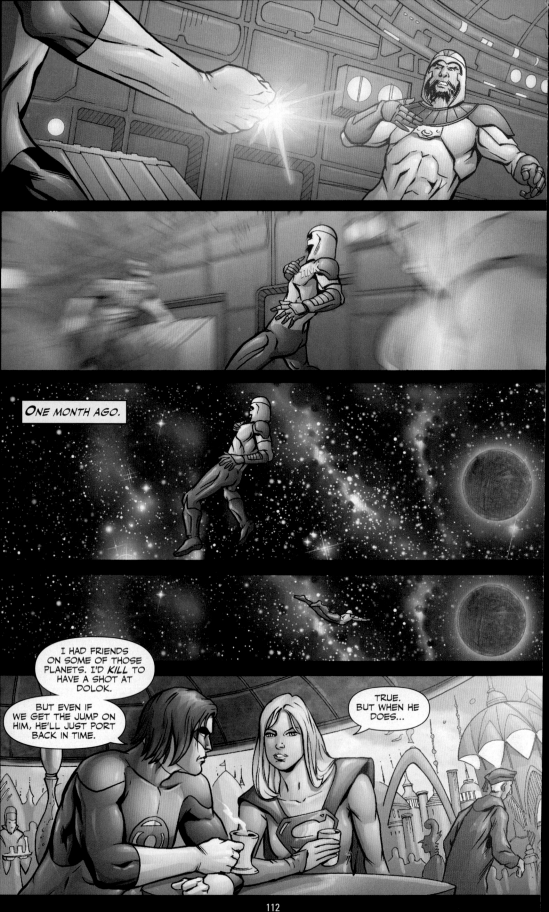

ONE MONTH AGO.

I HAD FRIENDS ON SOME OF THOSE PLANETS. I'D *KILL* TO HAVE A SHOT AT DOLOK.

BUT EVEN IF WE GET THE JUMP ON HIM, HE'LL JUST PORT BACK IN TIME.

TRUE. BUT WHEN HE DOES...

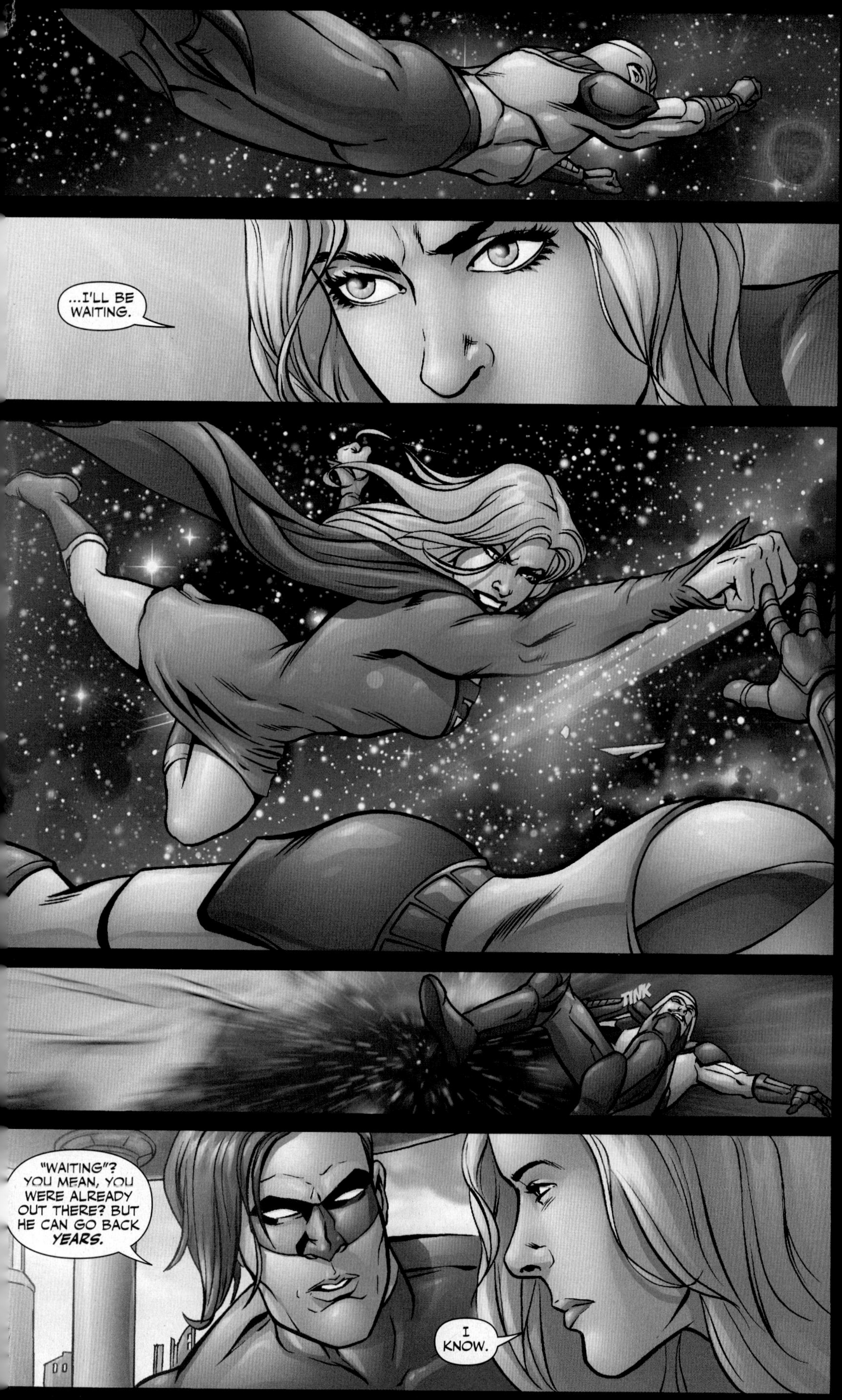

...I'LL BE WAITING.
TINK
"WAITING"? YOU MEAN, YOU WERE ALREADY OUT THERE? BUT HE CAN GO BACK *YEARS.*
I KNOW.

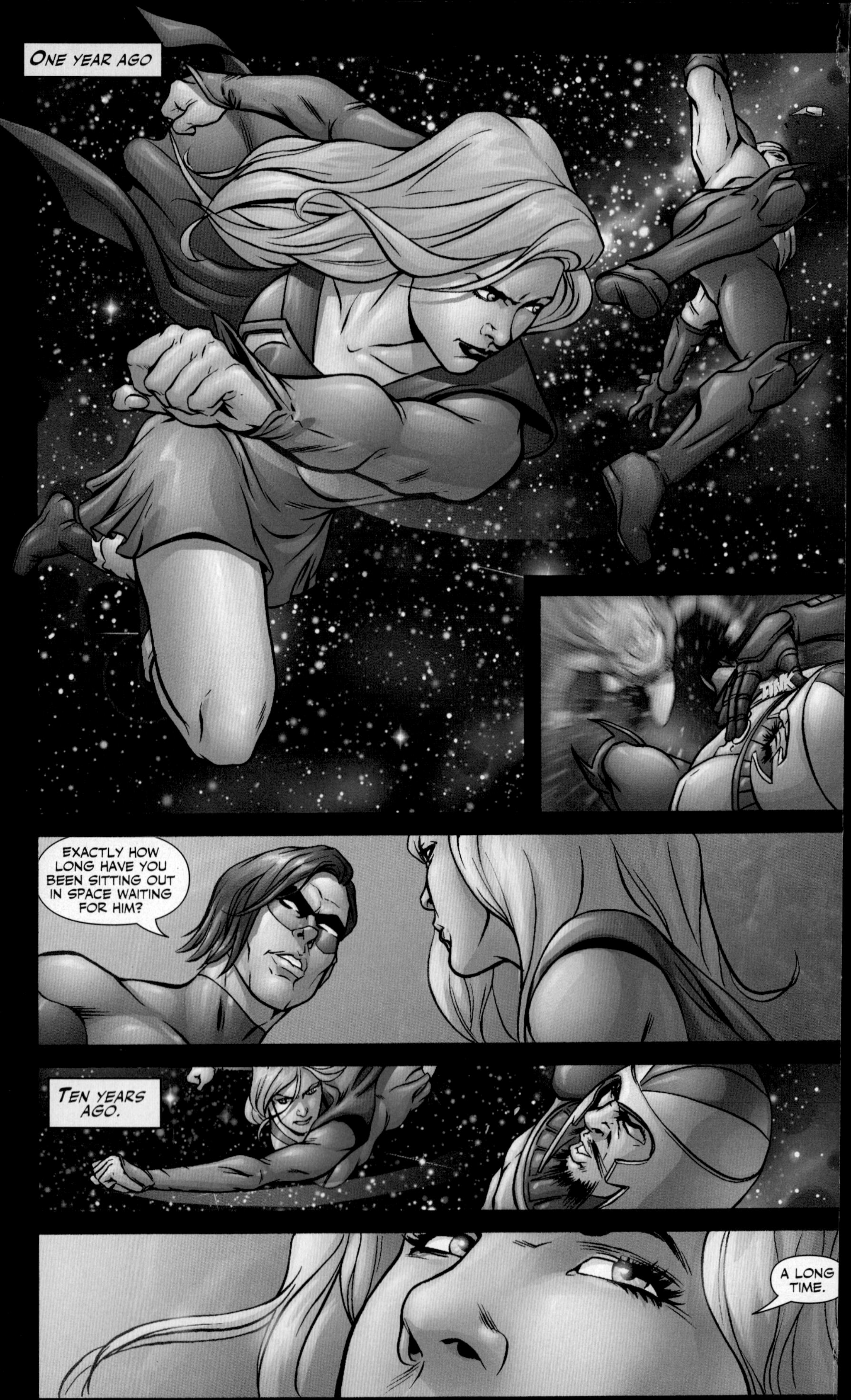
One year ago
TINK
Exactly how long have you been sitting out in space waiting for him?
Ten years ago.
A long time.

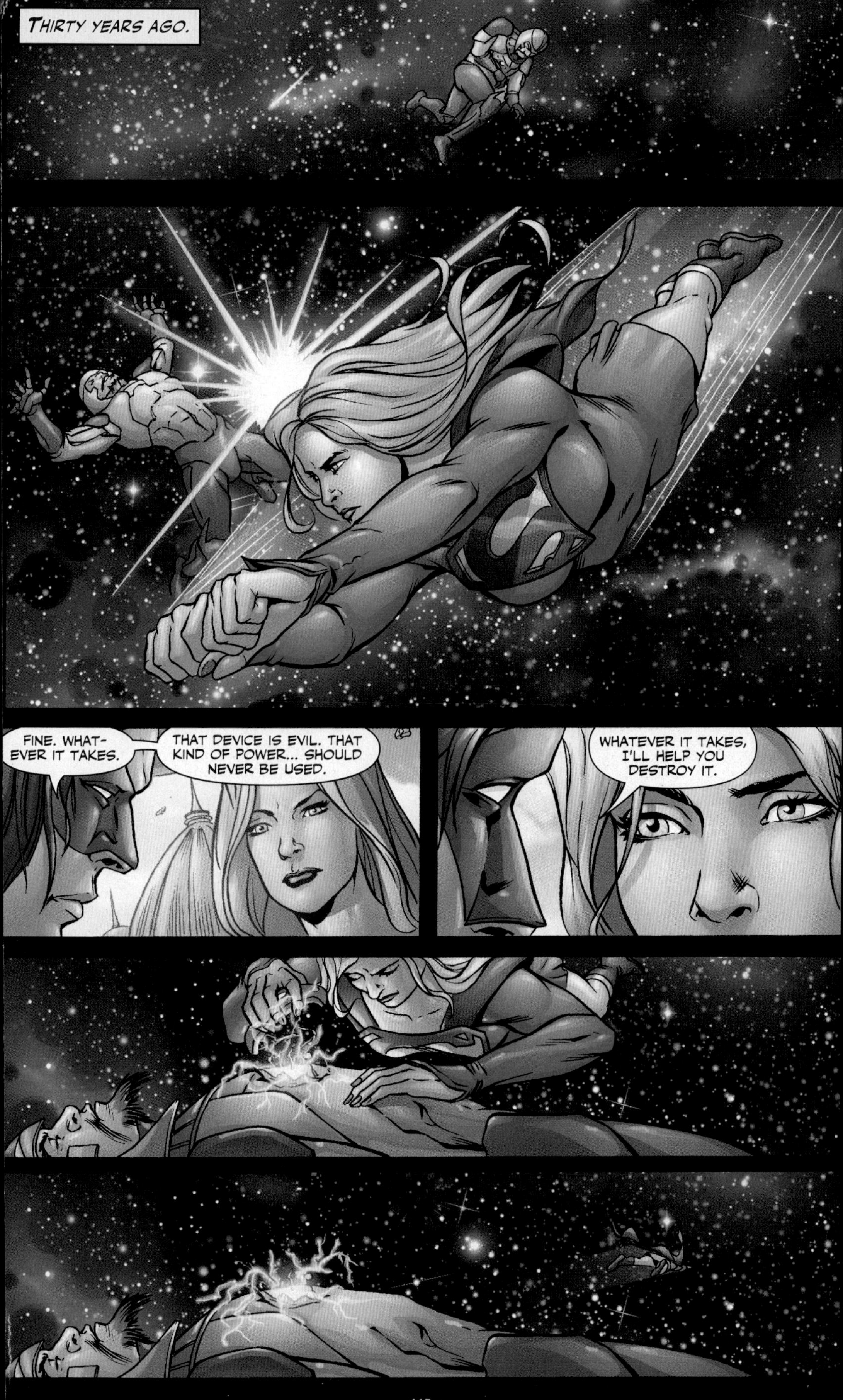

THIRTY YEARS AGO.
FINE. WHAT-EVER IT TAKES.
THAT DEVICE IS EVIL. THAT KIND OF POWER... SHOULD NEVER BE USED.
WHATEVER IT TAKES, I'LL HELP YOU DESTROY IT.

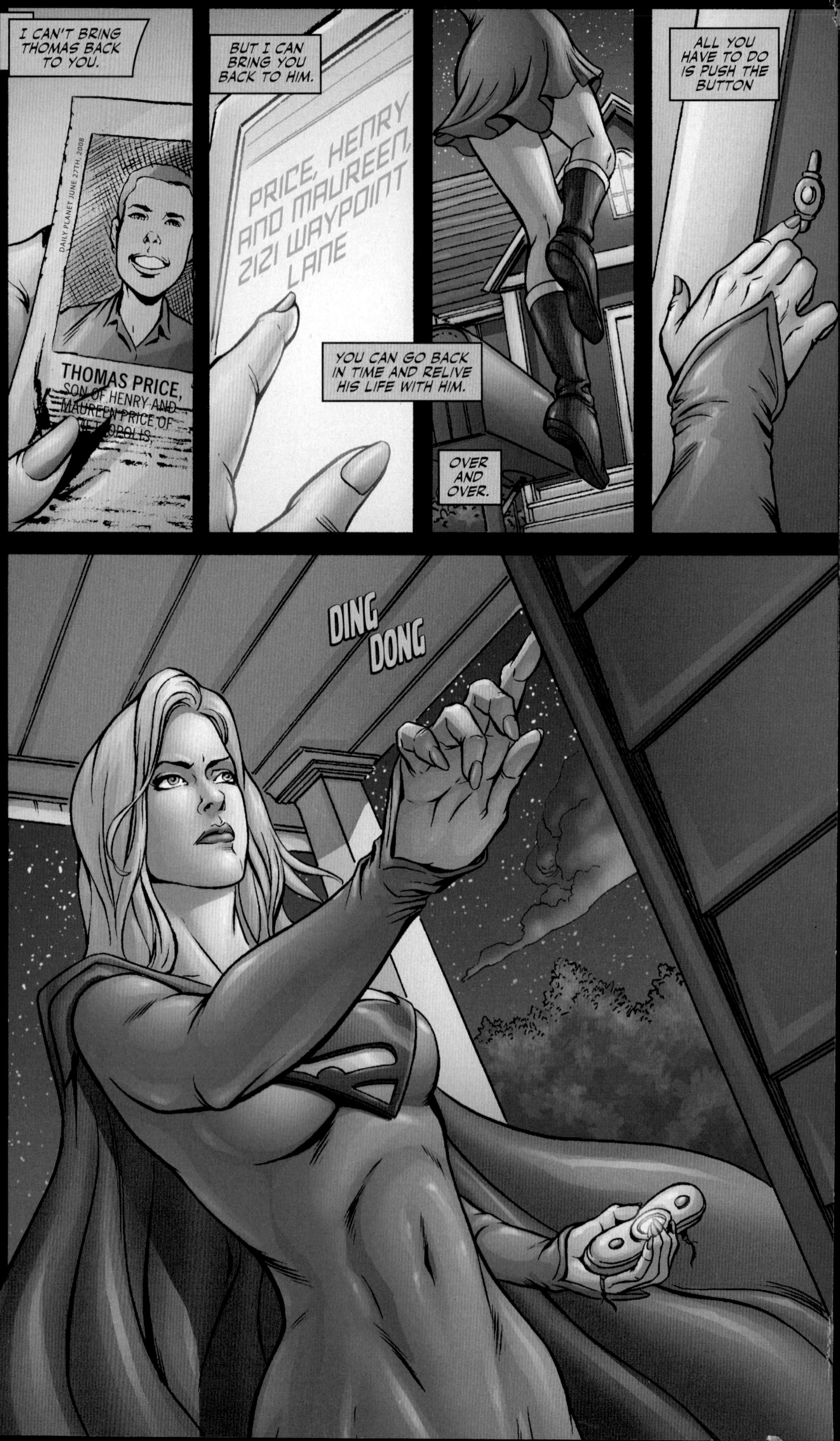
I CAN'T BRING THOMAS BACK TO YOU.
DAILY PLANET JUNE 27TH, 2008
THOMAS PRICE,
SON OF HENRY AND MAUREEN PRICE OF
BUT I CAN BRING YOU BACK TO HIM.
PRICE, HENRY AND MAUREEN, 2121 WAYPOINT LANE
YOU CAN GO BACK IN TIME AND RELIVE HIS LIFE WITH HIM.
OVER AND OVER.
ALL YOU HAVE TO DO IS PUSH THE BUTTON
DING DONG

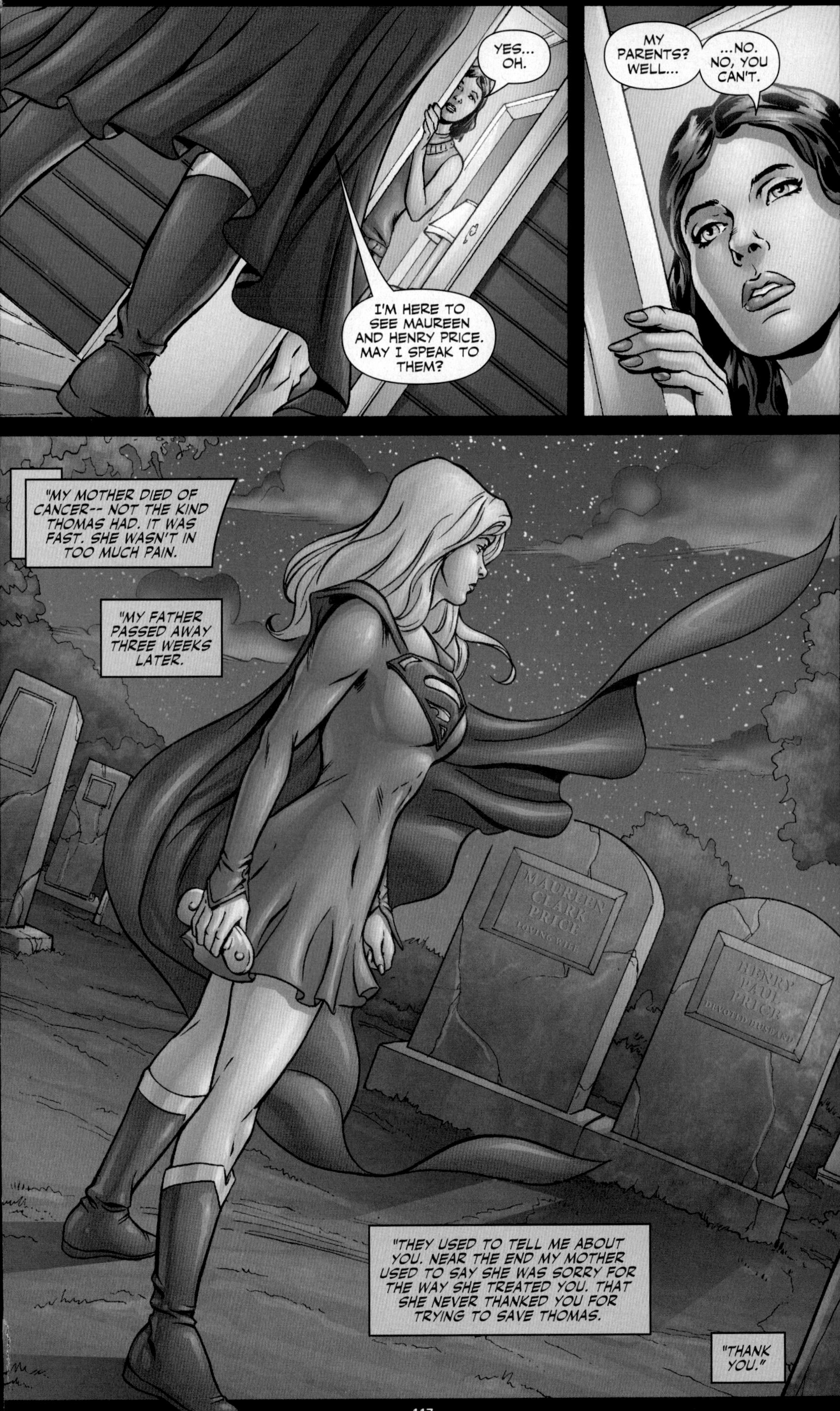

YES... OH.
I'M HERE TO SEE MAUREEN AND HENRY PRICE. MAY I SPEAK TO THEM?
MY PARENTS? WELL...
...NO. NO, YOU CAN'T.
"MY MOTHER DIED OF CANCER-- NOT THE KIND THOMAS HAD. IT WAS FAST. SHE WASN'T IN TOO MUCH PAIN.
"MY FATHER PASSED AWAY THREE WEEKS LATER.
MAUREEN CLARK PRICE LOVING WIFE
HENRY PAUL PRICE DEVOTED HUSBAND
"THEY USED TO TELL ME ABOUT YOU. NEAR THE END MY MOTHER USED TO SAY SHE WAS SORRY FOR THE WAY SHE TREATED YOU. THAT SHE NEVER THANKED YOU FOR TRYING TO SAVE THOMAS.
"THANK YOU."

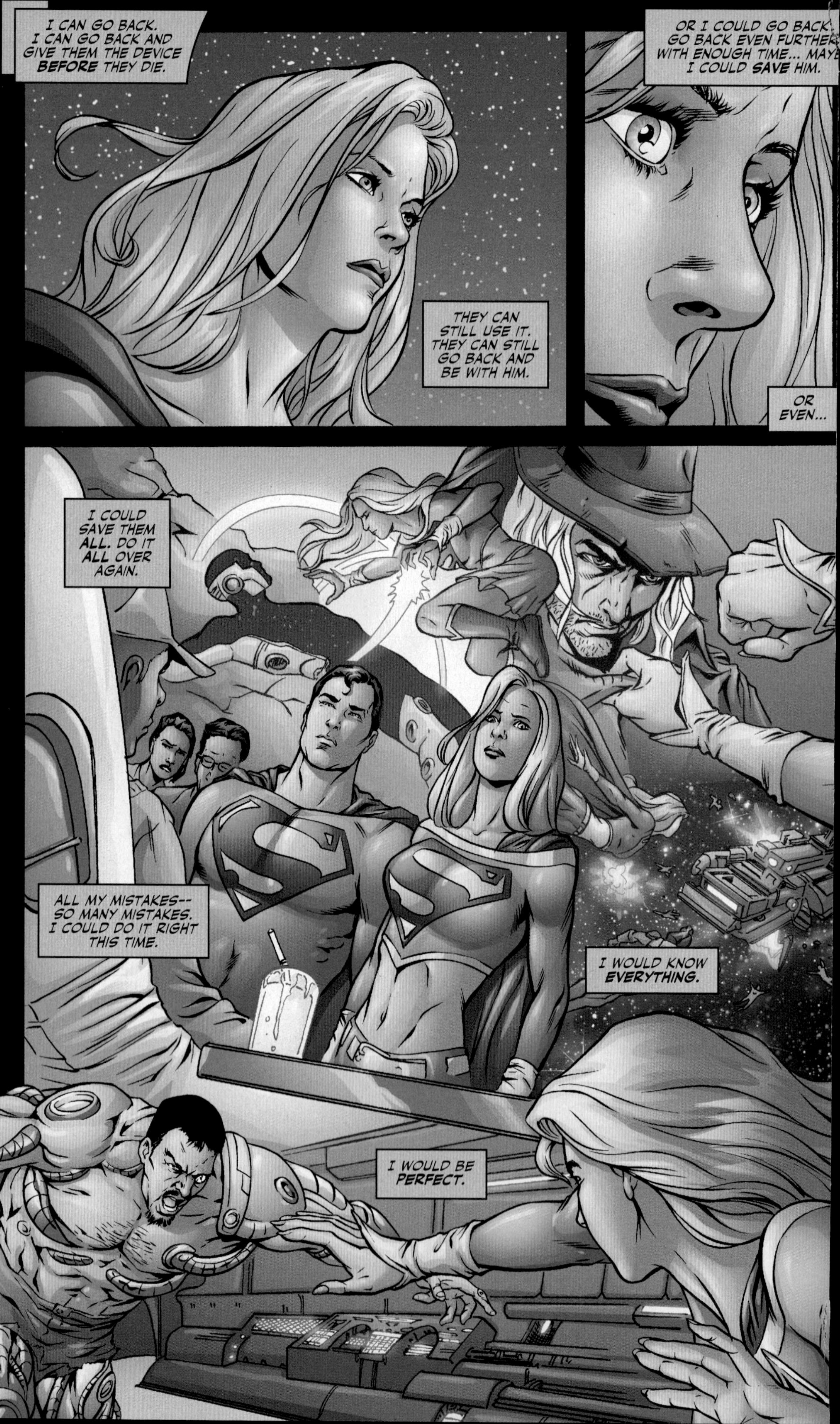
I CAN GO BACK.
I CAN GO BACK AND GIVE THEM THE DEVICE **BEFORE** THEY DIE.
THEY CAN STILL USE IT. THEY CAN STILL GO BACK AND BE WITH HIM.
OR I COULD GO BACK. GO BACK EVEN FURTHER. WITH ENOUGH TIME... MAYB I COULD **SAVE** HIM.
OR EVEN...
I COULD SAVE THEM **ALL**. DO IT **ALL** OVER AGAIN.
ALL MY MISTAKES-- SO MANY MISTAKES. I COULD DO IT RIGHT THIS TIME.
I WOULD KNOW **EVERYTHING**.
I WOULD BE **PERFECT**.

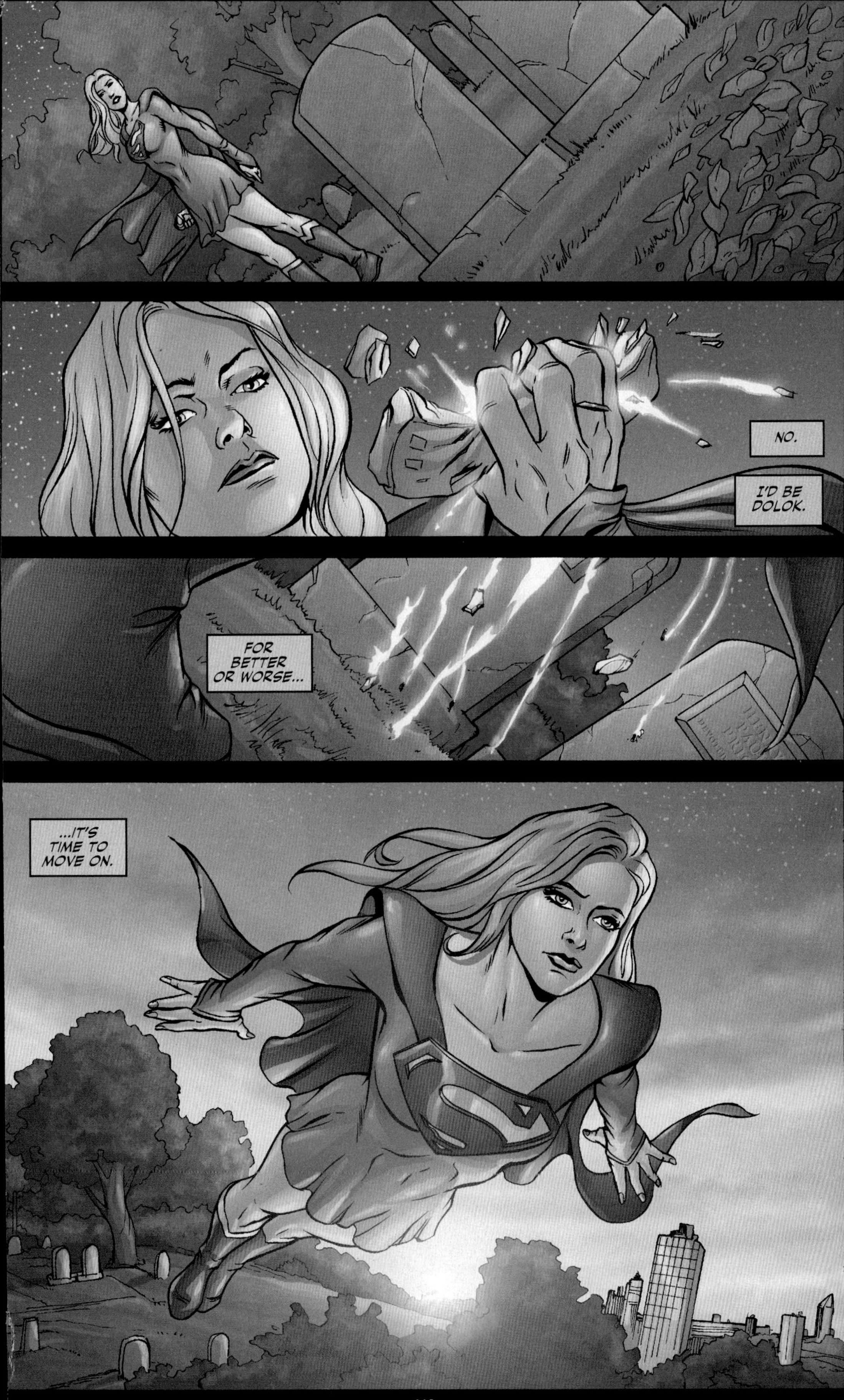
NO.
I'D BE DOLOK.
FOR BETTER OR WORSE...
...IT'S TIME TO MOVE ON.

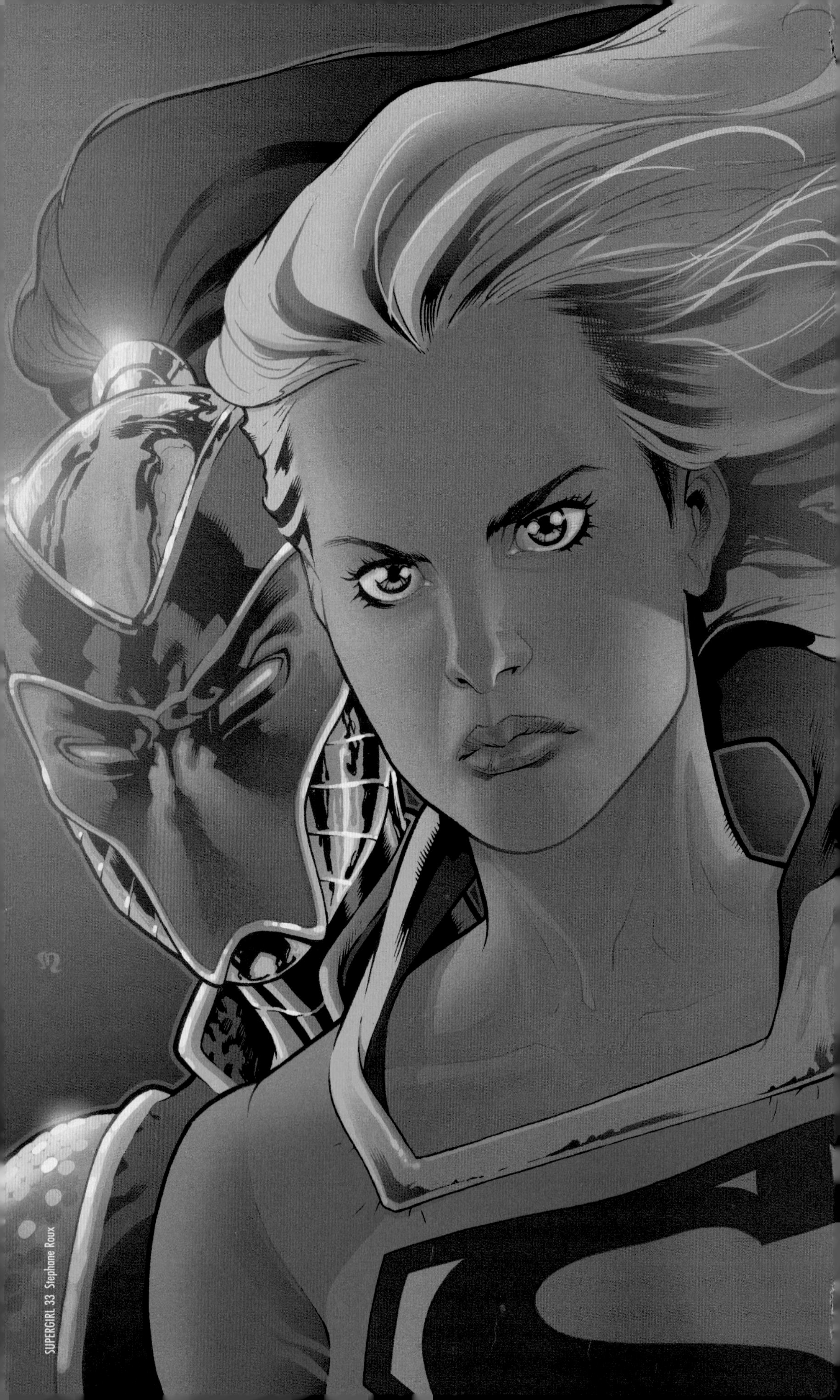

SUPERGIRL 33 Stephane Roux

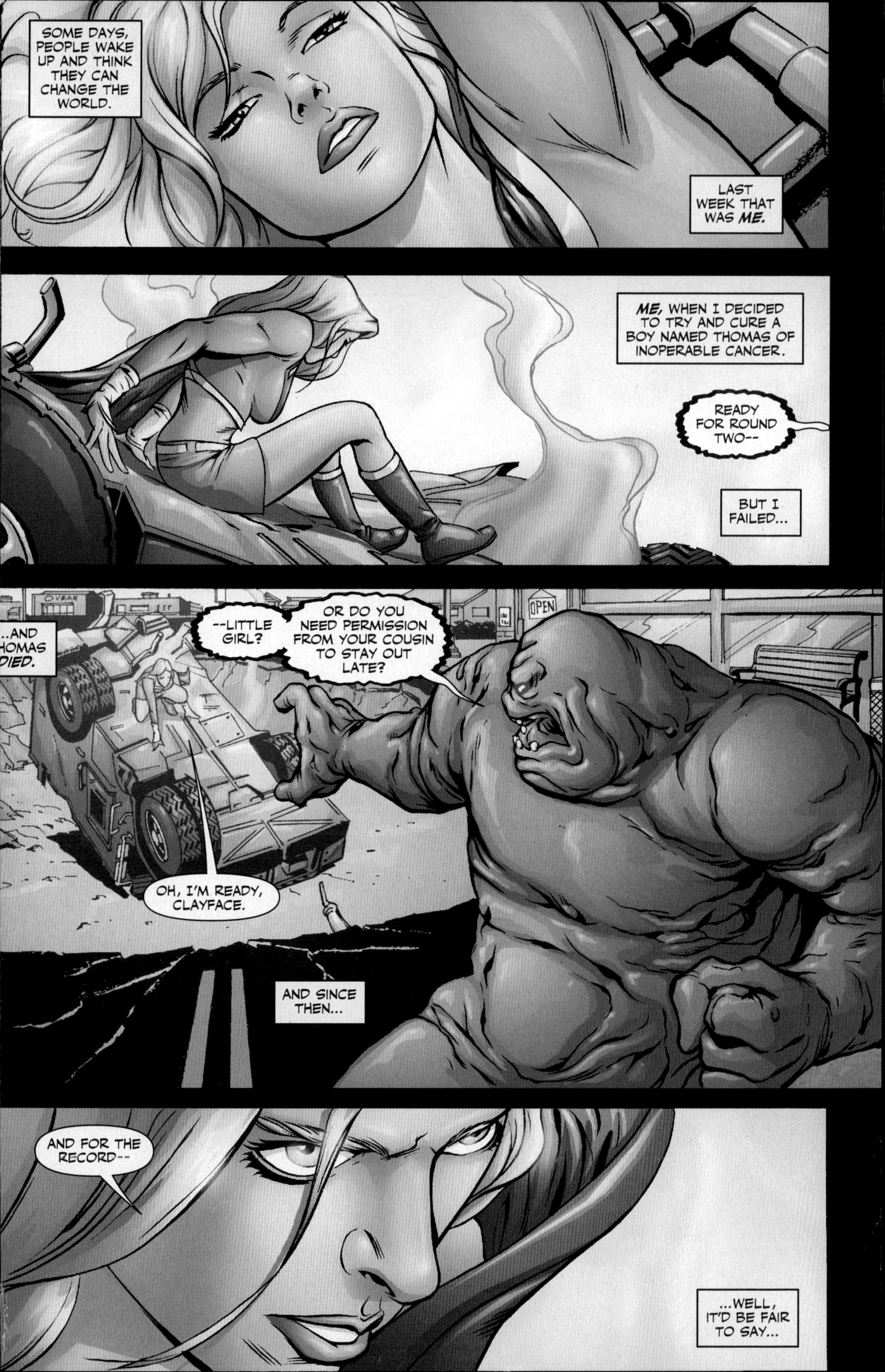
SOME DAYS, PEOPLE WAKE UP AND THINK THEY CAN CHANGE THE WORLD.
LAST WEEK THAT WAS ME.
ME, WHEN I DECIDED TO TRY AND CURE A BOY NAMED THOMAS OF INOPERABLE CANCER.
READY FOR ROUND TWO--
BUT I FAILED...
...AND HOMAS DIED.
--LITTLE GIRL?
OR DO YOU NEED PERMISSION FROM YOUR COUSIN TO STAY OUT LATE?
OPEN
OH, I'M READY, CLAYFACE.
AND SINCE THEN...
AND FOR THE RECORD--
...WELL, IT'D BE FAIR TO SAY...

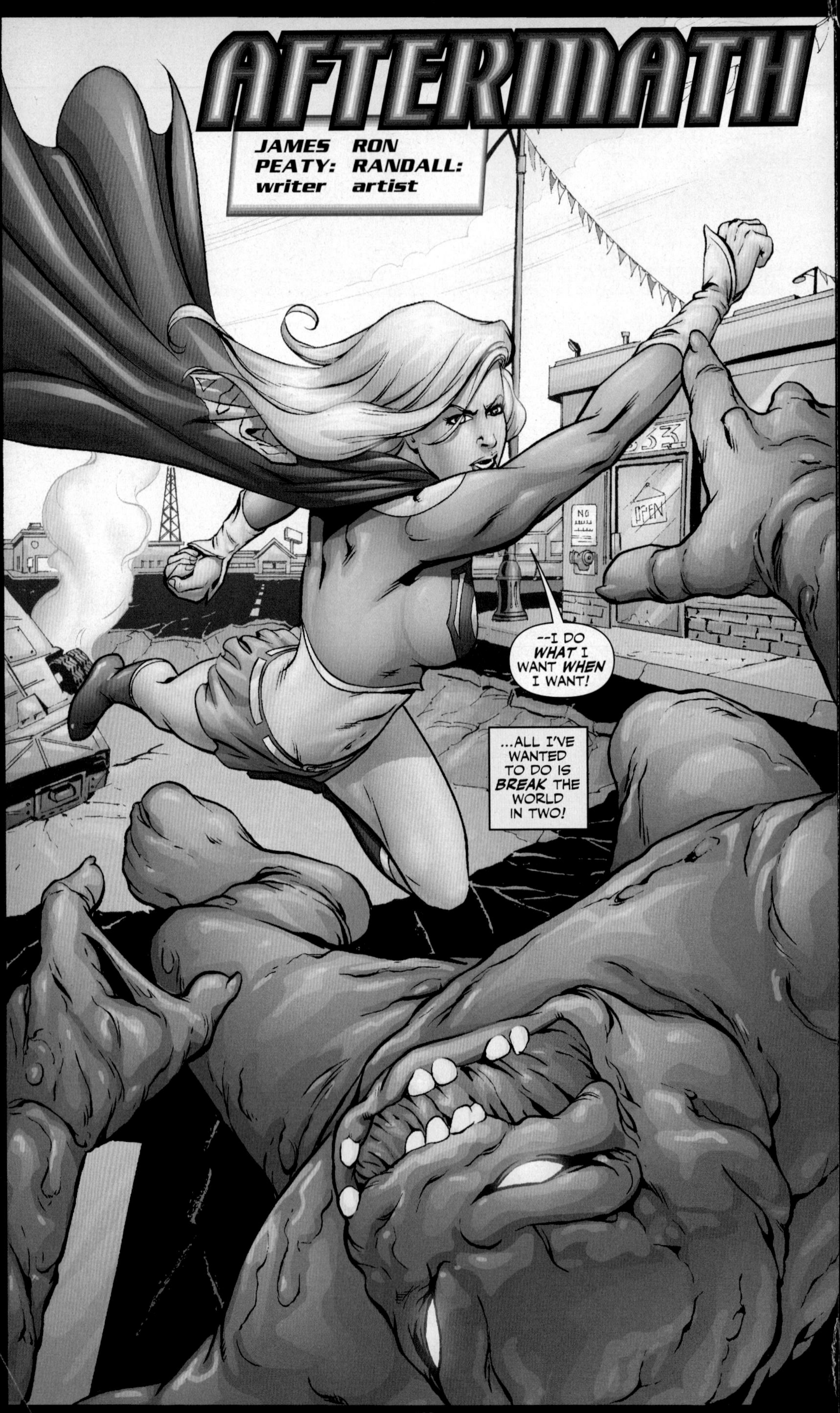
AFTERMATH
JAMES PEATY: writer
RON RANDALL: artist
--I DO WHAT I WANT WHEN I WANT!
...ALL I'VE WANTED TO DO IS BREAK THE WORLD IN TWO!

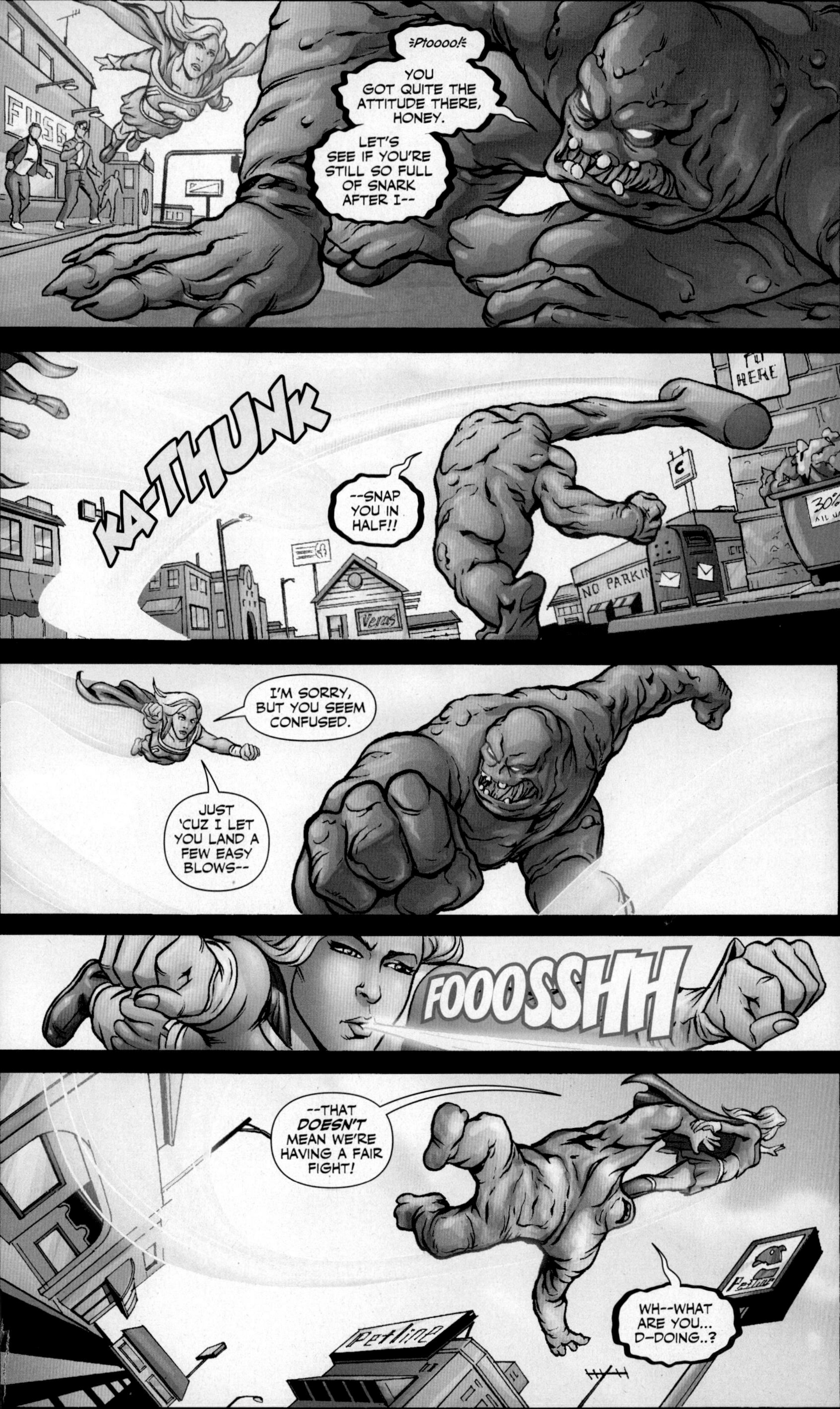

Ptoooo!
YOU GOT QUITE THE ATTITUDE THERE, HONEY.
LET'S SEE IF YOU'RE STILL SO FULL OF SNARK AFTER I--
KA-THUNK
--SNAP YOU IN HALF!!
NO PARKIN
Veras
HERE
30%
I'M SORRY, BUT YOU SEEM CONFUSED.
JUST 'CUZ I LET YOU LAND A FEW EASY BLOWS--
FOOOSSHH
--THAT DOESN'T MEAN WE'RE HAVING A FAIR FIGHT!
WH--WHAT ARE YOU... D-DOING..?
Petline

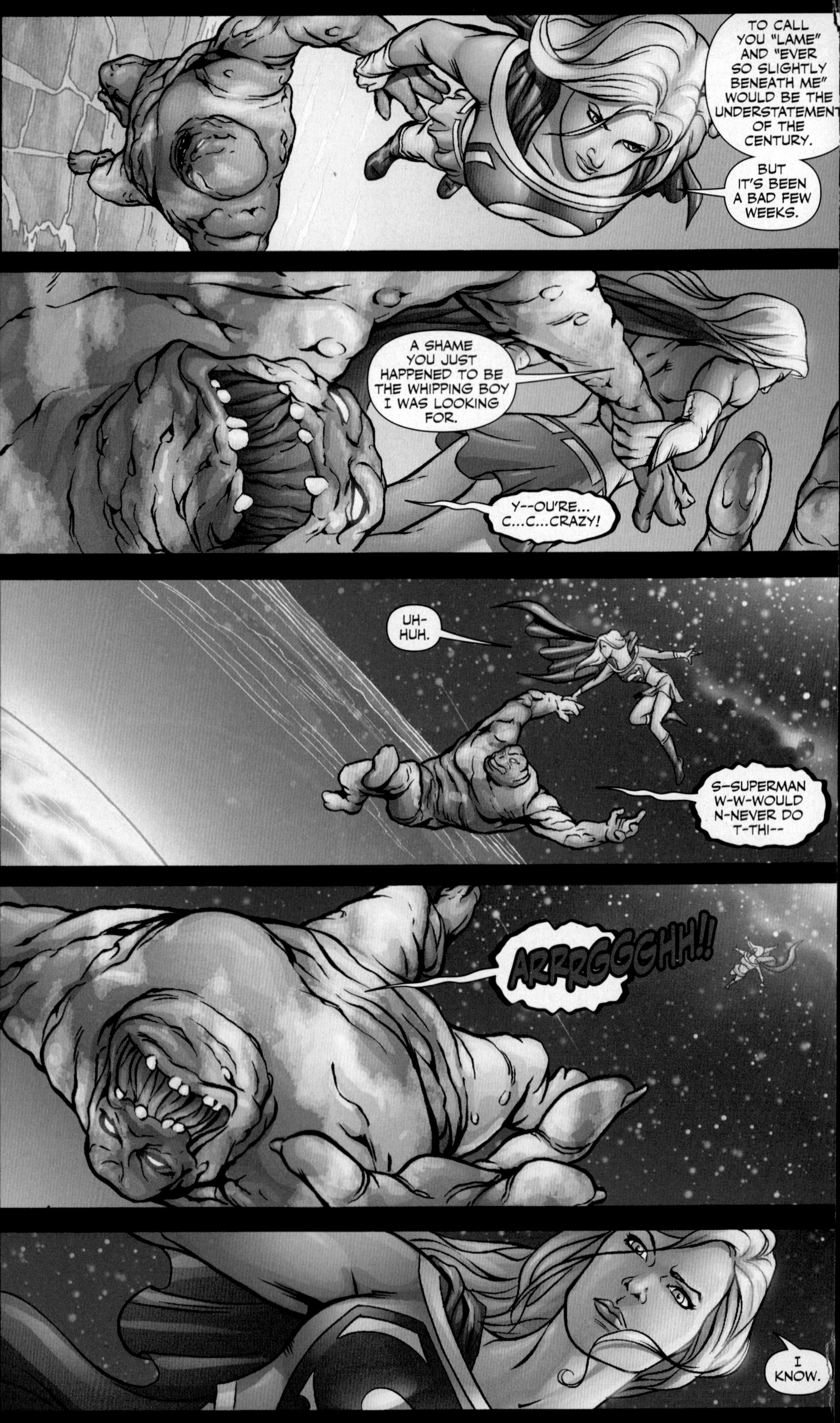
TO CALL YOU "LAME" AND "EVER SO SLIGHTLY BENEATH ME" WOULD BE THE UNDERSTATEMENT OF THE CENTURY.
BUT IT'S BEEN A BAD FEW WEEKS.
A SHAME YOU JUST HAPPENED TO BE THE WHIPPING BOY I WAS LOOKING FOR.
Y--OU'RE... C...C...CRAZY!
UH-HUH.
S-SUPERMAN W-W-WOULD N-NEVER DO T-THI--
ARRRGGGHH!!
I KNOW.

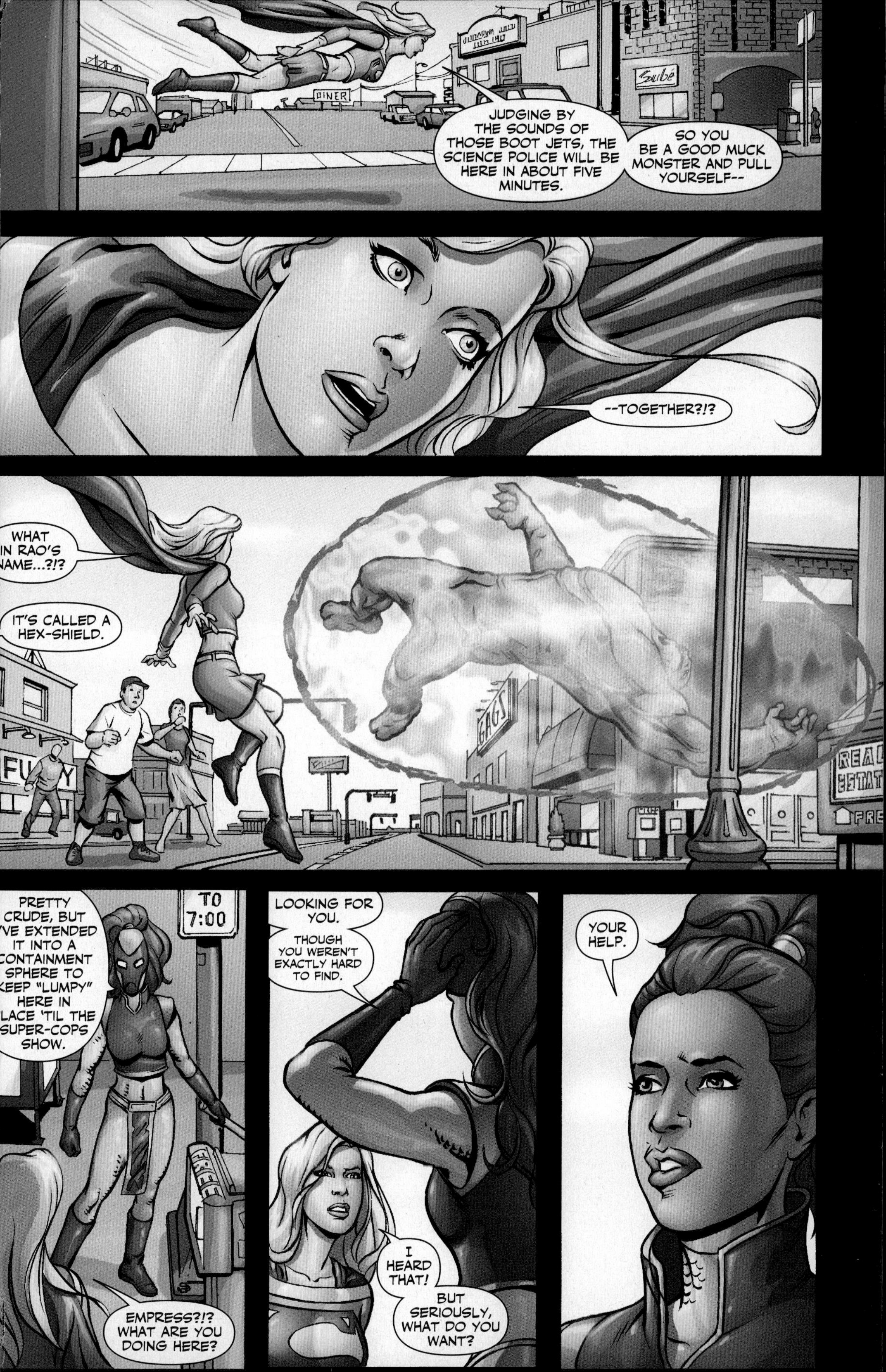

DINER
JUDGING BY THE SOUNDS OF THOSE BOOT JETS, THE SCIENCE POLICE WILL BE HERE IN ABOUT FIVE MINUTES.
SO YOU BE A GOOD MUCK MONSTER AND PULL YOURSELF--
--TOGETHER?!?
WHAT IN RAO'S NAME...?!?
IT'S CALLED A HEX-SHIELD.
GAGS
PRETTY CRUDE, BUT I'VE EXTENDED IT INTO A CONTAINMENT SPHERE TO KEEP "LUMPY" HERE IN PLACE 'TIL THE SUPER-COPS SHOW.
TO 7:00
EMPRESS?!? WHAT ARE YOU DOING HERE?
LOOKING FOR YOU.
THOUGH YOU WEREN'T EXACTLY HARD TO FIND.
I HEARD THAT!
BUT SERIOUSLY, WHAT DO YOU WANT?
YOUR HELP.

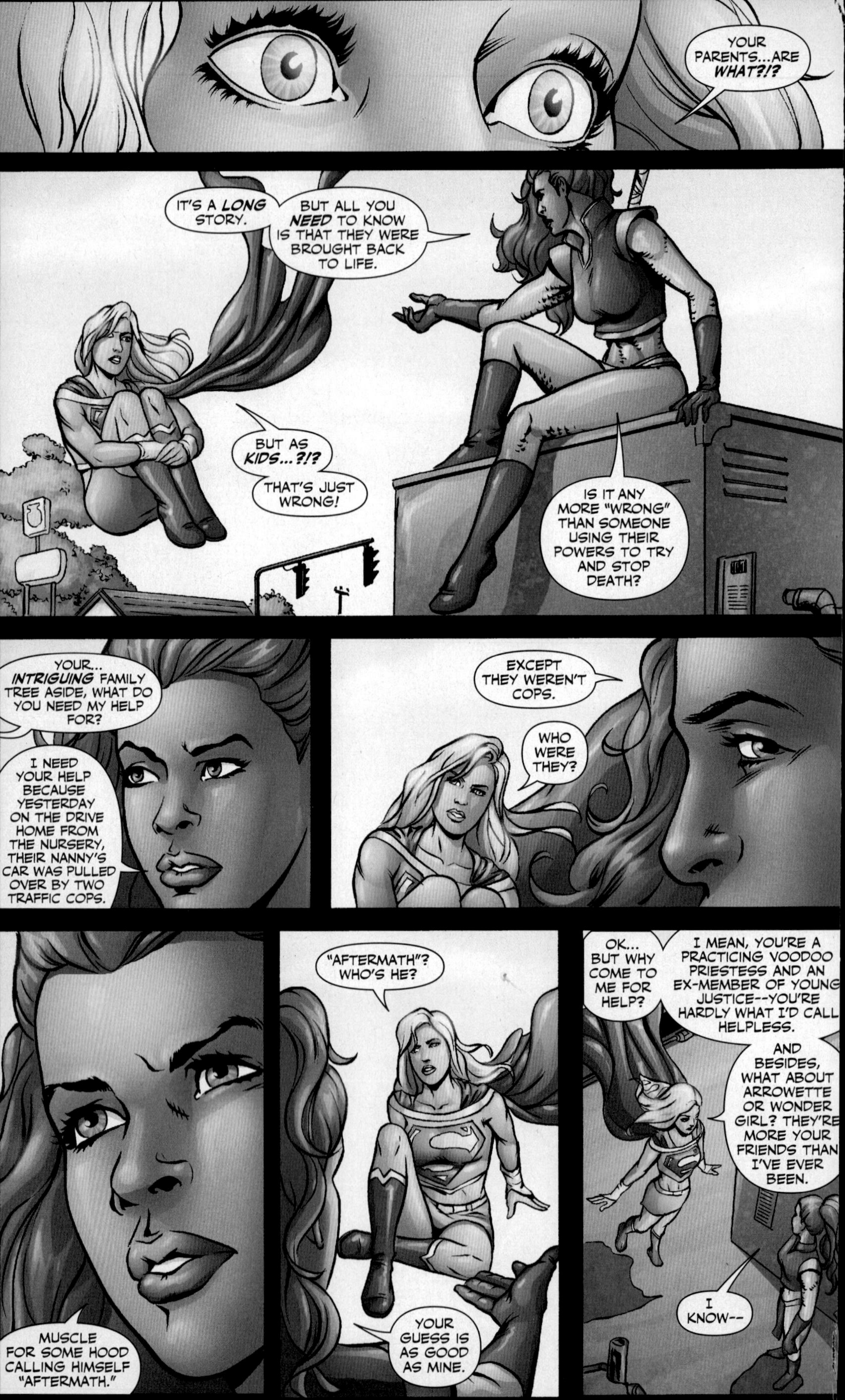
YOUR PARENTS...ARE *WHAT?!?*
IT'S A *LONG* STORY.
BUT ALL YOU *NEED* TO KNOW IS THAT THEY WERE BROUGHT BACK TO LIFE.
BUT AS *KIDS...?!?*
THAT'S JUST WRONG!
IS IT ANY MORE "WRONG" THAN SOMEONE USING THEIR POWERS TO TRY AND STOP DEATH?
YOUR... *INTRIGUING* FAMILY TREE ASIDE, WHAT DO YOU NEED MY HELP FOR?
I NEED YOUR HELP BECAUSE YESTERDAY ON THE DRIVE HOME FROM THE NURSERY, THEIR NANNY'S CAR WAS PULLED OVER BY TWO TRAFFIC COPS.
EXCEPT THEY WEREN'T COPS.
WHO WERE THEY?
MUSCLE FOR SOME HOOD CALLING HIMSELF "AFTERMATH."
"AFTERMATH"? WHO'S HE?
YOUR GUESS IS AS GOOD AS MINE.
OK... BUT WHY COME TO ME FOR HELP?
I MEAN, YOU'RE A PRACTICING VOODOO PRIESTESS AND AN EX-MEMBER OF YOUNG JUSTICE--YOU'RE HARDLY WHAT I'D CALL HELPLESS.
AND BESIDES, WHAT ABOUT ARROWETTE OR WONDER GIRL? THEY'RE MORE YOUR FRIENDS THAN I'VE EVER BEEN.
I KNOW--

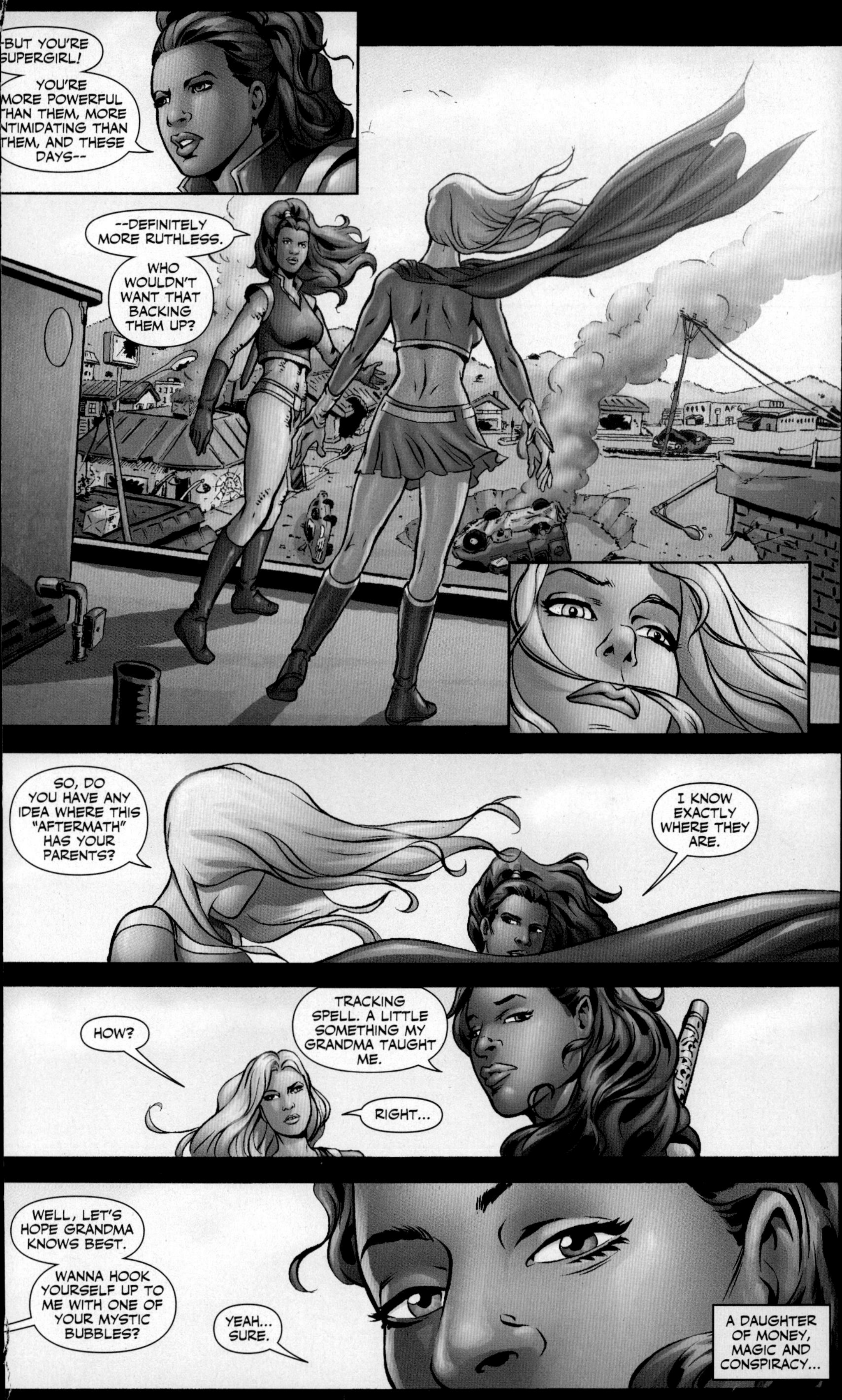
-BUT YOU'RE SUPERGIRL!
YOU'RE MORE POWERFUL THAN THEM, MORE INTIMIDATING THAN THEM, AND THESE DAYS--
--DEFINITELY MORE RUTHLESS.
WHO WOULDN'T WANT THAT BACKING THEM UP?
SO, DO YOU HAVE ANY IDEA WHERE THIS "AFTERMATH" HAS YOUR PARENTS?
I KNOW EXACTLY WHERE THEY ARE.
HOW?
TRACKING SPELL. A LITTLE SOMETHING MY GRANDMA TAUGHT ME.
RIGHT...
WELL, LET'S HOPE GRANDMA KNOWS BEST.
WANNA HOOK YOURSELF UP TO ME WITH ONE OF YOUR MYSTIC BUBBLES?
YEAH... SURE.
A DAUGHTER OF MONEY, MAGIC AND CONSPIRACY...

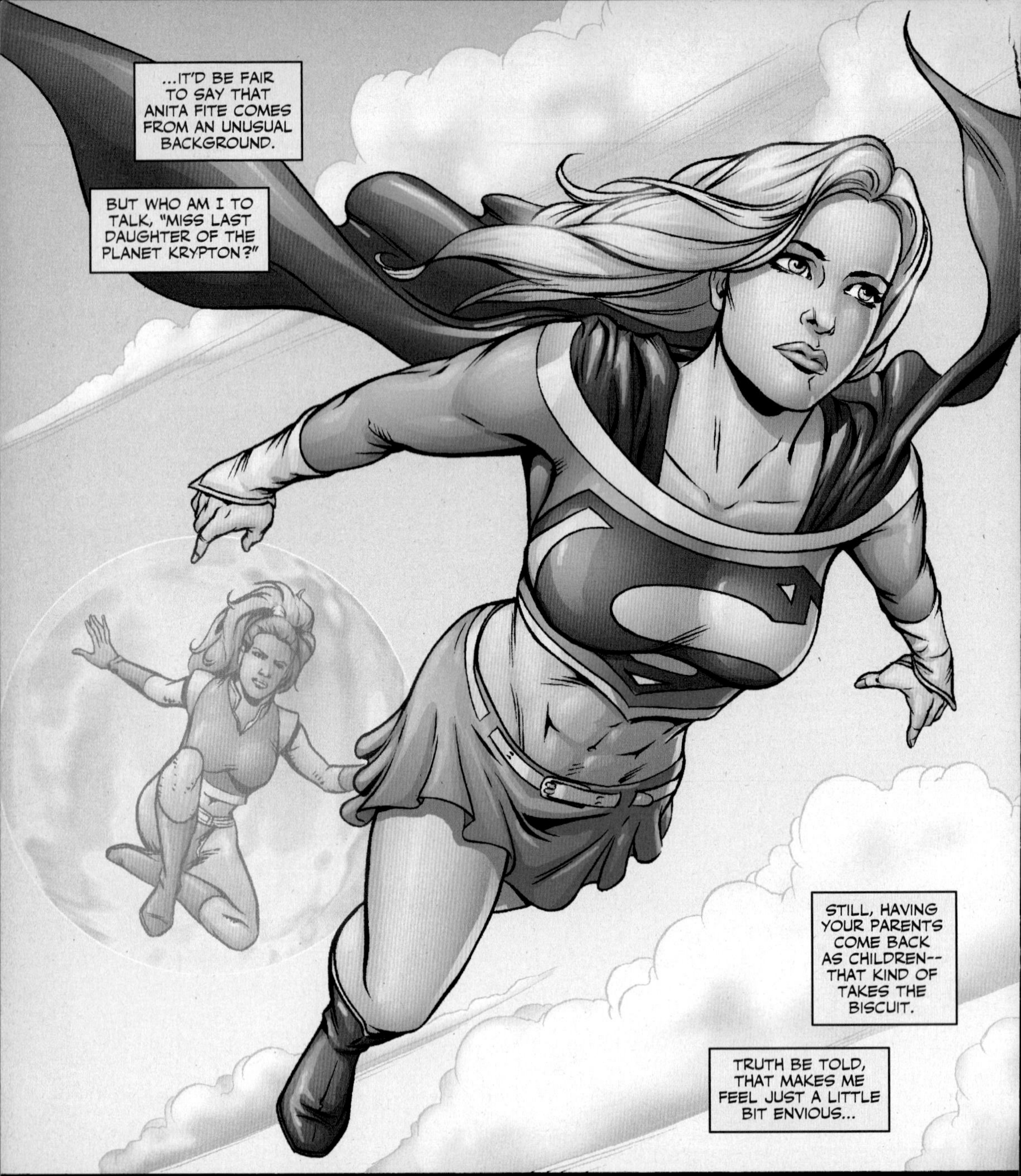
...IT'D BE FAIR TO SAY THAT ANITA FITE COMES FROM AN UNUSUAL BACKGROUND.
BUT WHO AM I TO TALK, "MISS LAST DAUGHTER OF THE PLANET KRYPTON?"
STILL, HAVING YOUR PARENTS COME BACK AS CHILDREN--THAT KIND OF TAKES THE BISCUIT.
TRUTH BE TOLD, THAT MAKES ME FEEL JUST A LITTLE BIT ENVIOUS...

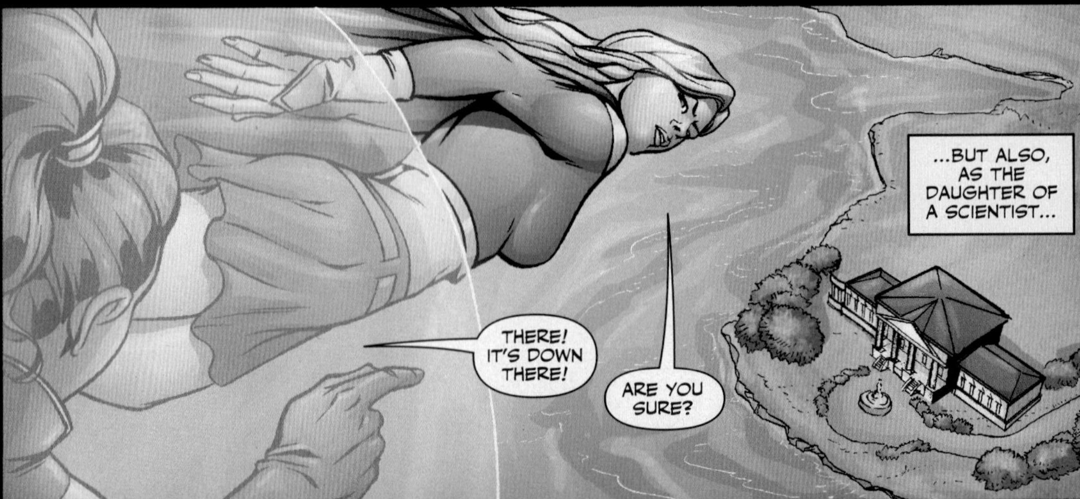
...BUT ALSO, AS THE DAUGHTER OF A SCIENTIST...
THERE! IT'S DOWN THERE!
ARE YOU SURE?

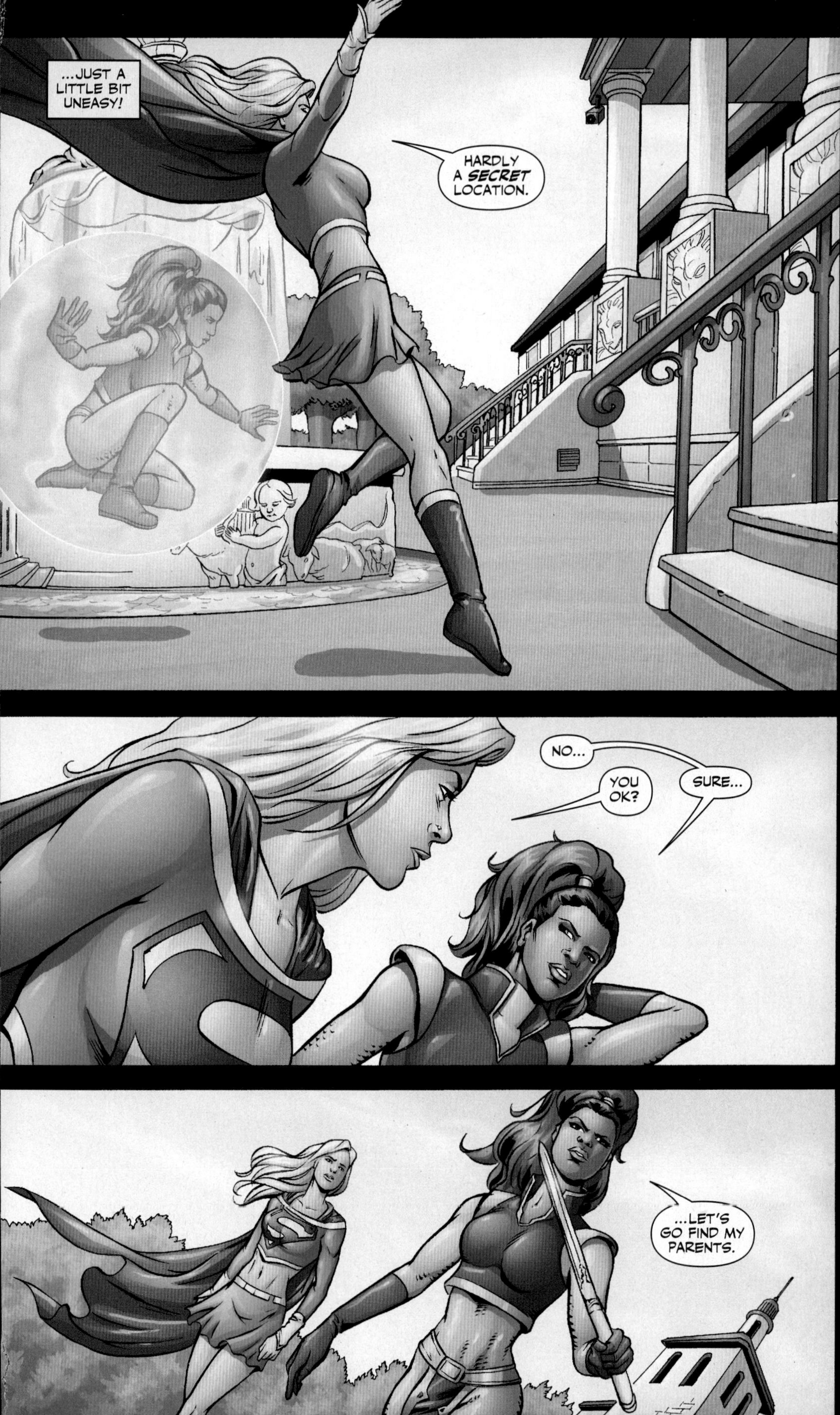
...JUST A LITTLE BIT UNEASY!
HARDLY A *SECRET* LOCATION.
YOU OK?
NO...
SURE...
...LET'S GO FIND MY PARENTS.

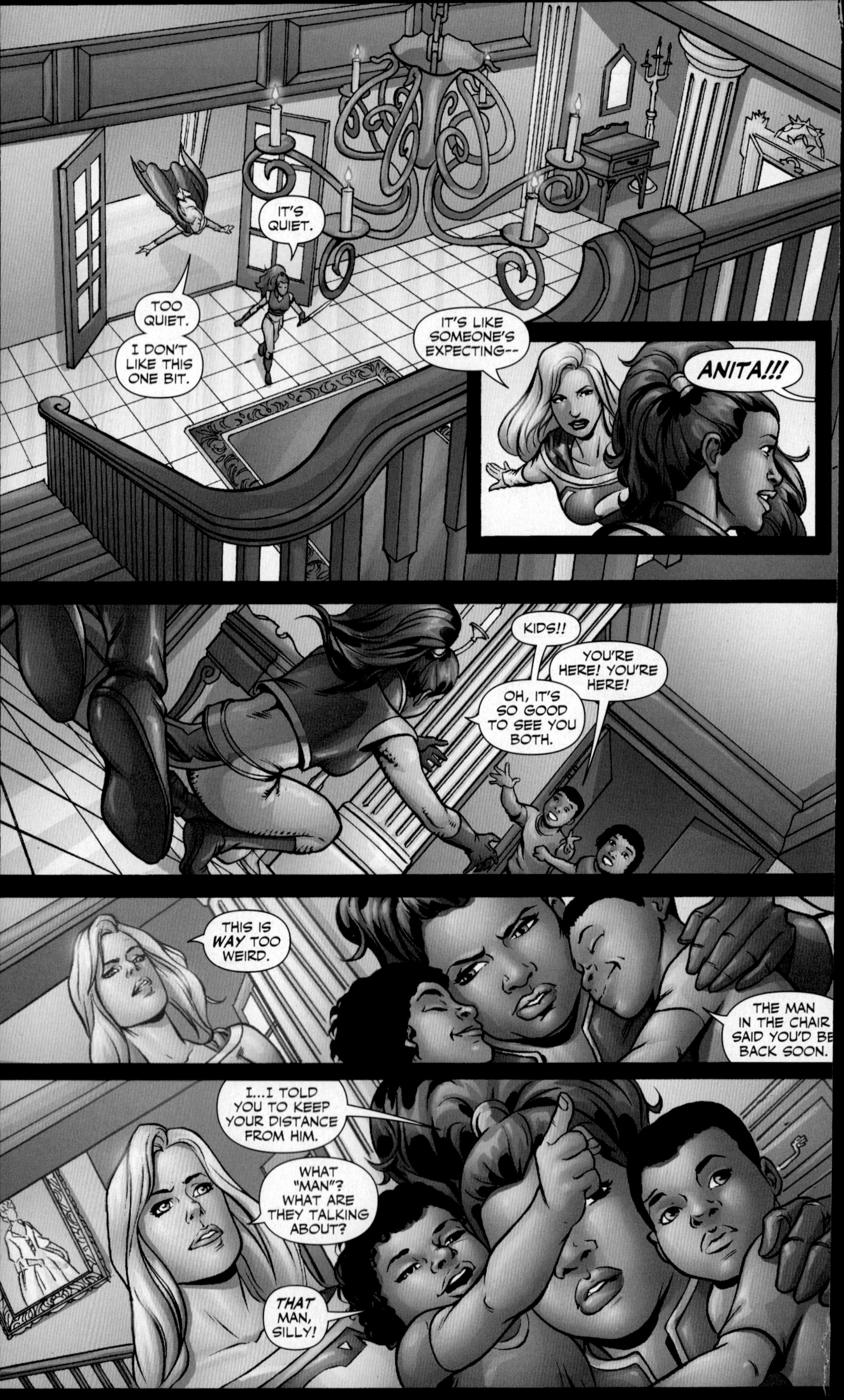
IT'S QUIET.
TOO QUIET.
I DON'T LIKE THIS ONE BIT.
IT'S LIKE SOMEONE'S EXPECTING--
ANITA!!!
KIDS!!
YOU'RE HERE! YOU'RE HERE!
OH, IT'S SO GOOD TO SEE YOU BOTH.
THIS IS WAY TOO WEIRD.
THE MAN IN THE CHAIR SAID YOU'D BE BACK SOON.
I...I TOLD YOU TO KEEP YOUR DISTANCE FROM HIM.
WHAT "MAN"? WHAT ARE THEY TALKING ABOUT?
THAT MAN, SILLY!

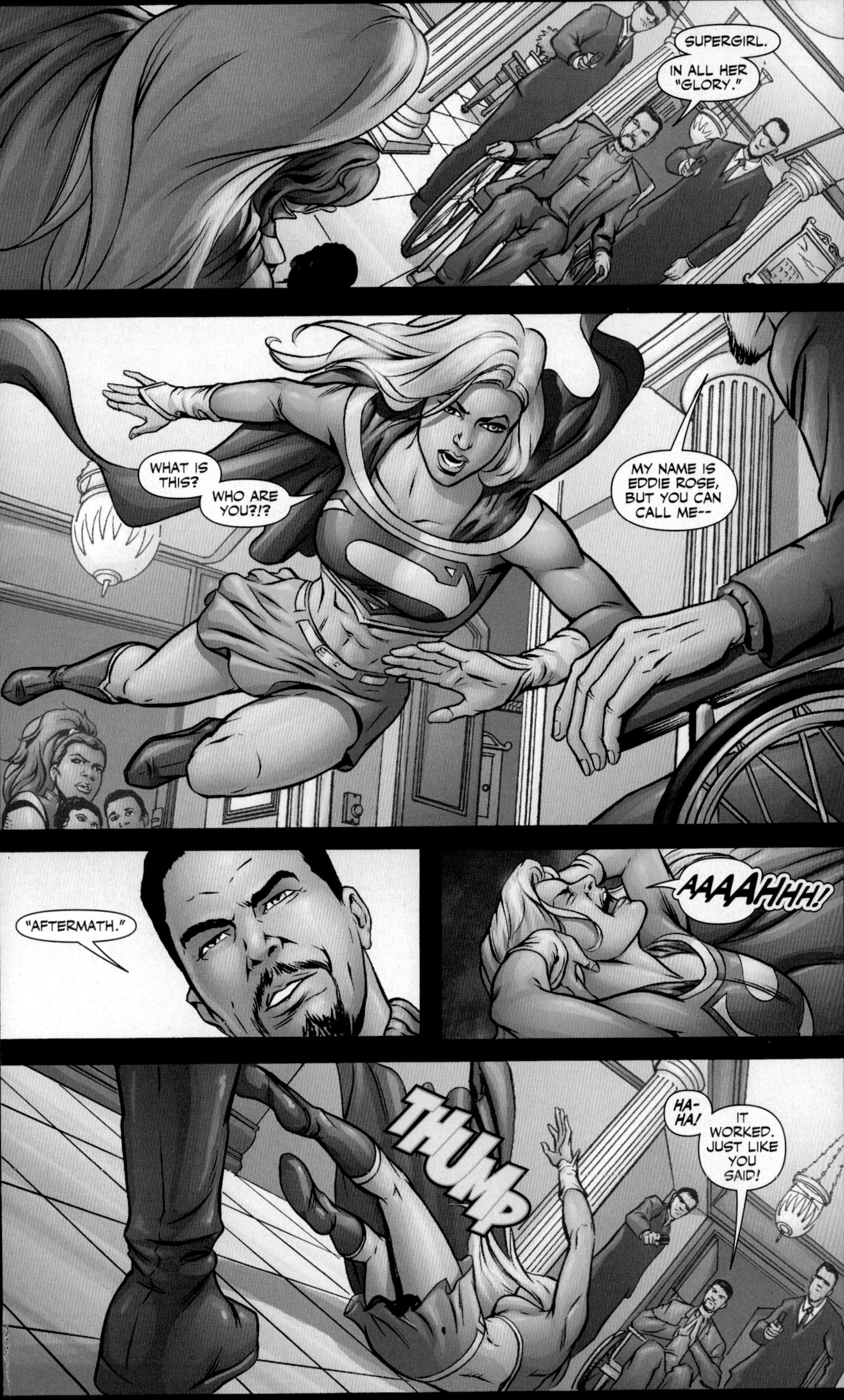
SUPERGIRL.
IN ALL HER "GLORY."
WHAT IS THIS?
WHO ARE YOU?!?
MY NAME IS EDDIE ROSE, BUT YOU CAN CALL ME--
"AFTERMATH."
AAAAHHH!
THUMP
HA-HA!
IT WORKED. JUST LIKE YOU SAID!

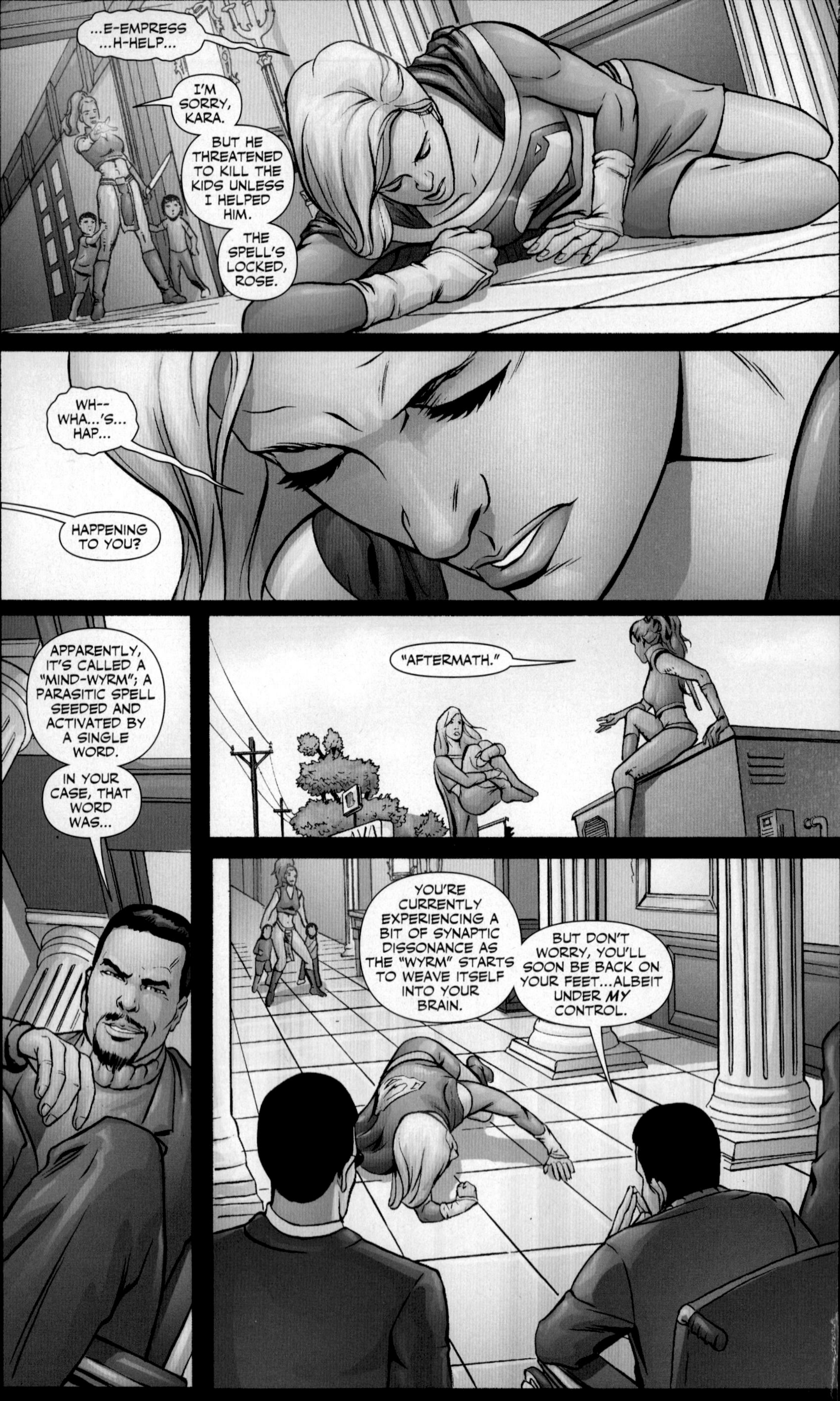

...E-EMPRESS ...H-HELP...
I'M SORRY, KARA.
BUT HE THREATENED TO KILL THE KIDS UNLESS I HELPED HIM.
THE SPELL'S LOCKED, ROSE.
WH-- WHA...'S... HAP...
HAPPENING TO YOU?
APPARENTLY, IT'S CALLED A "MIND-WYRM"; A PARASITIC SPELL SEEDED AND ACTIVATED BY A SINGLE WORD.
IN YOUR CASE, THAT WORD WAS...
"AFTERMATH."
YOU'RE CURRENTLY EXPERIENCING A BIT OF SYNAPTIC DISSONANCE AS THE "WYRM" STARTS TO WEAVE ITSELF INTO YOUR BRAIN.
BUT DON'T WORRY, YOU'LL SOON BE BACK ON YOUR FEET...ALBEIT UNDER *MY* CONTROL.

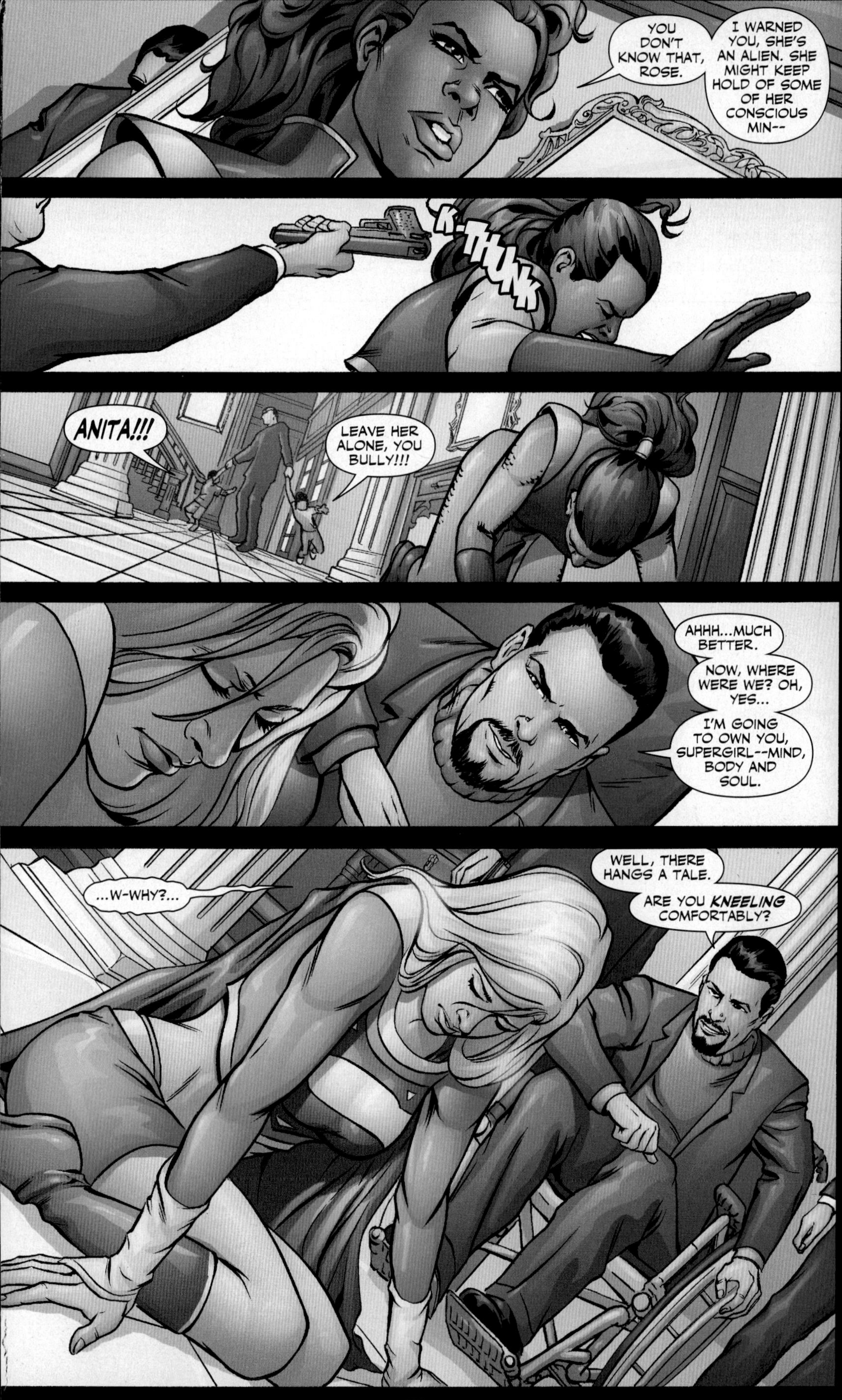

YOU DON'T KNOW THAT, ROSE.
I WARNED YOU, SHE'S AN ALIEN. SHE MIGHT KEEP HOLD OF SOME OF HER CONSCIOUS MIN--
K-THUNK
ANITA!!!
LEAVE HER ALONE, YOU BULLY!!!
AHHH...MUCH BETTER.
NOW, WHERE WERE WE? OH, YES...
I'M GOING TO OWN YOU, SUPERGIRL--MIND, BODY AND SOUL.
...W-WHY?...
WELL, THERE HANGS A TALE.
ARE YOU KNEELING COMFORTABLY?

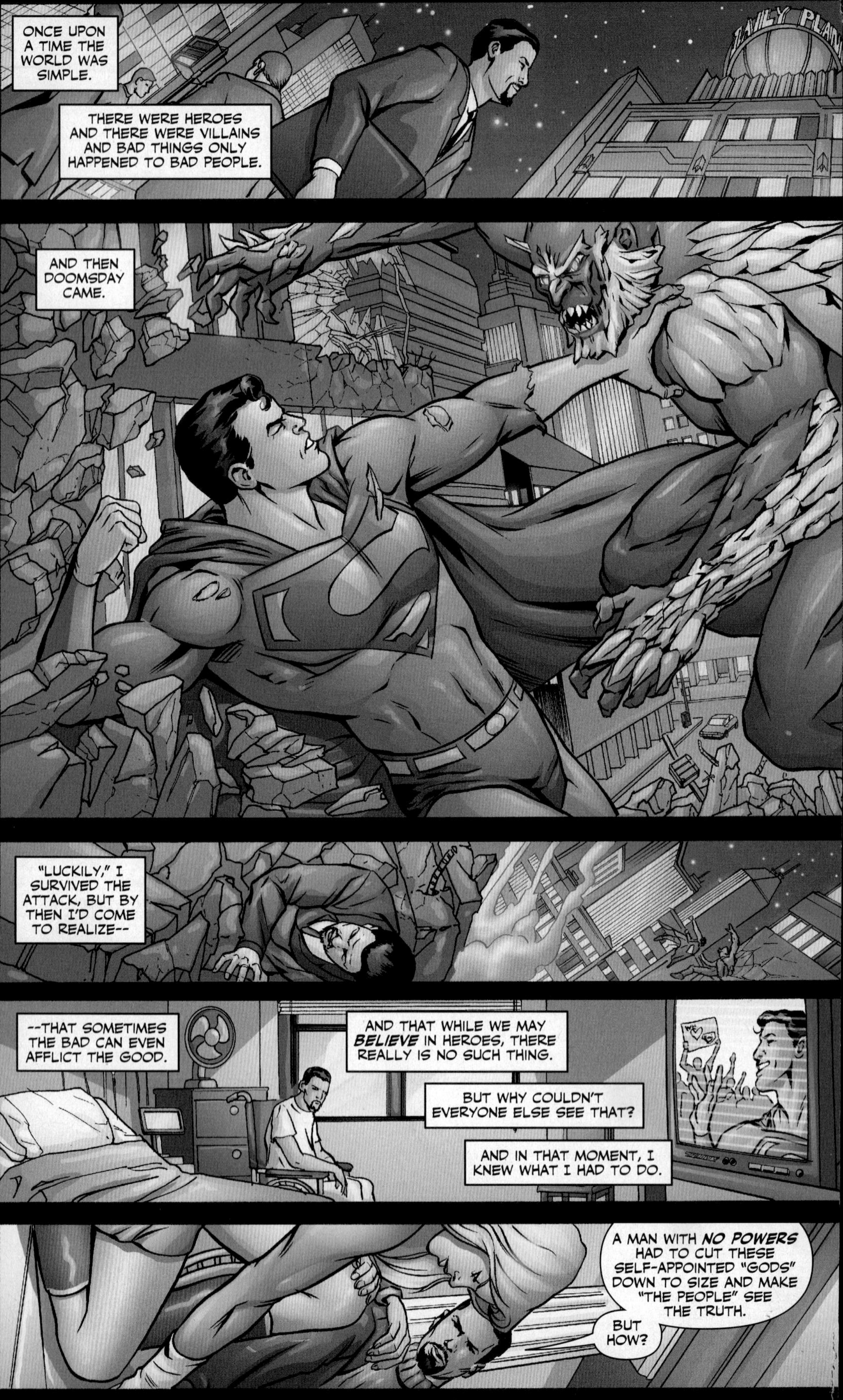
ONCE UPON A TIME THE WORLD WAS SIMPLE.
THERE WERE HEROES AND THERE WERE VILLAINS AND BAD THINGS ONLY HAPPENED TO BAD PEOPLE.
AND THEN DOOMSDAY CAME.
"LUCKILY," I SURVIVED THE ATTACK, BUT BY THEN I'D COME TO REALIZE--
--THAT SOMETIMES THE BAD CAN EVEN AFFLICT THE GOOD.
AND THAT WHILE WE MAY *BELIEVE* IN HEROES, THERE REALLY IS NO SUCH THING.
BUT WHY COULDN'T EVERYONE ELSE SEE THAT?
AND IN THAT MOMENT, I KNEW WHAT I HAD TO DO.
A MAN WITH *NO POWERS* HAD TO CUT THESE SELF-APPOINTED "GODS" DOWN TO SIZE AND MAKE "THE PEOPLE" SEE THE TRUTH.
BUT HOW?

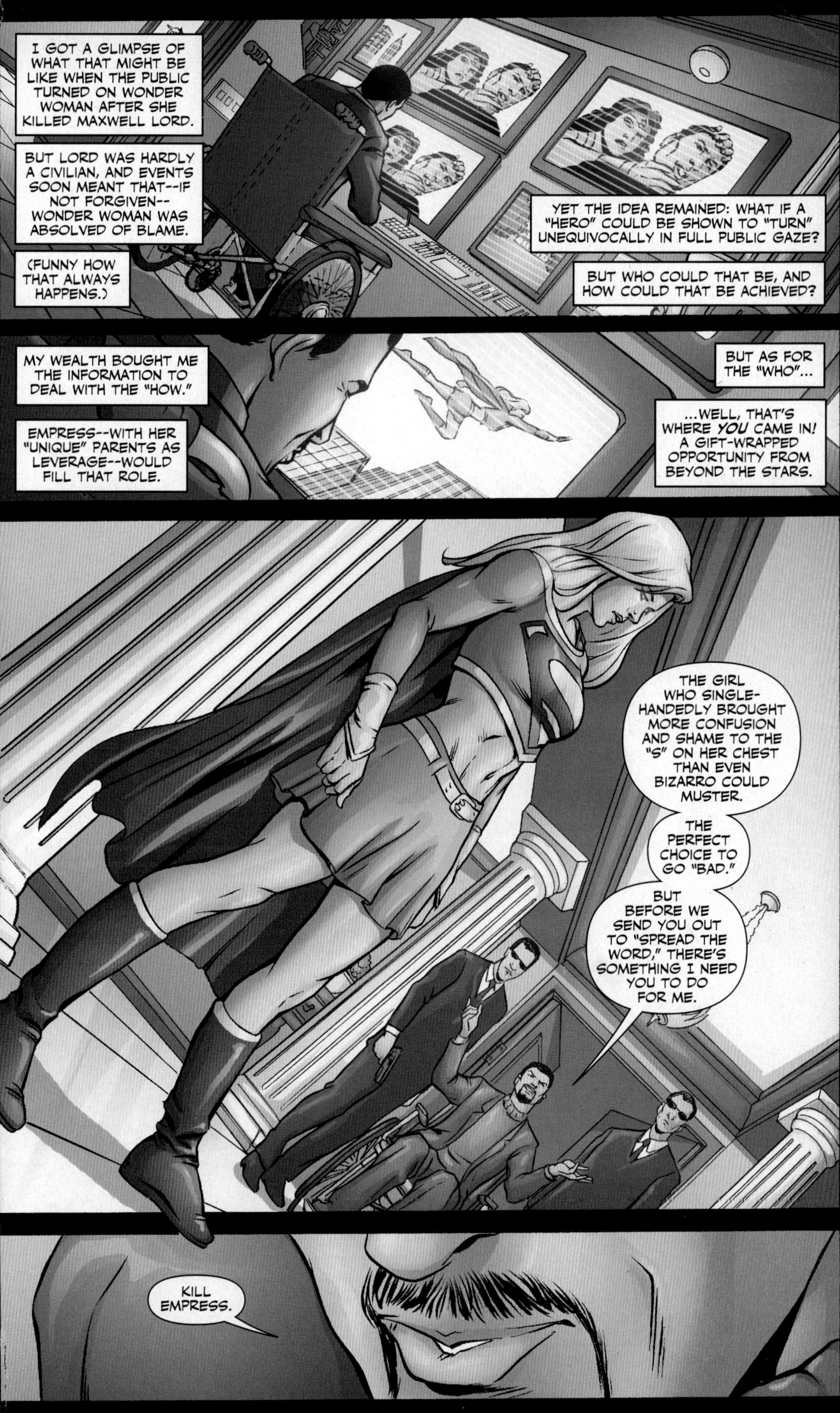
I GOT A GLIMPSE OF WHAT THAT MIGHT BE LIKE WHEN THE PUBLIC TURNED ON WONDER WOMAN AFTER SHE KILLED MAXWELL LORD.
BUT LORD WAS HARDLY A CIVILIAN, AND EVENTS SOON MEANT THAT--IF NOT FORGIVEN--WONDER WOMAN WAS ABSOLVED OF BLAME.
(FUNNY HOW THAT ALWAYS HAPPENS.)
YET THE IDEA REMAINED: WHAT IF A "HERO" COULD BE SHOWN TO "TURN" UNEQUIVOCALLY IN FULL PUBLIC GAZE?
BUT WHO COULD THAT BE, AND HOW COULD THAT BE ACHIEVED?
MY WEALTH BOUGHT ME THE INFORMATION TO DEAL WITH THE "HOW."
EMPRESS--WITH HER "UNIQUE" PARENTS AS LEVERAGE--WOULD FILL THAT ROLE.
BUT AS FOR THE "WHO"...
...WELL, THAT'S WHERE *YOU* CAME IN! A GIFT-WRAPPED OPPORTUNITY FROM BEYOND THE STARS.
THE GIRL WHO SINGLE-HANDEDLY BROUGHT MORE CONFUSION AND SHAME TO THE "S" ON HER CHEST THAN EVEN BIZARRO COULD MUSTER.
THE PERFECT CHOICE TO GO "BAD."
BUT BEFORE WE SEND YOU OUT TO "SPREAD THE WORD," THERE'S SOMETHING I NEED YOU TO DO FOR ME.
KILL EMPRESS.

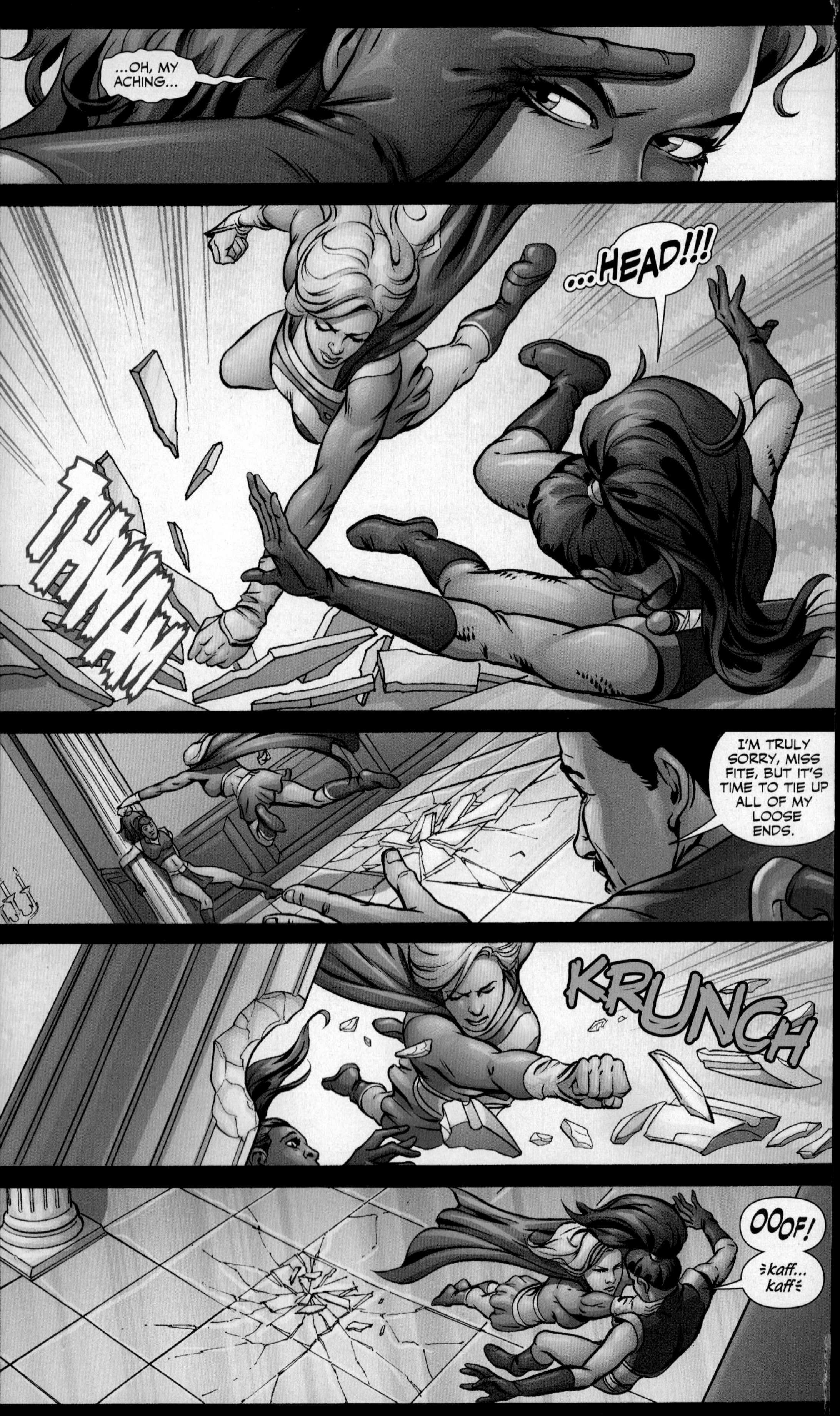
...OH, MY ACHING...
...HEAD!!!
THWAM
I'M TRULY SORRY, MISS FITE, BUT IT'S TIME TO TIE UP ALL OF MY LOOSE ENDS.
KRUNCH
OOOF!
kaff... kaff

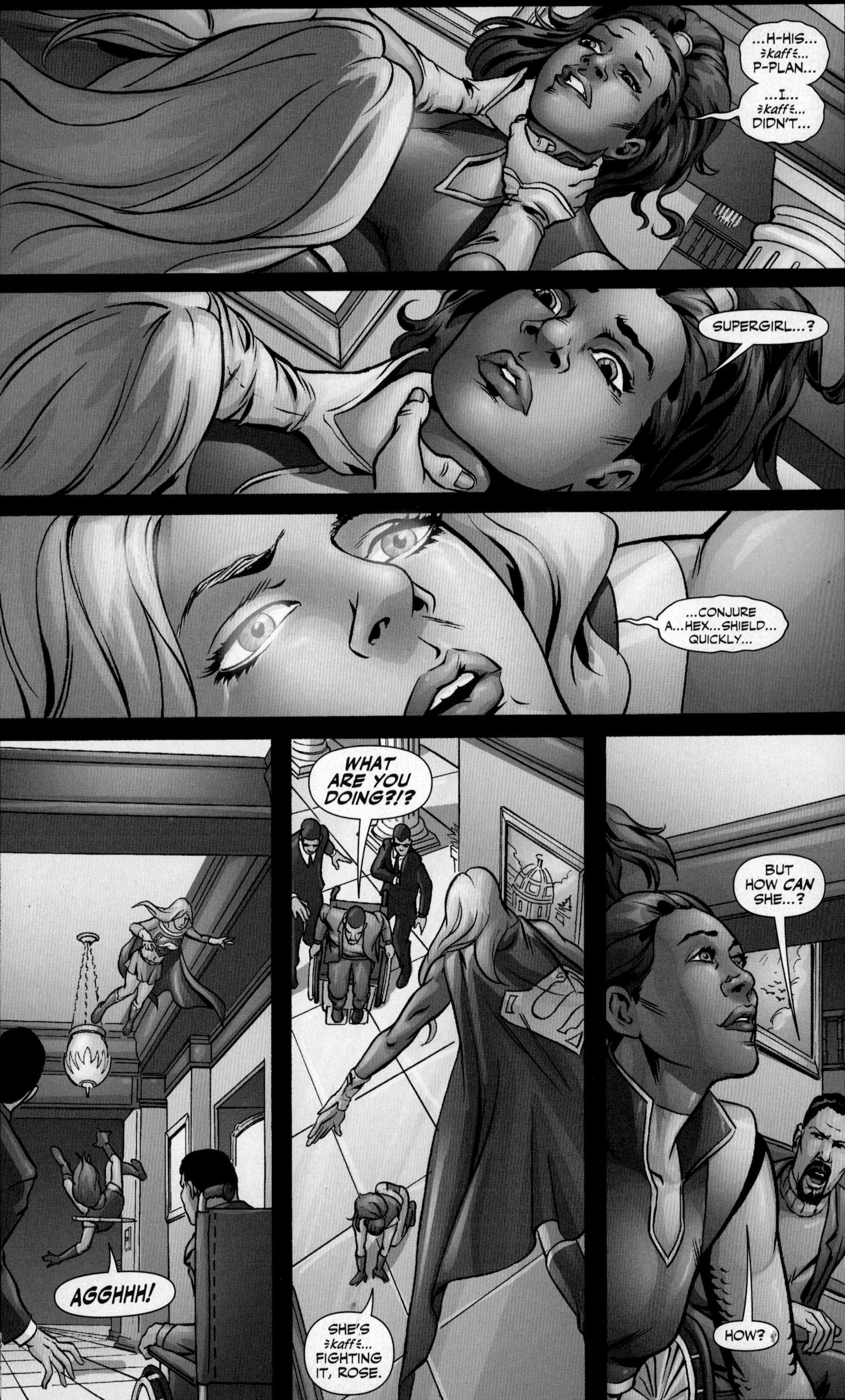

...H-HIS... ≷kaff≶... P-PLAN...
...I... ≷kaff≶... DIDN'T...
SUPERGIRL...?
...CONJURE A...HEX...SHIELD... QUICKLY...
AGGHHH!
WHAT ARE YOU DOING?!?
SHE'S ≷kaff≶... FIGHTING IT, ROSE.
BUT HOW CAN SHE...?
HOW?

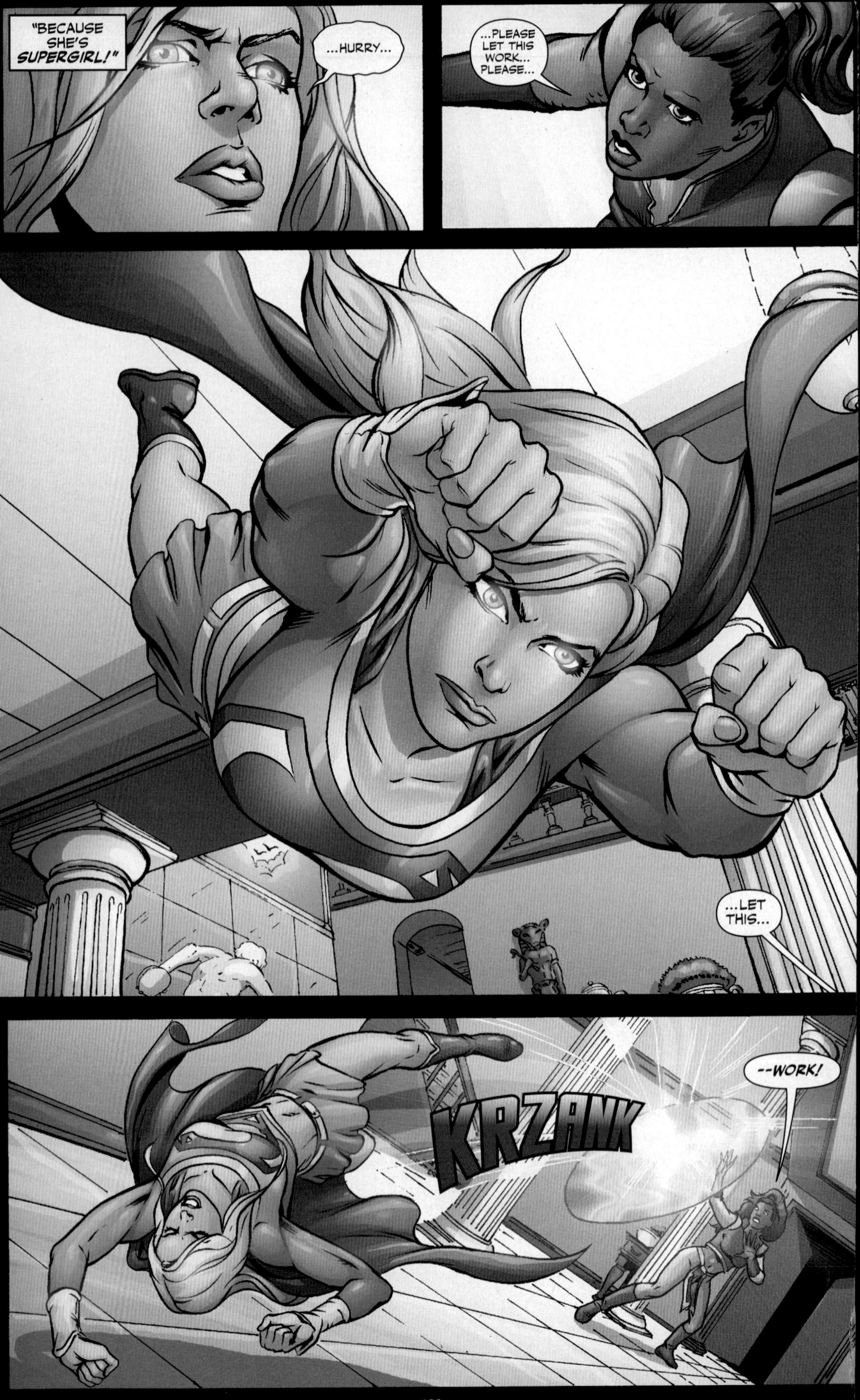
"BECAUSE SHE'S *SUPERGIRL!*"
...HURRY...
...PLEASE LET THIS WORK... PLEASE...
...LET THIS...
KRZANK
--*WORK!*

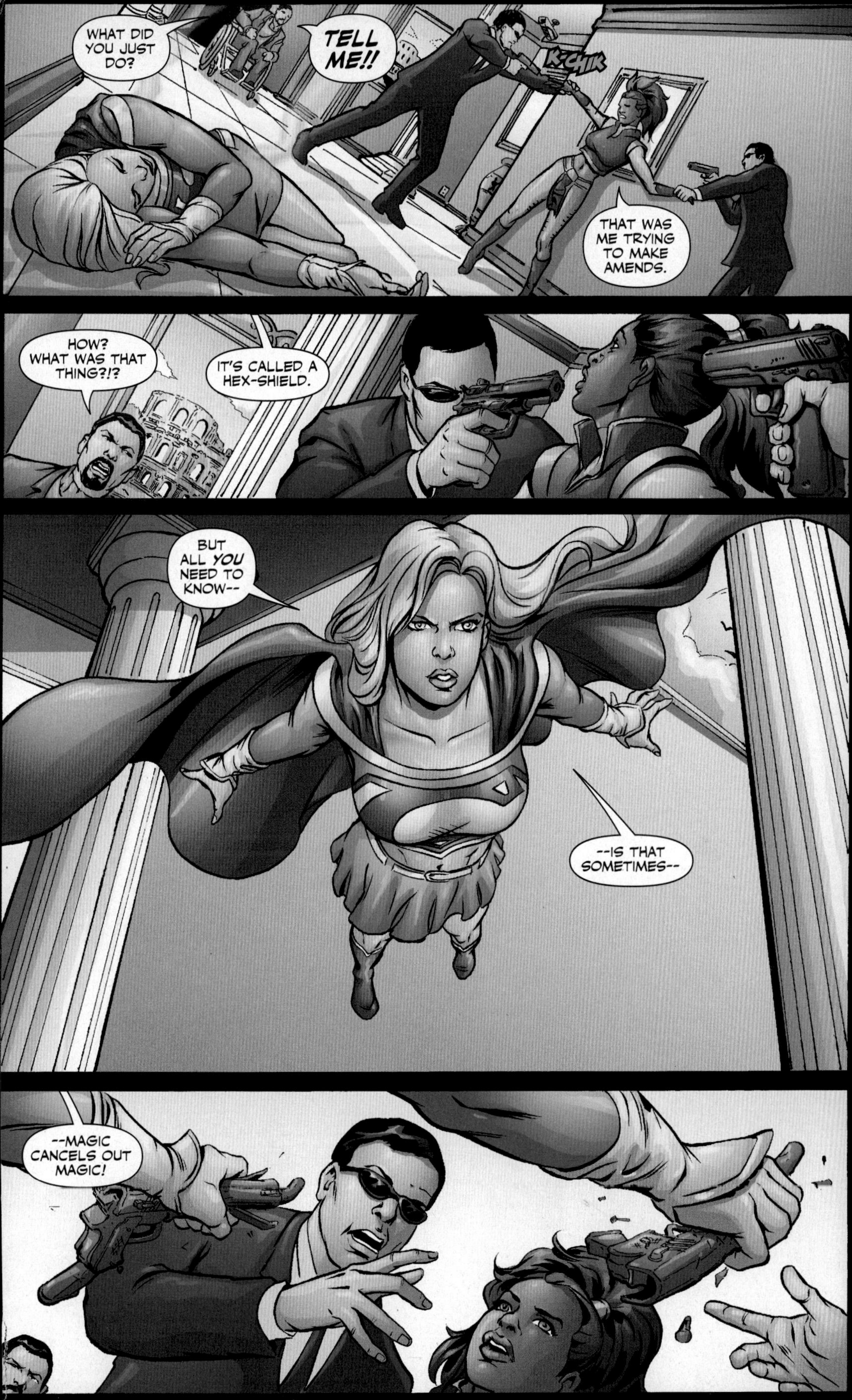
WHAT DID YOU JUST DO?
TELL ME!!
K-CHIK
THAT WAS ME TRYING TO MAKE AMENDS.
HOW? WHAT WAS THAT THING?!?
IT'S CALLED A HEX-SHIELD.
BUT ALL YOU NEED TO KNOW--
--IS THAT SOMETIMES--
--MAGIC CANCELS OUT MAGIC!

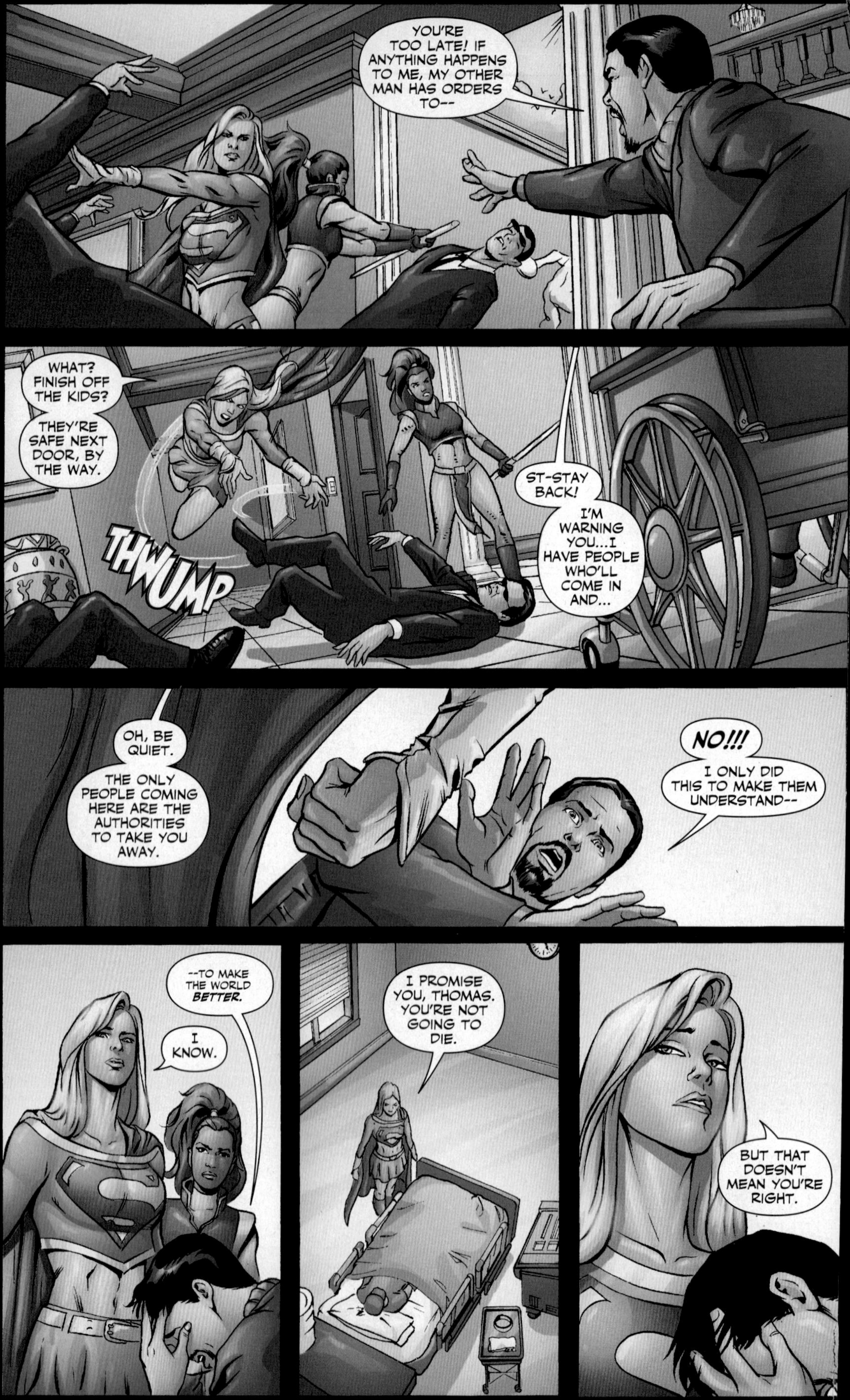
YOU'RE TOO LATE! IF ANYTHING HAPPENS TO ME, MY OTHER MAN HAS ORDERS TO--
WHAT? FINISH OFF THE KIDS?
THEY'RE SAFE NEXT DOOR, BY THE WAY.
THWUMP
ST-STAY BACK!
I'M WARNING YOU...I HAVE PEOPLE WHO'LL COME IN AND...
OH, BE QUIET.
THE ONLY PEOPLE COMING HERE ARE THE AUTHORITIES TO TAKE YOU AWAY.
NO!!!
I ONLY DID THIS TO MAKE THEM UNDERSTAND--
--TO MAKE THE WORLD BETTER.
I KNOW.
I PROMISE YOU, THOMAS. YOU'RE NOT GOING TO DIE.
BUT THAT DOESN'T MEAN YOU'RE RIGHT.

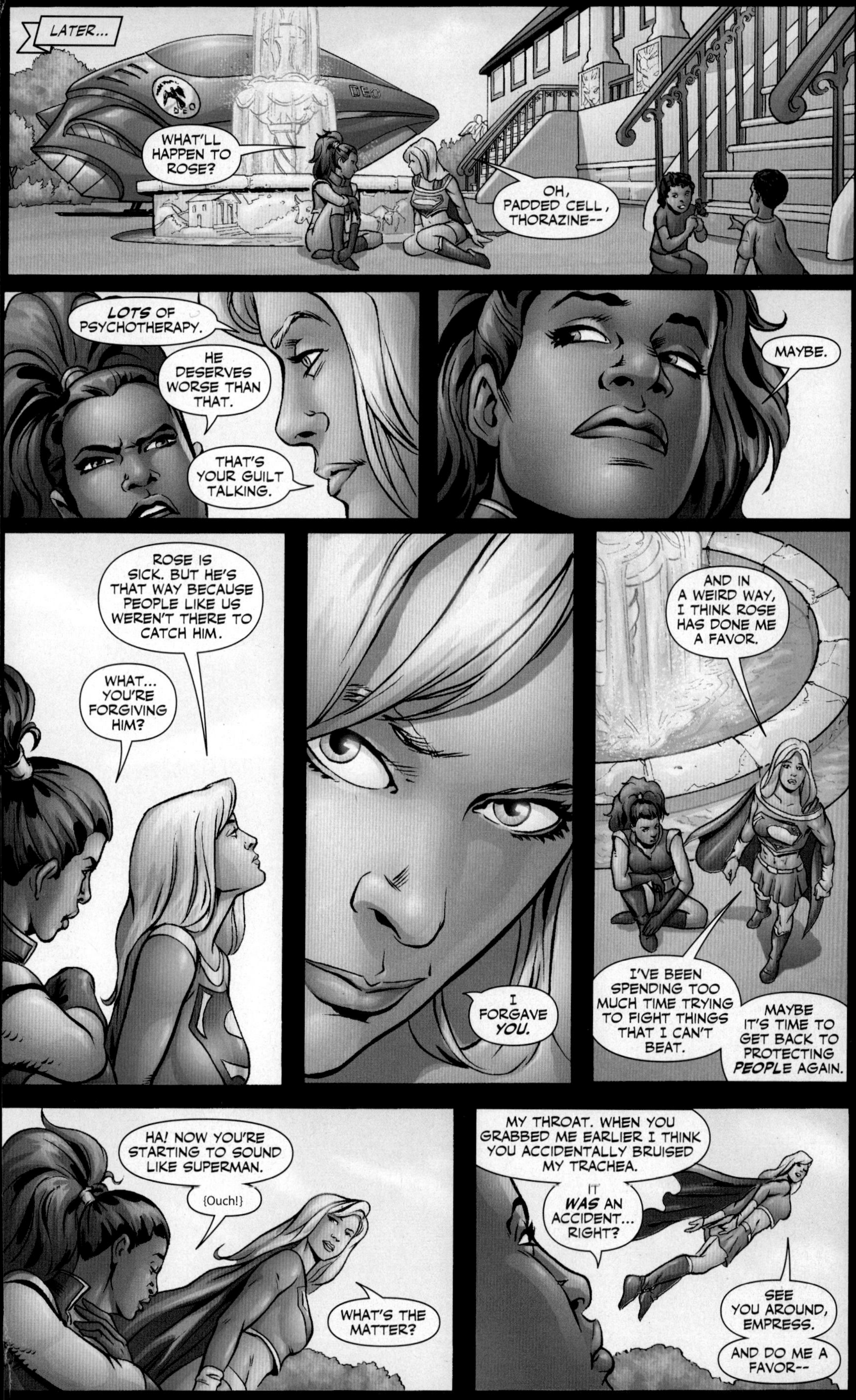
LATER...
DEO
WHAT'LL HAPPEN TO ROSE?
OH, PADDED CELL, THORAZINE--
LOTS OF PSYCHOTHERAPY.
HE DESERVES WORSE THAN THAT.
THAT'S YOUR GUILT TALKING.
MAYBE.
ROSE IS SICK. BUT HE'S THAT WAY BECAUSE PEOPLE LIKE US WEREN'T THERE TO CATCH HIM.
WHAT... YOU'RE FORGIVING HIM?
I FORGAVE YOU.
AND IN A WEIRD WAY, I THINK ROSE HAS DONE ME A FAVOR.
I'VE BEEN SPENDING TOO MUCH TIME TRYING TO FIGHT THINGS THAT I CAN'T BEAT.
MAYBE IT'S TIME TO GET BACK TO PROTECTING PEOPLE AGAIN.
HA! NOW YOU'RE STARTING TO SOUND LIKE SUPERMAN.
{Ouch!}
WHAT'S THE MATTER?
MY THROAT. WHEN YOU GRABBED ME EARLIER I THINK YOU ACCIDENTALLY BRUISED MY TRACHEA.
IT WAS AN ACCIDENT... RIGHT?
SEE YOU AROUND, EMPRESS.
AND DO ME A FAVOR--

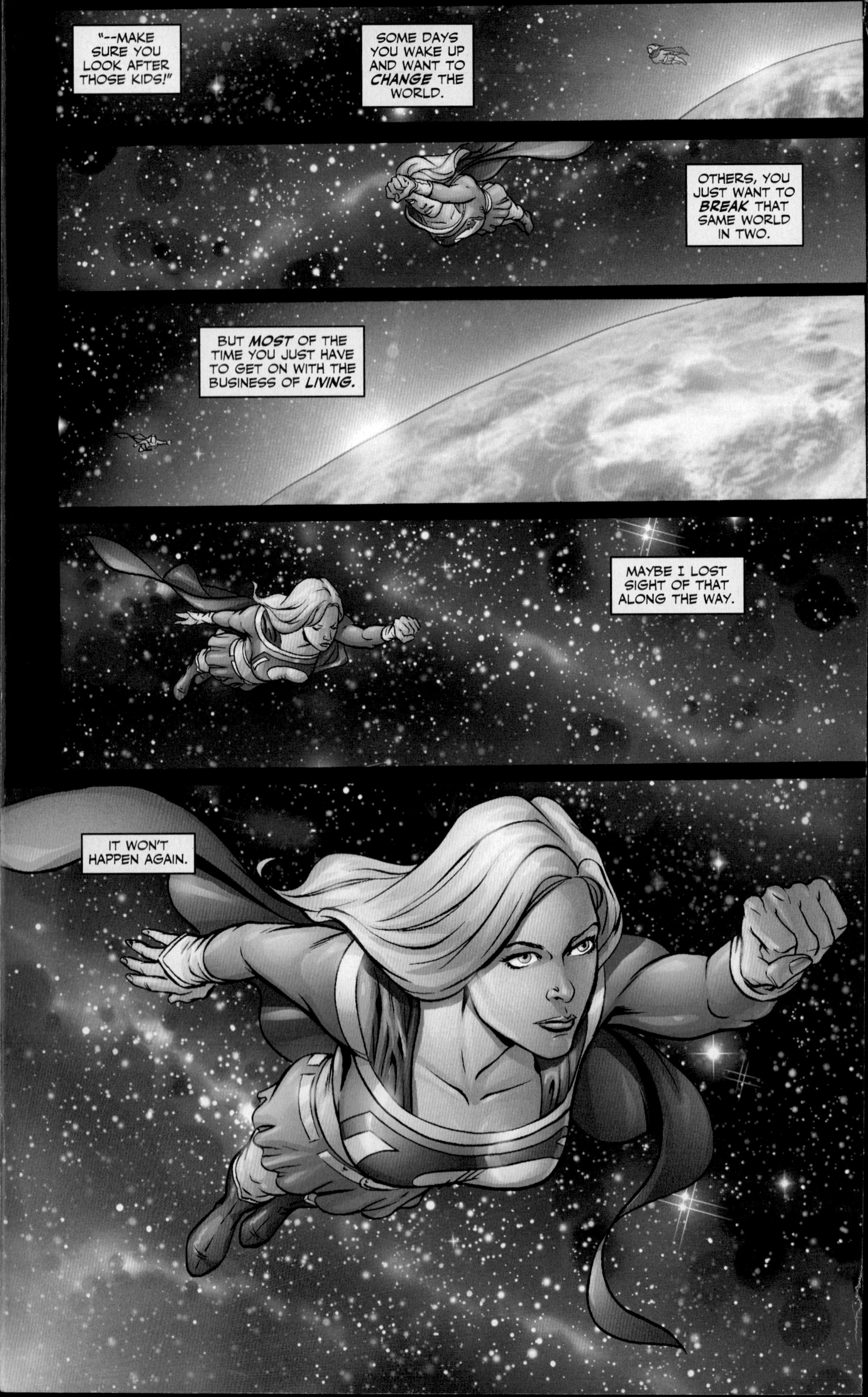
"--MAKE SURE YOU LOOK AFTER THOSE KIDS!"
SOME DAYS YOU WAKE UP AND WANT TO CHANGE THE WORLD.
OTHERS, YOU JUST WANT TO BREAK THAT SAME WORLD IN TWO.
BUT MOST OF THE TIME YOU JUST HAVE TO GET ON WITH THE BUSINESS OF LIVING.
MAYBE I LOST SIGHT OF THAT ALONG THE WAY.
IT WON'T HAPPEN AGAIN.

MORE CLASSIC TALES OF THE MAN OF STEEL

SUPERMAN:
THE MAN OF STEEL
VOLS. 1 - 6

SUPERMAN:
BIRTHRIGHT

SUPERMAN:
CAMELOT FALLS
VOLS. 1 - 2

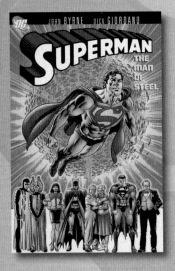

JOHN BYRNE

**MARK WAID
LEINIL YU**

**KURT BUSIEK
CARLOS PACHECO**

SUPERMAN:
OUR WORLDS AT WAR

SUPERMAN:
RED SON

SUPERMAN:
SECRET IDENTITY

**VARIOUS
WRITERS & ARTISTS**

**MARK MILLAR
DAVE JOHNSON
KILLIAN PLUNKETT**

**KURT BUSIEK
STUART IMMONEN**